150 THINGS EVERY MAN SHOULD KNOW

GARETH MAY

Published by Sourcebooks, Inc.
P.O. Box 4410, Naperville, Illinois 60567-4410
(630) 961-3900
Fax: (630) 961-2168
www.sourcebooks.com

Originally published in Great Britain in 2009 by Square Peg

Library of Congress Cataloging-in-Publication Data

May, Gareth.
  150 things every man should know / Gareth May.
     p. cm.
  1. Men—Life skills guides. 2. Men—Conduct of life. 3. Men—Humor. I. Title.
  HQ1090.M3846 2011
  646.70081—dc22

                              2011003718

           Printed and bound in Canada.
           TR 10 9 8 7 6 5 4 3 2 1

Dedication

For my Dad—the man I've always strived to emulate…

although I'm still holding out for the adoption papers.

Contents

How to iron a shirt like your mom

Whether you are a fisherman's wife or a bachelor running late for the office, the art of ironing a shirt is one which, once mastered, never fades, unlike a cheap short-sleever bought on sale. Here's how to do it the good old-fashioned way.

The best time to do the ironing is on a Sunday night, and to iron all the shirts for the week in one go. It'll be faster, as you'll get on a roll after the first one or two, and you won't have to do it again for a whole week. Stick on the radio or some football on TV—as usually nothing much is happening on the field, leaving you free to get on with the ironing.

Switch the iron on and allow to warm. If it's a steam iron, fill the water reservoir first. Most shirts are made of cotton and iron better when slightly damp and at a high heat, so select steam and the highest heat to give a crisper finish. If your shirt is dry, spray with water, roll up and leave to rest for ten minutes or so. If it's a dark color, iron inside out to save the brightness, and if it is white make sure the iron is clean so you don't mark the innocent pallor of your shirt. Here's how to iron out those creases like a pro.

* **Collar**—Lay it flat, lengthways across the ironing board, and iron in one single motion back and forth a few times. Fold it over at the collar, as you would when you're actually wearing it, and run the iron over it again. Lift up and check the line.

* **Back**—Place the shirt back, or yoke, on the ironing board, folded over just below the part which covers your shoulders and upper back. More often than not there will be a seam, so fold in accordance and iron with the point of the iron pushed up to the seam slowly moving towards the center.

* **Sleeves**—Line them up one at a time by folding at the seam and laying them lengthways. Run the point of the iron down their side and across with a smooth run. Use your

other hand to pull the fabric tight and iron the cuffs inside and out.

* **Front**—Place one side of the open shirt over the edge of the ironing board, with the end of the board sticking in the armhole and buttonholes facing widthways. Iron along the shoulder seam and around the collar. Then place the same side of the shirt, buttonholes lengthways, along the board. Lift and pull and iron until you come to the other side of the shirt. Iron in between the buttons with the iron point and you're done.

How to down a pint without being sick

Downing a pint in a bar can often lead to all subsequent drinks being bought for you. But get it wrong and you can find yourself covered in vomit and laughed at by strangers on the street. So if you want to take it on don't try to be a hero.

First of all choose the beer yourself and never agree to down a pint of cider—an amateur downer's mistake which could prove lethal. Don't go for something too strong, too cold, or too fizzy and let it settle for a while on the bar. When it's time, approach your challenge and your pint like a man. Employ a little theatrics, smack your lips and limber up as you get yourself in the zone. Pick up the pint, tip your head back, and slowly but surely take mouthful after mouthful until it's all down. Don't be tempted to gulp or hurry—you'll only panic, stop breathing and choke, death-by-lager style.

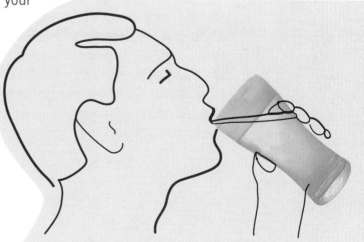

Breathe calmly, focus on the task in hand, and block out all distractions, Zen-like. Don't worry if people tell you to hurry up, just do it in your own time; a pint's a pint no matter how long it takes to go down. Pub folklore spins yarns of people who can just open their throats and effectively down the pint in one go without swallowing. Desert tribes drink their water like this as swallowing uses up too much energy, but remember, you're not in a desert tribe now so take it slow and reap the rewards.

How to undo a bra with one hand

Men made walls to keep out armies, women made bras to keep out men. But those walls have been breached and now, with one hand, those bras will be removed.

First off, mid-kiss, slip your left hand under her top and find the back of her bra. Run your fingertips along the strap until you find the 1¼–2 in. of rough fabric situated in the middle. This is the clasp you're going to have to undo; it is made up of hooks and eyelets. Your job is to move the hooks from the left to the right, so slide your middle finger underneath the right side of the clasp, with your nail facing her skin. Next, pulling the strap out ever so slightly—tact is required here, flicking a girl in the back will get you slapped—get your thumb and place it on the other side of the clasp, over, not underneath, the strap. Finally, rub your thumb and middle finger together like you're clicking your fingers and the clasp should come undone. Take a bow; the bra is defeated. You can now move on to even greater goals, like removing her underwear with your teeth!

How to hold chopsticks like Mr. Miyagi

"Man who catch fly with chop stick accomplish anything."—Mr. Miyagi

Customs are strange and wonderful things. In America, it's considered rude to eat before your host picks up his or her fork at a dinner party. Get your wires, or more specifically chopsticks, crossed in China, however, and you could be giving everyone around the table the sign of death.

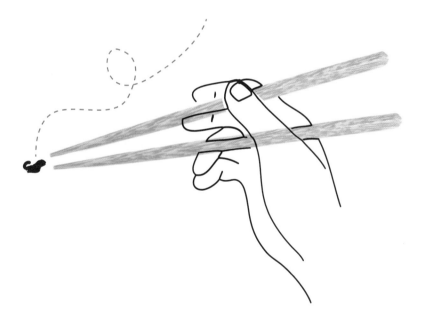

The people of Japan, China, Korea, Vietnam, and Taiwan eat using chopsticks; that's a lot of disappointed people if you always ask for a fork. Joining their ranks is simple-ish.

fig 1:   fig 2:

Pick up one chopstick like a pencil with the broad end resting into the V of skin where your thumb meets your index finger. Drop the narrow end down a finger so that it rests against the side of your end knuckle. It should fit there snugly and firmly. Pick up the second chopstick with your index finger and middle finger using your thumb to hold it in place. Adjust until their ends are touching and even. Do this swiftly and smoothly if you want to look like a real pro. When you start to eat the bottom chopstick should always stay still and the top chopstick should pivot. This is done by slowly moving the knuckle joint at the end of your middle finger; straighten to widen and bend inwards to clamp together. Only move your thumb when you need to realign the chopsticks.

As a beginner, you might find it easier to hold the chopsticks nearer to the middle or closer to the tips. As you grow in confidence however, you should hold them further towards the blunt end as it's considered polite to keep your hands as far away from the food as possible.

A few more things to consider:

* Picking up food should be done gently; don't apply too much pressure or be tempted to stab at your chow mein in desperation.

* When taking from communal bowls use the broad ends of the chopsticks so you don't pass on the germs from your mouth.

* When eating rice either use a shoveling motion or pack it together into a small mouthful. Don't be afraid to lift the bowl up to your chin.

* Noisily slurping up your noodles is perfectly OK.

A few cultural chopstick no-nos:

*   Don't lick, stab, rake, or point your chopsticks at fellow diners. This is a no-no-no.

*   Never stick your chopsticks straight down into the rice so they stand upright. It's bad manners because it will remind Chinese or Japanese diners of the incense burned when mourning a relative—not something too many people like thinking about while they're eating their meal.

*   Do not cross your chopsticks. In China this is a symbol of death and won't go down well with your foreign business partners.

*   It is usual to hold your chopsticks in your right hand. For some holding them in the left hand symbolizes dispute and could land you in the ER with a chopstick in the eye.

*   Do not pass food round the table with your chopsticks. In Japanese mourning rituals bones are passed between family members with chopsticks.

*   Resist tapping the edge of your bowl with your chopsticks. This is considered rude because it is what beggars do and might also lead you to break out in a verse of "Why are we waiting? Because we're salivating. Oh, why are we waiting…"

*   Try not to drop your chopsticks. This is considered bad luck and a little bit manky if you pick them up off the floor and continue using them to eat.

Remember—using chopsticks is like riding a bike. Once you get the hang of it, you never forget. Keep some chopsticks from your next take-away delivery and practice, practice, and practice again in the comfort and privacy of your own home until your chopstick prowess would make Mr. Miyagi proud. And what's more, you'll never have to buy a can of fly spray again.

How to shine shoes like an ROTC star

They say you can tell a lot about a man from the state of his shoes. So pay heed. Spitting on a piece of toilet paper and dabbing at the leather like your grandma trying to rid your cheek of ketchup won't cut it.

You will need:

* Newspaper
* Polish brush
* Black wax polish for black leather; brown for brown
* Horsehair shine brush
* Water sprayer
* Cotton balls—a piece of cloth wrapped around two fingers or a sock pulled over your hand will do.
* Shoe cloth (or use an old T-shirt or some nylon tights)
* Old toothbrush

Step 1.
Spread some newspaper out across the floor or table.

Step 2.
Remove the shoelaces. Use a brush or damp cloth to remove all dirt and dust from the shoe's surface. If your shoes are slightly damp, let them dry before putting the polish on.

Step 3.

Use the polish brush to apply the wax in small circular movements. Work round the shoe until the polish is spread evenly all over the leather.

Step 4.

Work the wax into the seams with the old toothbrush.

Step 5.

Leave to dry at room temperature for 15 minutes.

Step 6.

Take your horsehair brush and shine away like a madman until you've covered the whole shoe. This will remove all excess wax. Spritz the shoe with water from a sprayer once in a while to produce a better shine.

Step 7.

Put about a pea-sized amount of wax or polish directly on to a damp cotton ball. Massage the wax into the leather with small circular movements, paying special attention to the heel and toe. Repeat, using a fresh cotton ball each time, until you've got the right amount of shine on your shoe. Don't stop until you can watch TV in the reflection of the polish on your shoes. This could take up to 15 shines so be patient.

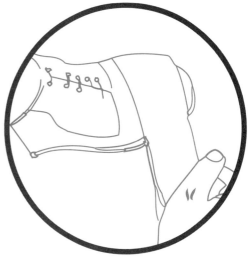

Step 8.

Use a clean cloth, a sock, an old T-shirt, or your girlfriend's nylon tights—when she's not wearing them of course—and buff up the shoe vigorously. Thread the shoelaces back through their holes, put the newspaper in the bin, and twinkle toes is ready for anything.

Choosing your polish:

For black shoes, use black polish. Find the correct shade of brown for brown shoes. Keep separate polish brushes for brown and black shoes.

Cream and paste polish—for fine leather. Keeps it flexible and moisturized, allowing it to breathe. Exaggerates color and extends shoe life.

Wax polish—easily covers scuffs and shines the best. Can dry out the leather.

Liquid polish—fast shine but can crack and dry out the leather.

Beeswax—melt in a tablespoon and apply as above. Similar effects to wax polish.

If the wax polish is hard and tough, strike a match and pass it over the wax until it catches alight. Once all the wax is burning place the lid over the tin and snuff out the flames. Remove the lid carefully and once the minuscule mushroom cloud dissipates you'll be left with a smooth wax ready for application.

Quick tip for shiny shoes in seconds:

If you're late for a party, peel a banana and dash the inside of the skin over the leather. Remove flecks of banana, tie your shoelaces and shoot out the door…not forgetting to eat the banana on the way.

The perfect shave

Chad Gillette was a funny old sausage. Despite being heralded as a "king"—of the shaving world at least—Gillette died a discontented and frustrated man.

A staunch socialist, in 1894 he wrote a book entitled *The Human Drift* which suggested competition was the root of all evil; this from the man who bought out smaller companies so that his would survive. He was a razor-sharp competitor who did not want to compete and in the end, with the Wall Street crash of 1929 and the knowledge that he had become a figurehead of capitalism, it was he who had lost. Here's a guide to the perfect wet shave.

How to shave:

1. Wash your face with a mild soap. This will remove any dirt and oil which may get trapped in your pores or reduce the impact of your razor. Pat your face dry but ensure it is still moist.

2. Preferably shave after a hot shower or smother your face with a warm washcloth. The warm water and steam will form a thin film between skin and lather, which allows the blade to "skim" over your skin rather than pull at the hairs. Warm water also softens your bristles, relaxes your facial muscles and opens your pores; all in all the perfect formula for a smoother, closer shave.

3. A little pre-shave oil can be used—this can help prevent cuts and irritation as it helps soften the stubble, giving a smoother shave.

4. Shave over a sink filled with warm water and steam your face while you shave. Lather up—soak your shaving brush in the sink of hot water, then take it out and allow all excess water to pour out.

5. Squirt a small amount of shaving gel—a thimble's worth is about right—into the palm of your hand or use a tub of shaving cream. Swirl the brush in circular motions in the foam in your hand, or directly in the tub, until a creamy lather is formed on the bristles.

6. Splash warm water on your face. Apply the foam with the brush using circular motions over your skin, against the direction of hair growth. Finish with an upward stroke—this will lift the hairs away from your skin, ready for trimming. This should take up to three minutes; a thorough lather leads to a thorough shave. Your face should now be covered in a thin but opaque layer of white foam.

7. Always use a sharp and clean razor. Blunt razors miss hairs and require you to go back over the same spot again, causing razor burn. Warm the razor in the sink or run it under the hot tap prior to shaving.

8. Shave in short strokes going with the grain, or in other words, in the same direction as the hair growth. If you shave against the grain, the hairs are pulled sharply away from your face, causing cuts, razor burn and ingrown hairs. Glide the razor lightly over the skin. You can hold your skin taut with your free hand, especially when it comes to doing your cheeks.

9. Do your sideburns first, followed by your jawline, then the neck. The area around your lips and chin should be left till last—these are the toughest hairs on your face so they need longer to become softened by the shaving foam.

10. Be guided by the contours of your face. Look at your face carefully in the mirror and see which way your hairs grow. Contours and grains change all over your face. No two faces are the same.

11. Rinse the razor in hot water after every stroke; hairs caught in the blades cause you to miss spots and you'll have to go over the same area several times.

12. If necessary, add a splash of warm water to your face and lather the area again with your brush.

13. When you have finished, splash cold water on your face to close your pores, reduce irritation and to remove any traces of shaving foam from around your ears and under your chin.

14. Pat your face dry with a soft clean towel. Don't scrub or rub your face or you'll end up looking like a beetroot.

15. Rinse, dry and put away your razor and brush

Advanced tips:

* Don't use a cheap or disposable razor; treat yourself to a decent one. Under no circumstances should you use your mom's or girlfriend's.

* Glycerine-based shaving creams cause less skin irritation than cooling gels as they don't close the pores mid-shave.

* If you shave every day, apply a moisturizer post-shave. Shaving removes the outermost layer of skin cells so give your skin a break once in a while and let the beard grow.

* Exfoliating your skin pre-shave will give you a closer shave.

* Some testify to re-lathering up and softly running the razor against the grain for the closest shave.

* Multi-blades offer control but don't follow the contours of your face as well as a single-bladed razor which requires more skill but will reward you with a closer shave.

* If you've run out of shaving cream, in an emergency you can use olive oil instead. Never use hand soap or Vaseline.

* Ingrown hairs should be pulled out with a pair of tweezers and then shaved over as normal and they should disappear within six weeks.

Aftershave tips:

* Despite Macaulay Culkin looking cool slapping aftershave on in *Home Alone*, you shouldn't actually scream in agony when you apply aftershave. If it stings, don't use it.

* Oily skin should be treated with aftershave that's made to keep skin dry. Dry skin should be treated with one that moisturizes.

* Alcohol-based aftershaves will tighten your skin and dry it out leaving you looking like Joan Rivers.

How to slow dance with confidence

As the lights dim and the music slows, unless your name is Patrick Swayze, the girl of your dreams won't be expecting you to grab her hand, say "Nobody puts Baby in a corner," and run onto the dance floor like in Dirty Dancing. *However, once you've politely asked the question and she's said "yes," taking a girl confidently by the hand and leading her up to dance with open shoulders and a powerful stride will fill her with awe and—hopefully—admiration.*

Once on the dance floor, get into position. Standing toe to toe is least complicated but if you're feeling adventurous place your right foot in-between her feet and encourage her to do the same. Or she might place both her feet inside yours. All of these are fine.

Next, place your right hand on the small of her back, and your left in her right hand at your shoulder height. **Your left arm should be bent at the elbow at roughly a 45-degree angle,** depending on the height deficit between you and your partner, whose left arm should be placed on your right shoulder. If, at this juncture, your grip keeps coming loose because either you or she has nervous sweaty palms, you can easily adjust to the Junior High dance stance. Lift her arms up so that they droop over your neck at the wrist before placing your hands on her hips—with hips not being a euphemism for bum. That said, God loves a trier.

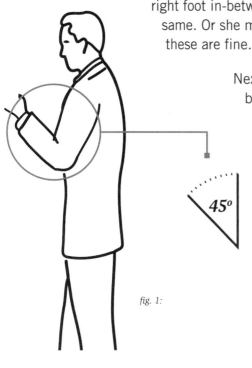

45°

fig. 1:

THE FOXTROT

■■■■□ Advanced

THE WALTZ

■■□□□ *Intermediate*

THE SHUFFLE

■□□□□ *Beginner*

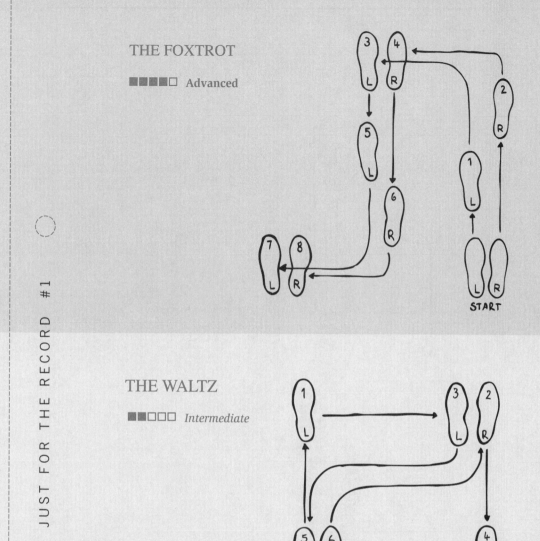

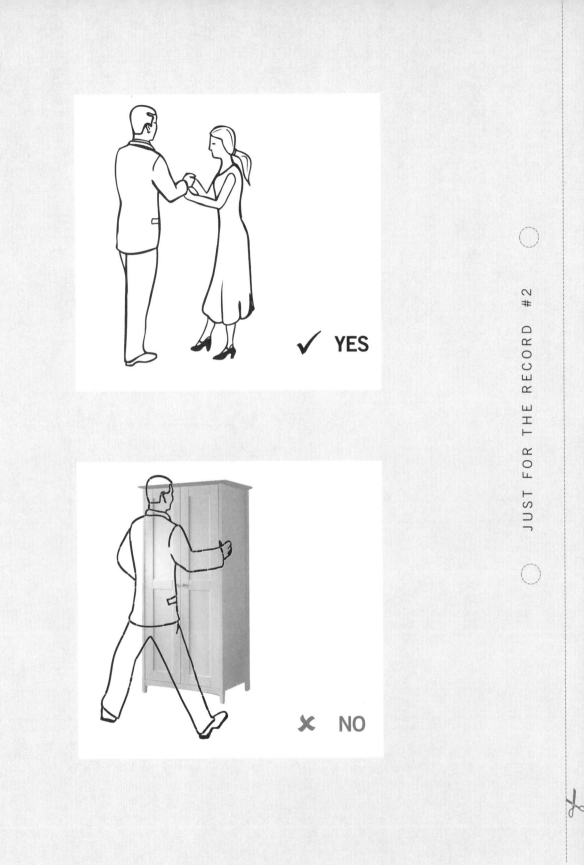

Slow dancing is an intimate position and can, if the right amount of chafing and rubbing ensues, result in a canoe magically appearing in your underpants. This should not be encouraged with grinding, nor should it be ignored. Despite her soft smiles and twinkling eyes, she's being introduced to your little soldier a little too early. If this happens, now might be the moment to offer her a drink and back away from the battlefield. This is also recommended if up close you discover that she has bad breath, smelly armpits or spinach in her teeth.

A waltz is the simplest of all the classic dance steps, and the rumba and Argentine tango are very erotic, but if you can't dance ballroom, now isn't the time to start experimenting with complicated moves picked up from Len Goodman. Simply move rhythmically in time to the music—one step per beat—leading your lady by gently pulling and pushing her right hand and taking small steps. Or, if the dance floor is polished, sliding your feet forwards and backwards, and from side to side, moving in a small square.

Patience is the key. Don't start to jolt and jerk her about like you're trying to move a wardrobe round the room; allow your weight to lead her and remember to smile. Whisper to her how beautiful she looks or stare into her eyes (but not too hard or too long, lest she starts to worry she's in the grip of a potential stalker). Holding out for two or three songs in this romantic stance will make her heart skip a few beats.

Know when to leave the dance floor and retire to a table: don't show foolish tenacity if the music changes tempo and "Come on Eileen" blasts out of the stereo. And definitely make a run for it before the conga starts up and you get lumbered with Old Granny Hubbard's rear end.

How to choose and smoke a cigar

Graduation. A new job. Brett Favre retires for the (supposedly) last time. A cigar is the emblem of celebration. Prepared properly, they should take anything from thirty minutes to an hour to smoke, so here's how. Sit back and enjoy without dissolving into a spluttering paroxysm of coughing.

Choosing your cigar:

* Cigars, like fine wines and brandies, come in different strengths: mild, medium-bodied and strong.

* Ask a reputable tobacconist for recommendations, or you might like to buy a six-cigar sampler box from a good brand to start off with.

* A simple rule when choosing a cigar is the color of the outer tobacco leaf, or wrapper. The darker the cigar wrapper, the stronger the taste. For the seasoned cigar connoisseur, stronger cigars have more depth and nuances of flavor. For the beginner, however, stick to the lighter and milder cigars.

* Longer, thinner cigars have a less intense flavor and strength, so are better for beginners.

* Some suggested brands for beginners are Baccarat Luchadores and Flor de Oliva torpedos.

* The price of cigars varies hugely depending on the brand, size, and country of origin. In general, Cuban cigars are considered best quality, and a Montecristo is la crème de la crème. Expect to pay anything between $16 and $64 for a single top-range cigar. The Gurkha "Her Majesty's Reserve" cigar comes in at a whopping $750 per smoke.

KNOW YOUR CIGAR

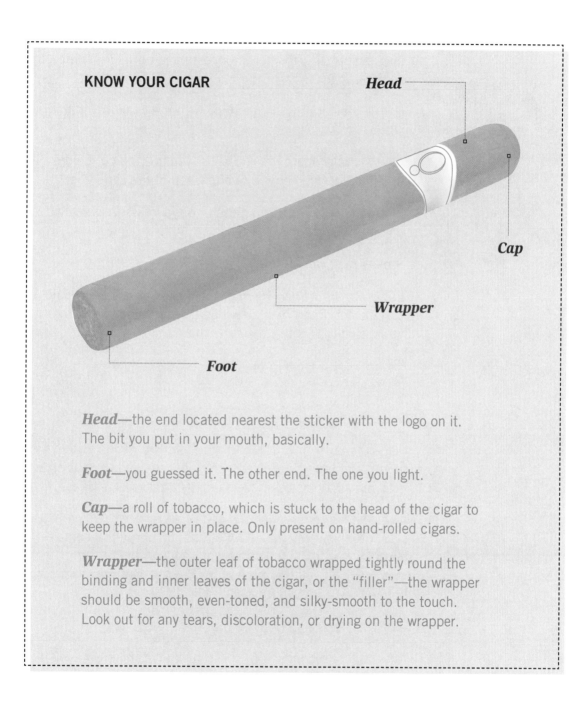

Head—the end located nearest the sticker with the logo on it. The bit you put in your mouth, basically.

Foot—you guessed it. The other end. The one you light.

Cap—a roll of tobacco, which is stuck to the head of the cigar to keep the wrapper in place. Only present on hand-rolled cigars.

Wrapper—the outer leaf of tobacco wrapped tightly round the binding and inner leaves of the cigar, or the "filler"—the wrapper should be smooth, even-toned, and silky-smooth to the touch. Look out for any tears, discoloration, or drying on the wrapper.

How to cut a cigar:

You might have seen it in the movies, but never bite the end off a hand-rolled cigar. Use a cigar cutter.

1. Grip the cutter with your strongest hand between thumb and forefinger.

2. Hold the cigar in your free hand with the head facing the cutter.

3. Find the line where the cap ends, you need to cut before this line, leaving about a quarter-inch of the cap intact.

4. Insert the cigar. You can close one eye to assist in your lining up the cigar properly.

5. Steady the cigar.

6. Cut down all the way through the cigar with a strong, quick, precise cut. Don't hesitate when cutting as any fumbling or indecision may cause the cigar to unfurl.

How to light a cigar:

1. Use a wooden match or butane lighter.

2. Place the cigar in your mouth, holding it between your thumb and index finger an inch from the head. If your cigar is as big as a baguette, use as many fingers as it takes.

3. Light the lighter or strike the match and place the cigar tip so it is hovering an eighth of an inch above the flame— don't let it actually touch the flame. Also, wait for the match to fully light and the phosphorous smell to disappear before taking it to your cigar.

4. Puff on the cigar and rotate it at the same time.

5. After twenty seconds or so the outer rim of the cigar should glow slightly. At this point you will be able to draw smoke.

How to smoke a cigar:

1. As you puff, rotate your cigar every thirty seconds or so.

2. Take the cigar smoke into your mouth slowly, but DO NOT INHALE, or you'll choke like you did when you took your first toke on that cigarette behind John's dad's garage. The whole point of cigar-smoking is to savor the taste in your mouth and NOT to inhale. The nicotine is absorbed through the mouth and nose's membranes and is so strong that you will get a buzz even though you are not inhaling the smoke into your lungs. See HEALTH WARNING below!

3. Savor the taste of the cigar in your mouth and then blow the smoke out.

4. Don't smoke too fast—you'll burn the tobacco and ruin the flavor—or too slow—you'll have to keep relighting it. About a puff per minute is perfect.

5. When the ash finger exceeds a half-inch it should fall off of its own accord. However, the longer the ash finger, the higher quality the cigar. Don't tap your cigar on the edge of the ashtray as you do when smoking a cigarette, but if the ash doesn't fall off by itself, lightly shake the cigar until it does.

6. Once you're down to the last two inches you'll begin to get an aftertaste and the cigar will get hotter. That's the end of the road for this cigar.

Don't stub out a burning cigar. Simply place it in an ashtray and it will automatically stop burning. Once the cigar is cold, empty the ashtray and dispose of the cigar stubs to minimize odors. Stubbing out a lit cigar will stink the whole place out with an acrid smell which will linger for several weeks.

Advanced tips for the novice cigar connoisseur:

* Smoke a varied selection of mild single cigars at first; you don't want to blow a whole month's wages on a box of Cubans if they make you throw up.

* Always inspect the wrapper—not the packet, the outer layer of cigar—for rips and tears. Roll the cigar between finger and thumb; if there are any hard areas the cigar might be "plugged" and unsmokable, any soft spots and it might not be packed tight enough and won't give a good draw.

* To prevent drying, only remove a cigar from its packet when you mean to smoke it.

* Have a glass of cold water at hand to sip between puffs. This will help cleanse your palate and might also help if the whole experience makes you feel sick.

* Brandy, Scotch, and coffee complement a cigar. If you're trying out several cigars don't vary your drink as this can affect the flavor of the cigar.

HEALTH WARNING

It is not unusual for novice cigar-smokers to feel sick or actually be sick as a result of their first taste of a cigar. This is due to nicotine overdose. An average cigarette contains 1mg of nicotine. A large cigar such as a torpedo or a Churchill, on the other hand, may contain as much as 400mg of nicotine, or the equivalent of smoking twenty cigarettes at once.

How to open a bottle of champagne without blinding an innocent bystander

When popping open an ice-cold bottle of bubbly, never aim it at the waiter, your granny's bottom, or the very expensive chandelier hanging in the dining room. A male nemesis, an unruly houseguest, or a strategically placed apple on Heidi Montag's head, however, are perfectly legitimate targets.

Here's how to open a bottle of Bolly like you've been drinking the stuff your whole life:

1. Remove the foil, revealing the wire cage covering the cork below. Loosen and remove the wire cage by twisting the ends until they become free.

2. Place a dish towel or fabric napkin over the bottleneck, fully covering the cork.

3. Angle the bottle towards a wall and firmly but slowly twist the cork out with your thumb controlling the pop—the cloth will help give leverage. Don't remove your thumb at any point—until you hear the pop. Don't pull the cork out once you feel it getting loose; just twist the bottle or the cork itself until it comes free.

4. When pouring champagne, angle the neck of the glass slightly to avoid getting a glass full of bubbles.

5. If the glass does fizz up with bubbles, simply place a clean finger in the middle of the champagne and the bubbles will miraculously disappear.

How to stop staring at other women

fig 1: Looking

Sex is everywhere. So, unless you walk around wearing a blindfold and doing your best impression of Mr. Bump, you're going to encounter attractive females. All perfectly natural. There is nothing wrong with wanting to look, or even looking. It's how you do it that matters. It's a fine line between looking and leching. Looking is an appreciative gander lasting anything up to three seconds. Beyond this watershed and you're leching.

If you recognize any of the above symptoms, fear not. There are several ways of curbing the pernicious ogling tendency.

fig 2: Leching

Wholesome diversion/distraction therapy. Channel your horn through a healthy and vigorous physical outlet like curling or bungee jumping. Avoid swimming until you are well and truly on the road to recovery.

Negative visualization therapy. Partake in the rather drastic remedy of picturing the girl you're looking at taking an extremely painstaking, time-consuming, face-contorting grunt.

Self-inflicted aversion therapy (figs. 3 & 4). If you're struggling to beat the urges, administer your own beating—wear an elastic band around your wrist, and snap it every time you take a cheeky peek or feel tempted to linger on a particularly eye-catching pair of buttocks.

Learn to appreciate what you've got. Send your girlfriend a nice text message at work and be more forgiving after arguments. At the end of the day, it's natural to find other girls attractive but it's a little self-destructive to act on the urges that often follow. And be aware of the dangers of vocalizing your ogling, or being caught in the act by your girl. A little self-control equals a lot of self-respect—something you'll have none of once you've been pelted with a handbag at thirty paces.

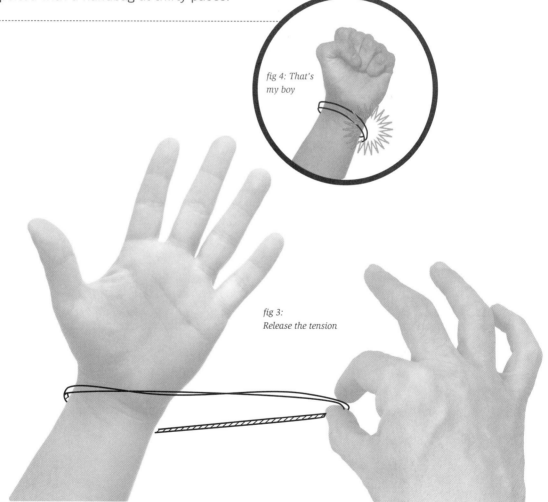

fig 4: That's my boy

fig 3:
Release the tension

How to rid yourself of the dreaded man-boobs

Man cans. Moobs. Chap baps. Big bones. Call them what you will, man-boobs are the bane of many a young chap's life. They're why you don't run for the bus, wear that tight-fitting T-shirt, or take your undershirt off in bed. They are the sole reason your sex-starved friends spike your pint, plonk a dress over your shoulders, call you Shirley, and cop a feel. Friends can be cruel companions. So too man-boobs. Here's how to banish them for good. The man breasts, that is.

Patience. The least active of all the options, suitable only for younger victims of unwelcome chest growth. During puberty, hormonal imbalance—a shift in your natural estrogen levels—can sometimes mean breasts where breasts should not be. With time the imbalance corrects itself and the body goes back to normal. But if your eighteenth birthday comes along and you can't lean over the cake to blow out the candles for fear of setting your tits on fire, it's probably time to consider some of the other options.

Exercise. More often than not man-boobs are a direct consequence of being overweight and underfit. The fatty tissue around your chest is just as easily banished as the fat elsewhere on your body. Aerobic exercise is your first port of call. Walking, swimming, five-aside footie, anything that gets you off your backside and running about. **Exercise for one hour three days a week. Throw in some chest exercises and you'll be kissing your sports bra goodbye after a couple of months!**

Strength Training. Specific upper chest exercises are perfect for turning your freak-show chest into a walking advert for muscle beach. Three sets of ten decline push-ups and incline bench presses twice a week will help you lose weight and develop your pectoral muscles.

Decline Push-ups. Lie flat on your chest with your palms facing the floor and your arms slightly more than shoulder width apart. Lift your feet up into an inclined position—the edge of the sofa will do fine.

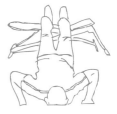

Keep your back straight and push yourself off the floor while breathing out. Inhale as you lower yourself. **Note: you must have your feet raised, as this puts pressure on the muscles in your man-boob region.**

Incline Bench Presses. First of all adjust the bench so it is at a 45-degree angle. Place some light weights on either end of the bar. Lie under the bar, with your back resting against the bench and your feet flat to the floor. Lift the bar with your palms facing towards your feet and your arms slightly out from your shoulders. Slowly lower the weight down onto your chest, breathing in as you do so. To complete one rep lift the bar vertically, exhaling at the same time, until your arms are almost fully extended, but make sure your elbows don't lock, and then lower the bar back onto your chest.

Don't "bounce" the bar off your chest—if the bar falls onto your rib cage man-boobs will be the least of your worries. **Note: you can use a dumbbell in each hand instead of a rack and bar.**

Diet. Cutting down on fatty foods and maintaining a low-calorie diet will ultimately make a difference over time. It's a tough decision but learn to pass on the McMan-breast to go. Estrogen compounds should also be avoided. They can be found in soya and, ironically, some nuts such as almonds. (And no, stuffing your girlfriend with macaroons and tofu will not give her a budget boob job.) Two-thirds of your daily food intake should be fruit or veg, and you should swap white bread for whole wheat and up your protein intake by eating more lean chicken and fish. Follow these guidelines and soon enough you'll be able to get your kit off in public without the police arresting you for indecent exposure.

Surgery. A last resort and one that can leave significant scarring to your body and bank account. Unless you're thinking of entering Mr. Universe or genuinely feel like your moobs are ruining your life this shouldn't even be an option. Explore all other avenues first. Exercise, exercise and more exercise. And keep away from the Family Bucket.

How to remove a zit before a first date

Bull's bile, ostrich eggs, olive oil, plant resin, flour and milk spread all over your face—ancient Egyptians really knew how to treat themselves, especially when acne was concerned, and they're not the only ones. The international quest for miracle cures is still going strong. Americans spend $100 million each year on treating the dreaded "zits." But if you've ever turned up to a date only to experience the torturous taunts of "Hey Rudolph" or "I thought Comic Relief *was next year?" you'll know $100 million is a drop in the ocean compared to emotional bankruptcy.*

You can help prevent pimples forming by keeping your skin clean using an anti-bacterial medicated face wash like Clearasil. Moisturize your skin every day with a light, non-greasy cream and, once a week, deep steam your face. To do this, fill a bowl with boiling water, add some drops of lavender oil if you like, **and hold your face over the bowl and cover your head and shoulders with a towel.** The steam will open up the pores and help clear impurities. Drinking water and not eating fatty foods all the time also helps. Stress can also contribute to bad skin outbreaks, so if possible try taking up a relaxing sport like swimming, running, or disc golf. If your spots are very bad and nothing seems to make a difference, see your doctor, who may prescribe antibiotics, an antibiotic lotion, or other medication.

If you still find yourself fending off the pen-wielding dot-to-dot fanatics before you go on a hot date, here's some drastic last-minute tips:

The night before your date, cover any spots with a generous blob of white toothpaste. This is a very effective trick used by supermodels. The toothpaste often completely dries up spots overnight. Lavender oil or tea-tree oil can also work wonders. Others swear by the soggy mulch on the bottom of the soap—apply directly to the spot and allow to dry.

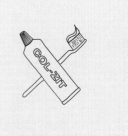

If the spot hasn't dried up and you wake up with a big yellow eruption on your chin or other facial extremity, you're going to have to get squeezing. **Squeeze in the morning to give your mini-Mount Vesuvius time to calm down.** Clean your hands first and use a folded-up tissue to gently squeeze the spot. Don't apply silly amounts of pressure or use your nails as you risk permanently scarring your skin. After squeezing grab a washcloth, soak it in hot water—not boiling, you don't want to burn your face off— and push it hard against the spot. This will reduce the soreness and make the blight on your otherwise-perfect face less visible. To avoid infection, get a cotton ball, dip it in fresh lime juice or tea-tree oil, and clean the spot. This will really sting but it's better than a could-be girlfriend calling the cops because you turn up smelling of toothpaste and wearing a balaclava.

Your face here

How to hit the bull's-eye in darts

They might not have the rugged good looks and muscle tone of an NFL quarterback or NBA all-star. They might not be picked to model topless for the new fragrance of Right Guard. And they might huff and puff their way up to the throw line and groan when they bend over to pick up a bounced-out dart, but for all that, darts players stand alone in the pantheon of sport's history, for darts is the only sport in which the training regime positively demands chugging limitless amounts of beer.

Grab your pint and step up to the throw line like a world champion.

Stance. Take a manly swig of your ale, then take position, standing side-on to the dartboard, with your leading foot on the throw line. Your other foot should be about shoulder width behind the front one. Distribute your weight evenly; don't lean forward as this will unbalance you. Stand up straight, shoulders back and in line with the board.

A steady arm is the key to accurate throwing. Keep both feet planted to the ground and try not to lift your heels as you throw. Instead, focus on holding your body fixed and steady.

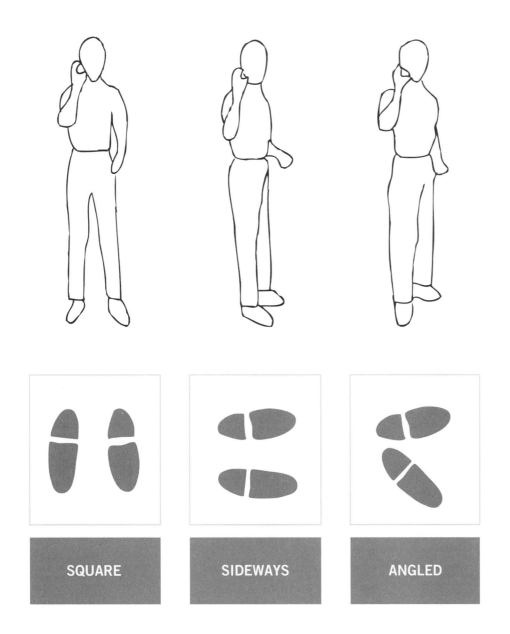

SQUARE

SIDEWAYS

ANGLED

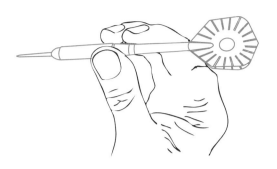

Grip. Balance the dart evenly in your hand and find where the center of gravity is. Roll the dart towards your fingertips with your thumb and place the pad of your thumb just behind the located center of gravity. Use only two fingers and your thumb to lightly grip the dart, your index and middle finger with your middle finger at the front. Bend all your fingers with the tips facing the board. Your grip should be firm but relaxed, so if your fingers start going white, you're holding the dart too hard. Fold any fingers that aren't gripping the dart away from the dart. Don't touch the flight, or you'll put spin on the dart and it will shoot off into somebody's pint. This will earn you a black eye, not a bull's-eye.

Set-up. Line up the dart with the bull's-eye. Hold the dart with your elbow straight, the dart held level and never at an angle. Keep it pointed straight at the board and never downwards, no matter what part of the board you are aiming for. Keep your eye, the dart and the target in one long line. Keep your elbow pointing at the floor. Your shoulders should be at an angle of 50–80 degrees to the board.

Pullback. The power for your throw comes from your wrist, fingers and arm. Pull your hand back towards your shoulder and aim the dart just above the bull's-eye. Arch your wrist slightly to elevate the dart. Bend your knees. Focus on your target and slowly move your arm into position. Pull back as far as is possible without slipping a disc.

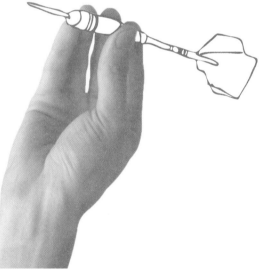

Release. Thrust your arm forward and release the dart. Except for your throwing arm your body should make no other movement. Your elbow will flex slightly at the highest point and towards the end of the throw—that's when you should release the dart, not before. Don't flick your wrist, just use your arm—the pros do this to increase acceleration but until you have the throw sorted it's best left to the experts. Always keep the dart parallel with the floor and release all your fingers at the same time.

Follow through. Your hand should point slightly below the bull's-eye and your arm should be straight. Hold this final stance—this doesn't help the accuracy but you'll look cool.

Advanced tips:

- Practice your throw. Try to hit the same spot several times in a row. Once you've nailed a good stance, grip, and throwing technique, with practice you will improve your accuracy.

- Watch the pros and study their grips and stances. Copy them until you find one that works for you.

- Check your stance by throwing with your eyes closed—you'll be able to tell if you're moving with the deftness of a Jedi.

- Check how far your dart is entering the board. The barrel should not be touching the board—if it is going in too deep, you are throwing too hard.

- Do some stretches before playing to relax and warm the muscles.

- Sandpaper the end of your darts to keep the tips sharp. Place onto the sandpaper and rotate like you're sharpening a pencil.

- Breathe—practicing your breathing technique as in yoga will help keep you centered, focused, and calm.

How to open a jammed jam jar like a Greek god

Hercules fought off the hounds of hell. Atlas held the heavens on his shoulders. Zeus...well, Zeus just sat around looking tough. But when the Greek gods gathered at the bottom of Mount Olympus, munching crumpets and drinking tea, there was one feat of strength that outdid all three: the mighty feat of opening the jammed jam jar.

Here's how to succeed where gods have failed, and enjoy your toast and jam:

1. Tap a spoon around the lid top or tap the lid against the table edge. This should release some air pressure and allow you to pop it open first try. If still resistant, use a teaspoon or flat-head screwdriver to lift the lid up slightly at several points around the lid to break the vacuum.

2. If you're still struggling, wrap a damp tea towel round the lid and have another go. If that still fails, wrap a thick rubber band round the lid edge to give you increased purchase.

3. Toast going cold? Still no jam? Run the lid under hot water for at least a minute. This should expand the metal so it will slide off with a twist.

If all else fails stab a sharp knife through the lid. This will break the vacuum, disperse the pressure, and allow you to have a jam sandwich at long last.

How to tell if a woman has had a boob job

Awestruck by a foreign woman's audacity to brave the frat boy-packed American beaches, we ponder: "Are they real?" Followed by, "I wonder what they feel like?" And, last but not least, "Would they explode on a plane?" Within minutes our girlfriend pipes up, "No, they're not real, they feel like sandbags, and, yes, they wouldn't last five minutes on a long haul. Now stop drooling and read your Tom Clancy."

If you're still curious, here's how to tell the difference:

Size. If she looks like she's smuggling watermelons they're probably fake. Or, she's smuggling watermelons.

Shape. Boob jobs look hard and muscular. Real breasts look soft and curve out slightly like a ski slope and are tear-shaped.

Position. If her cleavage is bigger than your fist or a space no wider than a quarter, they're fake. Normal breasts begin at armpit height but implants are regularly placed higher up the chest.

Movement. When a girl's lying down, her breasts normally fall to the side and do not stand to attention. While bending over, her breasts should give in to gravity and sag a little. Real breasts are made of fat so they jiggle like jelly when the lady runs.

Texture. Unless you were around in the blitz you might not know what a sandbag feels like, so think bag of sugar instead. If they feel harder than normal breasts, or unusually firm, they're probably about as real as Santa Claus. Oh, sorry. You didn't know?

Other clues. Nipples should point in the same direction and be in the middle of the boob, not on top or under it.

How to get rid of a love bite

Put a few wet spoons in the freezer for fifteen minutes, remove one, and press the rounded side against the hickey, applying a little pressure. Hold it there until it's no longer cold, then repeat with another cold spoon. This can help reduce the bruising.

* Some swear by white toothpaste—smear over the bite and leave it there.

* Break up the bruising with a circular lid—a lipstick lid is perfect—press it around the love bite.

* Apply arnica cream or take arnica pills. Arnica speeds up healing and is said to reduce bruises.

* Alternatively, wear a polo neck, scarf, or necktie, or all three. Tell friends and your mom that you're thinking of joining a bowling club if they get suspicious.

* If desperate, reach for some concealer. Add a few layers and blend in with a cotton ball.

How to get hold of a good contractor

The best way to extend the lengthy and painful process of remodeling your home is to try serving as head of the project yourself. Save yourself the energy, frustration, and six months of straight nagging from your wife—hire a contractor.

Save your sanity and find yourself an honest contractor:

* Get recommendations from friends and relatives or even next-door neighbors for a job that is similar to yours.

* Get other plumbers or builders to recommend someone. Hardware stores may also make recommendations. If you've bought a new sink from the local hardware store they might be able to inform you of a trusty tradesman.

* Feel free to ask for a list of references. Work your way from the middle of the list and call at least three or four people.

* Follow up word-of-mouth references also. If your Auntie Marjorie says your Uncle Steve said Great-grandma Hilda heard Father Lovecraft had his kitchen done by a nice guy from a few towns over, call the reference up and find out the facts.

* Get at least three quotes or estimates for the job.

* Get a written quote including a fixed deadline, an onsite assessment and sales tax. Never go ahead on a verbal agreement only; they could still be there after the Olympics.

* A good contractor is normally busy. If they're free straight away, be wary.

* Work out a payment schedule. Be dubious if they want you to pay in cash and deliver the money in a black trash can liner to a deserted garage out of town.

* Always being available via phone or email shows a commitment to new customers and an organized approach to work.

* Keep a file of work being done and receipts etc. This will help should you get into a dispute.

How to encourage a sexually self-conscious girlfriend to feel good about her body

Aphrodite's legs, Pamela Anderson's breasts, J-Lo's bum, and Christina Aguilera's tum. No matter what a girl is blessed with, thanks to size zero and celebrity idolatry, a body complex is normally close at hand. And when that complex spills over into the bedroom, the physical side of your relationship can take a turn for the worse.

If things have gone quiet under the duvet, a good way to give things a kick-start is to start by banning intercourse—contradictory though it may seem. Good sex needs mutual emotional and physical trust, so if this has been lost, go back to the basics. Remember that first breast you brushed your hand against in junior high? Remember how good it felt? You've got to get back to that place. Kiss for longer and prolong foreplay. And don't even think about having full intercourse.

Slow down your sex life to a stop. Touch her back, feet, arms, neck, hair, everywhere but her jubilees. Shower together and wash her body. The point is to get physical with one another so that she feels how much you love her and her body, no matter what her insecurities.

Use all five senses. The touch of a feather; the smell of lavender, the sound of the ocean, whisperings of when you first met. All these things will turn her on emotionally which, in turn, will turn her on sexually. A woman's largest erogenous zone is her brain. Remember that and you can't go wrong.

Put all thoughts of what you'd really like to do with her to the back of your mind. This is about reconnecting with her, so concentrate on finding out what she likes and what makes her respond and relax. This doesn't mean you should leave a questionnaire on her pillow—just follow her lead and stop if she feels embarrassed or uncomfortable at any point.

Take her away for a weekend, buy her some sexy underwear, and let your research do the talking.

If you still find she's reluctant to have sex with the lights on try to communicate further with her. Saying, "You're beautiful to me" or, "What does it matter what others think?" will not help, no matter how heartfelt your sentiments. Listen to what she has to say and how she is feeling about herself. This is something she has to address herself, so be patient and let her know that you adore her and you'll wait until she's ready.

Support her. Once she admits to having body image problems she can go about sorting them out. This might involve going to the gym or talking to a counsellor. Don't get impatient and start raising your eyebrows every time she reaches for the butter or an extra helping of mashed potatoes. Instead make it a joint effort by cycling or jogging together, and support her by laying off the booze and pizza for the time being when you're with her.

Where sex is concerned these things take time. You'll know when she's ready. Don't pester her. When you're having the best sex you've ever had with a woman you love, you'll never look back.

How to show your mom how iTunes works without strangling her with a USB cord

There's no doubt that mothers are the greatest thing since sliced bread. In fact, they probably sliced the bread in the first place. But that doesn't mean there aren't moments in our lives when we would sooner starve than give mother dearest a helping hand.

These situations normally involve technology and, more specifically, computers. Or worse still, the double whammy of computer and iPod. Brace yourself, take a deep breath and maybe a stiff drink—follow the step-by-step instructions below and before you know it you will have an eternally grateful mom loudly singing along to her Dido tracks and boasting about her downloads.

Download iTunes from their website: www.apple.com/itunes/download.
Choose your operating system, check the box and enter her email address to begin the download. Once downloaded, an icon called iTunes Setup will appear on her desktop. Double click and start installation. Follow the on-screen instructions, shushing your mom every time she asks you a question even a leading scientist at NASA couldn't answer. Now set up a desktop shortcut, make iTunes the default music player and apply for Apple software updates. Be considerate; remember that when it comes to computers your mom has the mental capacity of an orangutan. Actually that's probably a little unfair to the ape.

Once installed, iTunes will scan her hard drive for any music files and import them. Get your mom to fetch her favorite CDs and open iTunes. Making sure you're online, insert each CD and wait for the computer to connect to the Internet. iTunes will then automatically collect information from the Compact Disc Database (CDDB for short) and display each CD's name, artist and song titles. This will make your mom say, "Oh. How did it do that?" Just ignore her and click on the bottom right-hand corner button marked "Import." The CD will now be imported. You will know the process is complete when her computer chimes, to which your mom will respond by saying, "Oh. What was that?" You will smile fondly and say nothing.

Connect her iPod via a USB port. Make sure she knows where to plug it in—and follow the instructions. iTunes will download all the songs in the library on to her iPod. Don't do anything else while it does this, just be patient and glare at your mom. She can now make some choices about what content she wants to sync by clicking the tabs at the top of the iPod window. Click "Apply" at the bottom right-hand corner of the window once she has finished and her James Blunt, Neil Diamond, and Barbra Streisand albums will be transferred to her iPod.

Create an iTunes Store account. Choose the iTunes Store option in the left-hand menu and click "Sign In." Choose "Create New Account." Agree to the iTunes Store's terms. On the next screen enter your mom's email and get her to give you a password. Suggest your mom chooses a member of the family's date of birth for her password as this is a good way to guarantee she'll never forget it. Either that or Drake Hogestyn, *Days of our Lives*, or Michael Bublé should suffice. For the secret question, type in, "Which amazing son helped you install iTunes?" and tick the newsletters option. Click "Continue" and enter your mom's billing details including her address, her card number and security code. At this point you can also get her to make you a cup of tea, write down her card details and get your dad into a whole lot of trouble. "But darling, I swear I've never even heard of barbarasbigbouncyones.com."

How to sell all of your old toys on eBay

Grab your He-Man, Thundercat, Stretch Armstrong, or Space Hopper, give them a good cleaning and a kiss and prepare them for their big send-off. Avoid eye contact. They're never going to forgive you for this; all those years of joy sold for $8.00 plus postage and handling.

Register with the site. Get online and click "register" to create a seller's account. Choose an online ID. This is the name other people will see you as so don't choose an embarrassing nickname from school. "Pissy Pants" or "Twinkle Nuts" won't inspire customer confidence. Once you've filled in the registration form you'll receive an email asking you to confirm your account. Confirm, return to the site, register your billing with PayPal and you're done. Now you're ready to start selling.

Research. Search for similar items on eBay and note down selling prices and info. This will help you with the title, description, price, payment method, postage cost and photo forms you'll need to fill in.

List your toy for sale. Use key words in your "Listing Title," including the make and model of the toy, any other key details such as the color and the recommended age range of the toy, dimensions, interesting features and any damage, repairs, etc.—you are limited to fifty-five words, so make them count. The more key detail you add, the better chance of a sale. See below for eBay jargon.

Take a photo of your toy. You will need a digital camera for this part. Use a plain white or dark wall as a backdrop (pin up a white sheet if necessary). Keep the photo clear and clean, and shoot the item head-on with no other items in the picture other than the toy you are selling. Use this shot as your "Gallery Photo." Take a few more photos at different angles, zooming in on particular features or any damage or repairs. Make sure the lighting is right—shoot the toy outside in good light if possible, or if not, take the photo in a bright room in daylight and light the shot with a few desk lamps inside. Try to avoid shadows and switch off the flash on your camera.

Add a photo. Download the pictures on to your hard drive, choose the "Bring your item to life" option on the "Sell your item" section of the site and click "Add pictures." Browse to select the pictures on your hard drive, then select and click OK.

Once listed. eBay will automatically categorize your item. The total cost of selling the item is the Insertion Fee; this is the charge eBay makes for listing your item on their site and is matched to the starting price. Unless you're selling a priceless Steiff bear, keep the starting price for your cuddly friends reasonable. Chances are your Stretch Armstrong's emotional value won't always translate into hard cash.

The sale. When a listing is successful you'll get an email from eBay detailing your buyer's payment method and postage address. Once you receive the money, package the items carefully and take them to the post office.

Wave goodbye to childhood innocence. Get thinking about how to blow the proceeds in a suitably grown-up fashion.

SOME EBAY SELLER JARGON:

New in Box (NIB). Informs the buyer the original packaging has not been either tampered with or opened since purchase Effectively, brand new and mint condition.

Gently used (GU). Taken out of the box but well looked after with no marks or damage. Pretty much original condition.

Excellent. Well kept, clean but may have small scratches and marks.

Very good. Scratches but no major dents or discrepancies.

Good. Some scratches and dents.

Fair. Well used and therefore well worn, toys with dents and many scratches.

Poor. Highly damaged and possibly even broken but may be good for spare parts.

How to win an arm wrestle

Winner

Settling a dispute like a man can be a nasty pursuit. Sometimes it's best to turn tail and shout, "Leg it" at the top of your voice. Other times, if you're feeling particularly upbeat about your chances of outdoing a fellow male, why not challenge him to an arm wrestle to settle the argument? Just don't wimp out at the last minute and ask for a thumb war instead.

Here are the key factors to ensure you bring this one home:

Feet. Sit as close to the table as possible and if you're right-handed put your right foot firmly on the ground as far as is comfortable in front of your left, left in front of right if you're left-handed. Hook your other foot around the chair leg for added support as you wrestle.

Grip. "Wrapping" your thumb is the most effective way to grip the opponent's hand. Reach for their hand, grip as normal but rather than having your thumb resting over both your and your opponent's hand tuck, or "wrap," it under your fingers.

Arm placement. When you place your elbow on the table keep your upper arm close to your chest. This gives stability and limits shaking and also aligns your arm with your body to give you added power. Keep your arm straight in front of your shoulders. Never let your arm leave this position.

Use your shoulders and upper torso. Don't push with your arm alone, but use all the power from your upper body. Your arm merely channels that power. After all, your biceps are nothing in comparison to all the muscles in your shoulders and back unless you're Rafael Nadal, who has abnormal biceps the size of a young child's head.

Arm-wrestling moves:

Back pressure. Pull your opponent's arm across the table towards you. With his body stretched, and with the side pressure you're placing on his arm, he'll lose the power of his body and have to fight you with his arm alone. Be quick, otherwise he'll use the same move on you first.

The Hook. Curl your wrist around your opponent's hand—the most common form of arm-wrestling move—and maneuver your body over your arm. Keep wrist contact steady as you wrestle so that the power is delivered through the wrist rather than your arm.

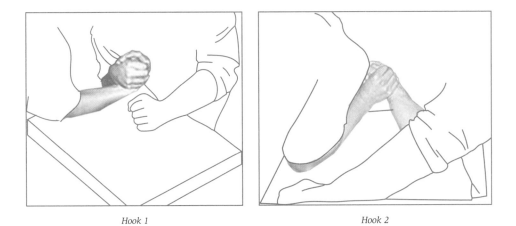

Hook 1   *Hook 2*

Press. Best technique if you have a stronger upper body than your opposite number. Keep your arm close to your body and use wrist pressure to maneuver your opponent's hand so that his palm is facing the ceiling with your hand on top. Then force his arm down using your shoulder and triceps strength.

Top roll. With this move you're using guile, not muscle. At the start of the match, spread his fingers wide and attempt to open out his hand. Wiggle your hand out of his grip, walking your fingers to the edge of his hand—the closer to his fingertips the better. His hand should be wrapped around your wrist and your hand should be sticking out the top of his—similar to when your girlfriend refuses to hold your hand properly because you wouldn't wait for her hair straighteners to heat up. At this point push against his hand and while he's attempting to regain his grip, nail the match.

Top Roll

Advanced tips:

----

*   If you're competing in a tournament, vary your tactics—this will rest certain muscles between rounds and also confuse your opposition.

*   Shake hands with your opponent before the match to gauge how strong they are.

*   Try to prevent your wrist from being bent backwards. It is harder to win from this position.

*   Don't twist your shoulder and look away from the table. Keep your head and shoulders facing forward and pivot round by exerting pressure from the whole of your upper body.

*   Look your opponent in the eye and smile. Blowing kisses is probably a bit over the top though.

Know your beef

Used to eating our beef in ground form in a hamburger bun, few of us actually know one end of a cow from the other, let alone recognize a piece of chuck if it were to hit us in the face. And that can be problematic when you're in the queue at the butcher's doing some shopping for your lady or mom.

Here's how to tell your rump from your rib eye and your chuck from your shank—and how to cook them when you get home:

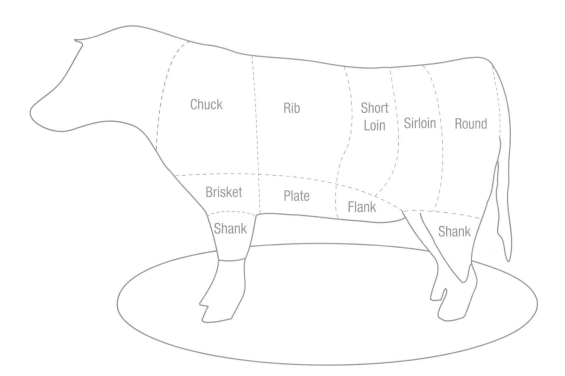

Chuck. Chuck steaks are particularly popular for use as ground beef. Chuck steaks are usually cooked with liquid as a pot roast or stew. Good for braising and long cooking as the meat is nicely marbled with fat and will flavor and moisten the dish as it cooks.

Rib. Very tender rib meat—contains part of the short ribs, rib eye steaks, prime rib, and standing rib roasts.

Plate. The plate contains the other part of the short ribs as well as skirt steak, which is great for fajitas.

Flank. The flank is used primarily for grinding, but also produces the long, flat flank steak, best used in a London broil.

Brisket. A cut frequently used in barbecue. Also used for stewing, braising, and salting, for example in pastrami.

Shank. From the foreleg of the cow. Needs very long, slow cooking. Usually used for stews and soups. Veal shank is used for the classic Italian dish *osso bucco*.

Sirloin. Less tender but more flavorful than the short loin, the sirloin is where you find top and bottom sirloin steaks like the tri-tip, as well as beef tenderloin.

Short Loin. Get your short loin bone-in and you're treated to deliciously massive T-bone and Porterhouse steaks. If you go boneless here, you'll have a nice N.Y. strip and filet mignon.

Round. Lean, slightly tough, and lower fat cuts. These meats, round steak, eye of round, and roasts, require moist cooking.

To braise a piece of meat, first seal it off in a very hot pan for thirty seconds or so on each side. Then add cooking liquid to the pot—beer, wine, stock, etc.—and cook on a very low simmer until the meat is tender and easily torn apart with a fork.

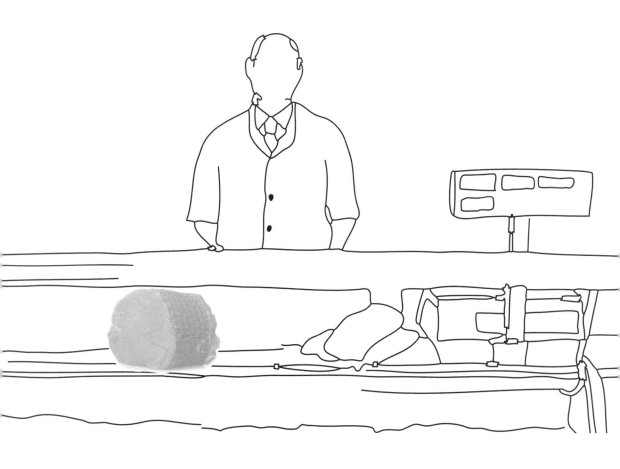

Know your penis and condom size

Penises can be more trouble than they're worth. Sure, they give us the most pleasure on earth. Yes, we love nothing more than to get it out and wave it around after a few drinks. It's our fifth limb, chief of staff, and second brain. But it can also be the bane of our life.

Here's how to get to know your little fella:

Corpora cavernosa. This is the part of your penis that becomes engorged with blood when erect.

Glans penis. Informally known as your helmet, this is the main sensory hub of the penis.

External urethral orifice. The departure lounge of your penis.

Corona. The outer rim of the glans penis, not to be confused with the Mexican beer of the same name.

Frenulum. Also called the banjo string.

Corpus spongiosum. The spongy tissue below the corpora cavernosa.

Urethra. The tunnel your semen and urine travel through.

Scrotum. Probably the worst piece of divine mechanics in the inventory of God's achievements. Baboon's bright red ass, take a back seat!

Condom size, or how to measure your penis:

Knowing your condom size doesn't mean you should pull out a tape measure and mark up in the middle of Superdrug. You're much better off measuring yourself in the comfort and warmth of your own home.

How to measure your equipment properly:

* Get an erection. Use visual aids if necessary (browse your mom's *Victoria's Secret* catalog if you've no top-shelf magazines at hand).

* Grab a ruler. Hold your pride and joy at a right angle away from your body, and place the end of the ruler at its base, close to the pubic bone. Record the length to the tip of your todger.

* Now, with a tape measure, measure the width of your shaft halfway down. If you have no tape measure at hand, wrap a piece of string or a strip of paper round your girth, then measure the string/paper length in inches with ruler.

* Zip up, put ruler away and, depending on your measurements, cheer loudly or meekly log on and Google "penis enhancers."

The average penis length is roughly 3 inches or 7.5cm at rest and 5½ inches or 13.5cm erect, but if you measure between 3-9 inches erect all condoms and brands on the market will fit you fine. On the other hand, if you've got an unusually small or large girth, condoms will stand a good chance of either falling off or, if they're too tight, splitting, leaving you in a mess—in more ways than one. Check the packaging for the "nominal width" using the guide on the next page:

Not to scale

Condom width guide:

Thin penis. 2 in. nominal width condom will stretch to fit a penis of 4¾ in. girth or less. (Snug or trim fit—although this may not appear on the packaging.)

Average penis. 2¼ in. nominal width condom will fit a penis of 4¾ in.–6 in. girth. (Standard fit—most condoms on the shelf are this size.)

Pringles tube penis. 2¼ in. nominal width condom will stretch to fit a 6 in. plus girth. (Large fit—Trojan's Magnum condom is this size.)

If you still can't find a condom that works for you, ask your GP or visit your local GUM clinic for advice on which condom is best for your unique appendage.

Know your condoms:

Extra safe. Best for peace of mind, you could wear one of these in a nuclear reactor and come out unscathed.

Featherlight. Best for male sensation. Less peace of mind about splitting but still high protection.

Ribbed. "Ribbed, for her pleasure." And perfectly safe too.

Tickler. One for the ladies, but less protection, so save this for when you're in a long-term, stable relationship.

Natural lamb. Made from sheep's innards and suitable for allergy sufferers. More natural sensation but less protection against STDs and HIV, and could put you off your roast lamb for life.

Novelty condoms. Edible, color, flavor, tingling, and heat—not always safe to use during sexual intercourse.

Latex vs. polyurethane. Most people use latex condoms, but those who are allergic to latex use polyurethane which is equal in the protection stakes but not as elastic.

How to throw a strike in bowling

The ten-pin bowling shoe. With seams as thick as the crimps on the crust of your mom's apple pie and leather as shiny as a disco ball, no self-respecting gent would be seen dead wearing a pair outside the bowling alley.

Here's how to make sure your strikes get all the stares instead:

Step 1. Pick up your ball with both hands and rest the weight in your left hand. Place your thumb in the biggest hole, lay your palm flat against the surface of the ball, and slot your middle fingers, not your index finger, in the two remaining holes. Your choices of grip are:

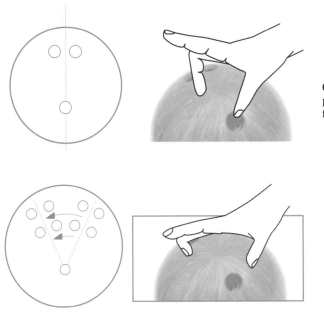

Conventional grip—more purchase on the ball, best for beginners.

Fingertip grip—more scope for the hook ball.

Step 2. Start your approach four steps back from the foul line and slightly to the right of center. Lift the ball to your chin, with your thumb pointing towards your face, and stare down the pins over the ball.

Step 3. Keep your shoulders and hips square to the foul line and step forward with your right foot. Simultaneously push the ball out the length of your arm. Keep your arm straight and let it swing back naturally with the weight of the ball.

Step 4. By the third step the ball should be behind you and your knees bent slightly.

Step 5. As the tip of your left foot lands near the foul line the ball should have swung back in the same arc and you can release. Try to release the ball onto the polished wooden floor in a fluid motion so it glides along the surface; don't throw it.

Step 6. The follow-through should see your arm up in front of your face and your right leg off at an angle like a ballerina.

Where to aim:

To score a strike you need to aim at the "pocket"—the space between pin 1 and 3. By knocking pin 1 over, the ball will crash into pin 3 and fly through to pin 5 before smashing into pin 9. Hitting the pocket maximizes internal pyramid damage and picks off the periphery pins, sending your skittles to the great big bowling alley in the sky.

Mastering the hook ball:

Hook balls curve the path of the ball giving you more chance of hitting the pocket. Use a fingertip grip so your thumb is released first. This disrupts the stability of the ball as your fingers come out a little later, coupled with twisting or rolling your wrist from left to right the spin on the ball will cause it to curve or arc towards the pocket.

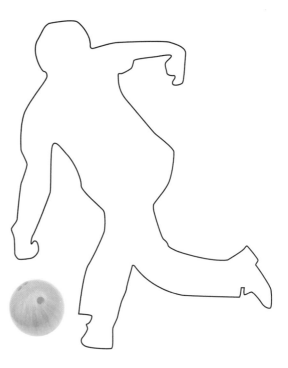

How to choose a bowling ball:

Bowling pros keep their own balls wrapped up in cotton wool and secured in a large leather handbag. Amateurs on the other hand coolly grab the first one they come across, not realizing it's a 16 lb electric-blue-monstrosity that will put their shoulder out of joint after two throws.

Heavier balls knock more pins over but lighter balls are more accurate. Try several balls for weight and size. As a rule, you should opt for the heaviest ball you are comfortable with, but remember you'll be swinging it several times so don't hit above your weight or your arm will get tired very quickly.

Your fingers should fit snugly, but not too snugly, and the space between the holes should be no more than the length of your palm. Once you've found the perfect ball for you, remember it, and use it every time. Balls will usually be color-coded for weight, and they also will have a serial number on them.

A 12 lb ball is perfect for a ten-pin virgin.

An American's guide to playing rugby league

Don't write off rugby just because it's not played much in these parts. A little like football but without the padding, it's one of the manliest games around. A worldwide winter sport, the gentleman's game complements the cold snap of the westerly winds with biting tackles and ice-cool runs. But the arrival of a searing sun doesn't mean the oblong balls have to be relegated to the changing room. Find a clearing on a sandy beach or soft grassy field and you've got yourself a field. Follow these quick, rough-around-the-edges (and somewhat improvised) rules and you've got yourself a game.

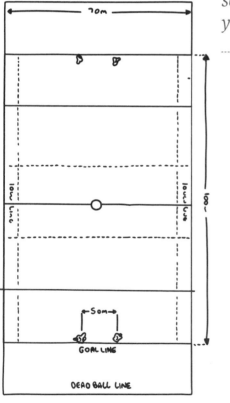

* Separate the teams evenly and mark out the playing field's parameters (including a halfway line) with scores in the sand or with T-shirts.

* Flip a coin. With the rest of his team behind him, the loser of the toss kicks to the opposing team from the halfway line. This is also the procedure from a restart—the team that conceded the try must kick to the scoring team.

* When in possession always pass backwards and, whenever you're tackled, hit the deck. When tackling, be sure to ground the player and then release and allow them to roll the ball back between their legs to a fellow teammate.

* Possession switches to the other team when the ball is lost in contact, kicked under pressure or put down for a try over the line.

* The ball also gets turned over (i.e. possession switches to opposite side) after six consecutive tackles.

* Penalties are not awarded due to the absence of a referee. However, ungentlemanly conduct can be punished with a wedgie.

* To make things easier, lineouts become simple uncontested throw-ins.

* Conversions are also obsolete owing to a lack of goalposts. A tall friend standing with his arms held out like a human Y will be a worthy substitute, but he'll probably get a broken nose and a mouthful of rugby ball for his troubles.

* Tactics: stay in a line, shuffle the pack with varying lengths of passing and make the ball do the work. After this punishing workout, you'll need a drink. Head straight to the nearest boozer for a pint.

Urinal etiquette

At the heart of urinal etiquette is self-preservation. When we are naked, or at least have our pride and joy peeping out of our trousers, it's only natural that we feel vulnerable. Indeed, it is perhaps in the urinal that we men feel most threatened. So, we create personal space by choosing to pee as far away from another man as possible and deny our existence by ignoring the norms of society such as greeting with a nod and a smile.

And if someone dares to stand at the urinal right next to us or say "hello," we shuffle our feet. We clear our throats. But we are trapped, caught in a Freudian field day where small penis syndrome pervades our consciousness. Under such frightful conditions, is it any wonder that, no matter how much we strain, those first drops of pee remain embarrassingly elusive?

So, here are some essential rules of urinal etiquette:

*   Show empathy to fellow urinators. If the bathroom is fairly empty, choose one of the end urinals, and don't take the urinal right next to the only other man in the place. However, if you're weeing at work be prepared for some small talk, especially if the boss wanders in.

*   Acceptable topics while you're brandishing your pecker include: football scores, women troubles and, as clichéd as it may sound, the weather. Never attempt to broach: sexual conquests, work concerns or, and in particular, penis size.

*   Control the power of your pee. Backsplash is embarrassing enough on your own shirt let alone your boss's.

*   If you suffer from stage fright, don't stand there for hours waiting for the stream to start or others will notice. Use the cubicles, try another location, or give up and come back later.

*   Remember: the sinks are for washing your hands and nothing else—you're not in your halls of residence now.

*   Don't stand far back from the urinal or start experimenting with your aim (unless you are in halls of residence).

*   Whistling while you work, so to speak, is only acceptable in solitary confinement. Two grown men caught humming the *Baywatch* theme tune side by side at a urinal will result in security being called. And security isn't as nice as Pamela.

DO NOT chance a glance at the next man's penis or compare sizes. It won't allay your concerns. Conversely, if you have a big one, intimidate other users by putting one, or if you're really blessed, both hands on the wall in front of you, secure in the knowledge that the weight of your penis will ensure the stream is directed down into the bowl or trough. Show them who's Daddy, but don't be surprised if they think you're a bit of an idiot.

*   It is totally unacceptable, in so many ways, to operate a BlackBerry at a urinal, especially during a video conference call.

*   To avoid conversation, ALWAYS read the advertising and graffiti or look at pictures above the urinal.

*   Don't loiter. Be quick—this is a toilet, not an art gallery.

*   If there are cigarette butts in the trough, only chase them along to the drain hole with your pee if no one else is present. Doing this in company makes you look a) childish b) very drunk.

*   When you shake, remember you're holding your penis, not a sparkler, and don't try to write your name.

*   Wash your hands when you're done. Or at least pretend you did when your girlfriend asks.

What to look for when you buy your first second-hand car

Cars are like children. You clean them, look after them and even christen them. Unlike children, you can also buy and sell them, and most of the time they do what they are told.

Here's how to choose a used car that won't misbehave like a toddler after two cans of cola:

☐ Check the exterior of the car thoroughly. Walking around with a clipboard and checklist is probably going too far, but look for any recently done paintwork or dents that could knock a small amount of money off the asking price.

☐ The tires should have good tread depth, with no bald patches or bulges.

☐ Check for rust damage—the wheel wells are particularly susceptible so get down on your hunkers and get a good look.

☐ Inspect the interior for tears, rips and scratches and make sure the mileage corresponds with the car's condition. If there's low mileage but the steering wheel is shiny and the foot pedals are worn, the car has probably done more miles than Jeff Gordon.

☐ Ensure there's a substantial amount of time to run on the inspection certificate and that there is a registration. If there isn't a registration, don't buy the car. Without the registration the car's history cannot be checked, and the car could be stolen, cloned, or a cut-and-shut (when two different cars are welded together)—which all amount to you buying a car you won't actually legally own.

☐ Carfax checks are a useful way of checking a car's financial and document history. They're available online. All you have to do is enter the car's registration and you'll find out whether there is outstanding finance—money still owed to the company the seller bought it off—as well as any serious previous damage the seller may not have notified you of. If the car was a previous write-off—declared a "total loss" by insurers after an accident—it may have previously been beyond repair. Carfax will tell you if it's still legitimately roadworthy.

☐ Finally, if everything's in order take your new baby for a test spin. If the driving glove fits, pay the man his money, shake his hand, and pray the wheels don't fall off at the bottom of the drive.

o As good as new
o Only one owner previous
o Low mileage

Essential painting and decorating tips

Michelangelo. Painter. Sculptor. Teenage Mutant Ninja Turtle. The ultimate Renaissance man. The ceiling of the Sistine Chapel—his greatest achievement—took him four years to complete, the time it will take you to decorate your living room if you're going it alone. From stripping to cutting in, here's the idiot's guide to decorating from scratch.

Your tools:

Buy your tools from a good trade counter—pay by cash and buy in bulk and you can expect a good discount.

Good quality paint brushes. Buy the best quality brush that you can afford. Pure bristle brushes (horse and Chinese boar) are considered best quality, give a good finish and will last a long time if looked after.

Paint rollers. Choose lambskin, mohair or synthetic rather than foam which gives an uneven finish. **NB: The smoother the surface, the shorter the pile of roller.**

* use a short ½" pile for applying emulsion to fresh plaster or flat walls and ceilings.

* use a ¼" nap for glossy walls.

* use a medium ½" pile for textured or uneven surfaces such as woodchip, and on ceilings.

* use a long pile head for embossed papers and bare brickwork.

You will also need:

* Paint tray.
* Coarse sandpaper.
* TSP and sponge.
* Stepladder.
* Dropcloths and tarpaulin—old bed sheets work well.
* Rags for wiping.
* Masking and duct tape.
* Paint thinner.

Decorating tips:

* Use one dominant color in flat and emulsion paint for the main walls, another for the ceiling and use a gloss color, usually white, for the window frames and base board.

* **Light colors make a room look bigger and—you guessed it— dark colors make a room look smaller. Painting the ceiling white will make it appear higher.**

* Use a strong, statement color to paint one contrasting wall in a large room for a dramatic effect.

* Take photographs of the room and adjust the wall color on Photoshop.

* If you're painting over a darker color with a lighter one, use primer and leave for a day before painting in your main color.

* Estimate the amount of paint you'll need. As a general rule, one gallon of paint covers between 150 and 300 square feet of wall. However, to make sure you don't go over budget, or run out of paint, measure the height and width of the walls you're painting and round them up. There are many free paint coverage calculators available online and once you put in the measurements you'll be told how much paint you'll need to get the job done.

Always buy one extra can of paint—you don't want to get to the end of the job and have to run out for some more.

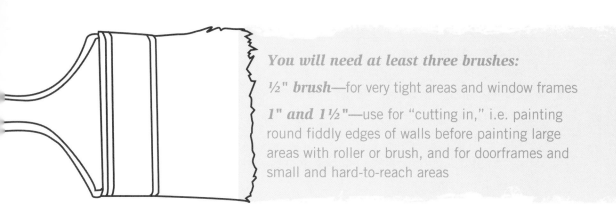

You will need at least three brushes:

½" brush—for very tight areas and window frames

1" and 1½"—use for "cutting in," i.e. painting round fiddly edges of walls before painting large areas with roller or brush, and for doorframes and small and hard-to-reach areas

How to prepare a room for decoration:

1. Stare at the wall for several minutes, shaking your head and tutting. Clap your hands together loudly. Well done. You've earned your first tea break.

2. Remove shelves, mirrors and hooks from the wall. Wrap light fixtures with black garbage can liners and seal the top with a wrap of duct tape.

3. Remove any chipped paint and sand smooth before painting over.

4. Dust off the walls and ceiling, then clean with warm soapy water—work from the bottom up to stop streaks of dirt marking the wall. For very dirty walls and windows in kitchens, use a heavy duty cleanser to remove all grease before painting.

5. Remove any mold or mildew with a 50% water, 50% bleach solution. Wear rubber gloves and scrub the wall clean. Rinse with cold water.

6. Cover carpets and flooring with tarpaulin. Tape the edges and make sure there are no bubbles or creases, as this will allow paint to seep through.

7. Move all furniture into the center of the room and cover with dropcloths.

8. Windows should be shut but keep the room ventilated with a fan.

9. Fill in any nail holes with filler, smooth over and let dry for two hours. Sand off the top and paint the patch of wall with primer.

10. Use masking tape to mark off the edges of the ceiling and on light switches and windows to give a clean, sharp edge and avoid smearing.

11. One lump or two? Time for another tea break.

Painting tips:

The correct order for painting a room is ceiling, walls, and lastly, woodwork. Always try to finish an entire wall or area in one go—a half-finished wall will leave a drying mark which will remain visible on the finished surface.

1. Always read the paint instructions carefully. Shake the can, open and stir. Pour a quarter of the paint into the tray or holder; never dip a brush or roller straight into the tin.

2. Cut in. Use the smaller brush to paint a border of a couple of inches at the edges of the walls and around any taped fixtures. Don't leave jagged marks, keep vertically or horizontally in line with the wall.

3. When using the roller, roll it several times in the tray to load it evenly on the roller. Don't overload it with paint. When painting, use a sweeping stroke, and start a foot from the edge and bottom of the wall. With only a little pressure—any more could damage the rolling cloth—roll upwards at a slight angle and paint a capital W on the wall, stopping a couple of inches from the ceiling. Fill in the spaces in-between with gentle up and down brush strokes.

4. Spread the paint you've just applied by gently rolling over it.

5. Always leave a wet edge. By painting on top of a wet edge you won't see any overlapping marks. Repeat until the entire wall is coated.

6. Never leave the edges to dry, so always complete a wall before taking a break.

7. Once finished, roll up and down over the whole wall without any paint on your roller—get as close to the edges as possible but don't allow the roller to touch them. This will blend the layer of paint smoothly.

8. For the ceiling, work away from the window and work across the width of the ceiling in three-foot-wide bands. Reapply paint at the beginning of each new band.

9. Leave the paint to dry for 24 hours, then remove all the masking tape by pulling it off gently at a 90° angle.

Stand back and take in your handiwork.

How to clean your roller and brushes:

For water-based emulsions, clean immediately under cold running water until all traces are removed. Hot water can damage some brushes. For oil-based paints, clean immediately with paint thinner to remove all paint then wash in warm soapy water. For latex paint run under warm water until all flecks of paint are gone.

Scrape any excess paint from rollers with an old kitchen knife. Wash with warm water and detergent, scrub away with your fingers and rinse until the water runs clear.

Resist the temptation to soak your brushes in a bucket of water; the wood will expand, then shrink. This leaves the metal casing enlarged and results in loose bristles.

Allow the brushes to dry completely, straighten out the bristles and store in a brush keeper or hang upside down. Don't keep bristles down in a jam jar as this bends the bristles.

Saving money on car maintenance

Make sure the rubber on the wiper blades isn't splitting; the exposed metal could scratch your windshield and you'll need to fork out for a new one.

The correct tire pressure is important. Check your handbook, or there are often stickers on the doorframe. Alternatively, most gas stations have a sign on the wall telling you each car make's tire pressure. Keep your tires at the right pressure and you'll use less fuel.

In winter, mix antifreeze with the water in the windshield washers—25% antifreeze to 75% water, roughly—and frequently check the engine's water in the summer months.

Wash the wheel wells with a pressure washer, as this will prevent the build-up of mud which attracts moisture and cause rust.

Most car manufacturers recommend getting a service every 15,000 miles. And after every new set of tires get a wheel alignment check so they'll wear evenly and last longer.

You also need to get a new cam belt about every 70,000 miles, so keep an eye on the mileage counter.

.06 in.

The little dents in the tire, the tread, should be .06 inches deep. You can check this by getting a dime and putting it sideways on in the tread. The tread should cover the edge of the coin to a depth covering the circumference of the coin as shown. If not you could be liable to a fine of $1,800 and points on your license.

Finally, remember to check your oil regularly. Park on a flat service, pull the dipstick out, wipe it clean, put it back in and pull it back out again to see what the level is. There are lines showing min and max; it should always be just below max.

How to organize the greatest bachelor party in history

Bells chime in the background and glorious sunshine filters through the church's arching doorway as you walk down the aisle sharing nods and checking your pockets for the ring. Your clammy hands search your waistcoat, your fingertips preempting the warm halo of gold imprinted against your chest. Shit. You've left it on the bed stand. Best man becomes worst man. Here's how to nail the bachelor party at least.

- [ ] *Plan ahead.* Draw up a list of attendees with the groom. Set a budget and make sure everyone can afford it well in advance. Consider age, travel implications, convenience, accessibility, style, finance, calendar, transport, dress codes, and paperwork. You're the one in charge so be prepared and organized.

- [ ] *Location.* The days of the small party the night before the big day are long gone. So make the most of the big wide world and think further afield.

- [ ] *A cabin.* There are few things more manly than a bunch of dudes hanging out in a cabin on a lake for the weekend. Wake up, fish, drink, grill, party, sleep, and repeat.

☐ *Miami.* An up-and-coming rival to Vegas in the bachelor party scene, Miami's extensive nightlife will surely keep any groom occupied.

☐ *Las Vegas.* Like Disney World on steroids for adults, Vegas is the ultimate grownup play land. Casinos, strip clubs, and excessive partying make The Strip the crème de la crème of bachelor locales. Thankfully for the groom (and any of his married friends), whatever happens there, stays there.

☐ *Daytime activities.* You need to have activities prepared for the day because drinking for twenty-four hours straight will result in liver disease; not the best send-off for your best friend. Sporting or outdoor activities make drinking all day virtually impossible and furnish conversation for the evening; especially if some of the invited either don't know and/or hate each other.

☐ *Evening activities.* In the evening, book a restaurant and then after-dinner entertainment. If you're a big group, a private room may be best as things will likely get a tad rowdy before the end of dinner. Make sure the restaurant knows what to expect so they can give all their waitresses fair warning about the "fun" group of guys they'll get to serve that night.

Daytime:

- 4x4 Off-Roading
- Brewery Tour
- Clay Pigeon Shooting
- Kite Buggying
- Sky Dive
- Golf
- Go-Karting
- Archery
- Paintballing

Evening:

- Burlesque Cabaret Night
- Lap Dancing Club
- Comedy Club
- Fancy Dress Pub Crawl—dress up and hit the locals
- Greyhound Races
- Beach Party
- An Ice Bar

One more word of warning, if the bachelor party is staying away overnight, book accommodation in advance and try not to arrive at the hotel too outrageously drunk: you might be turned away and tied to a lamppost naked instead of the groom-to-be.

How to split up with your girlfriend without being a complete bastard

Whether you do it in a stuffy car scattered with fast-food cartons or on a rain-soaked pavement mirroring the stars, the scene of the ending of a relationship is seldom glamorous. Nor is the role you'll play as love's executioner.

Plan A:

It's not you, it's me...

But you don't have to behave like a total bastard. Here's how to make things as pain free as possible:

Plan B:

I think you're a lovely girl— but we're just not compatible

* You can limit the length her heart will remain broken by being straight from the start. Don't um and ah your way out of it—uncertainty is just unfair.

* Don't take her to a flash restaurant and do the deed in front of the whole world—choose neutral ground.

* Now comes the bit where you have to explain. And you *do* have to explain. Don't be mean, don't ask to be friends and don't lead her on. Give her all her stuff back, don't get drawn into a circle of abuse, don't say, "It's not you, it's me"—even if it is.

Plan C:

You deserve someone who can appreciate you for who you really are deep down...

* Saying you can't handle a relationship at the present moment will normally result in them saying, "I'll wait." Tell them you're not worth it. Don't give the hope that one day her time will come because it won't and you know it. Just explain why you don't want to be with her any more; unless it's something shallow like the size of her breasts, in which case you really should reassess your values, or offer to pay for breast enlargement.

* If you're really struggling for words try: "I think you're a lovely girl but we're just not compatible. You'd be better suited to someone who can really appreciate the person

you are deep down." Straight from the Casanova school of let-downs.

* Be brave and do it face to face, not by email, not by phone, and, heaven forbid, not by text. UR DUMPED BCOZ I 8T U. B8CH.

* Don't get dragged in to "talking it all through." Girls are much better at arguing and at remembering minute details and past grievances, so avoid entering this trap.

* If you don't really love her or want to be with her, you're doing the right thing. Hopefully she'll take it in a dignified manner. If you awake to a doll's head in your bed, or a burning effigy of your penis on the front lawn, she hasn't. Psycho exes are a rare species and should be treated with the utmost care. Do not antagonize or provoke. Put up with her behavior for as long as you can and then, when it gets to the point when you're going to jump off a cliff (or worse, push her off one), don't answer her calls. Attention seeking, when ignored, will dissipate eventually. In the unlikely event of things getting out of hand, there's always 911. Or an easy jet flight to Bratislava for a week of reflection.

* Whatever you do, don't undo what you've done after a couple of weeks. Manfully resist the temptation to meet up with her for a quick fumble under the nightdress and don't ring her up for a drunken conversation late at night. Post-split girls always look a lot hotter than they did when you were going out, so be warned, you'll probably want her back the next time you see her. But keep your desire locked deep down inside and don't tell her you still love her, even if you do. Breaking someone's heart is hard enough the first time; having to do it twice will just make you feel like the bastard you tried so hard to avoid being in the first place.

A beginner's guide to horse racing

The office trip to the races. A confusing, drunken affair that's never complete until you've lost your month's wages and won a hangover. Here's how to make sure you don't place all your hard-earned cash on a "nightmare."

Racing terms to know:

Furlong. The length of a race is measured in furlongs. One mile equals eight furlongs. The shortest races are run over five furlongs. The longest, the Grand National, is run over four-and-a half miles (7.2km).

Pace. The speed set by the leading horses at the start and the middle of the race.

Blown up. When a horse begins to wane during a race.

Length. The length of a horse, used when describing the distances between horses during the race and at the finishing line.

Winning by a nose or a distance. A short head is minimal whereas a distance is up to 30 lengths or so.

Hacked up. Used when a horse wins easily.

Penalty. A weight added to a horse to even out the chances. Weights are allocated according to past performance in handicapped races.

Pulling. Horse that is using energy fighting with the jockey rather than running to win.

Stayers. Horses with good stamina and therefore better for longer races and heavy-going conditions.

Other racing terms:

The "going." The condition of the course. Some horses perform better on firm courses, while others thrive on soft or muddy courses. Depending on the condition on the race day, the going is classified as either hard, firm, good to firm, good, good to soft, soft or heavy.

Claiming race. A race where horses are entered for a certain amount of money to ensure no amateurs take part.

Handicap. Race where penalty weights are placed on horses running.

Sprint. Race of seven furlongs or less.

Steeplechase. Race with fences and water hazards.

National hunt. Race with hurdles and fences. August—May traditionally. Unusual to be run on all-weather surfaces.

Flat. Normally summer but can be all year round—run on all-weather surfaces.

Maiden race. The runners are all horses that have never won a race.

Colt. Male horse four years old or younger.

Filly. Female horse four years or younger.

Rabbit. Horse which is entered in a race to set a fast pace, but won't last the distance.

Claimer. Apprentice flat race jockey.

Apprentice. Young jockey with a trainer.

Reading a racing card:

Understanding how to read the race card will help you make an informed guess on which horse to bet on. It gives information on the horse, its age, and any penalty weight it will carry in the race. Also listed are the rider, the trainer, and the owner's name, and most importantly codes which give information on how the horse has performed in recent races, or its "form."

> **Odds can be long or short**
>
> *200-1* **are long odds and mean the horse is less likely to come in winner.**
>
> *2-1* **are short odds and indicative of a potential winner or at least a good place.**
>
> *Odds on* (favorite)- **where the odds are less than evens or less than even money.**

* Time, name and distance of race.

* Prize money—this is split among the jockey, owner and trainer. Prize money is also awarded to horses in second or third place.

* Horse name—punters with less experience, often place a bet on a horse with a name they like. The country the horse comes from may be in brackets after the name.

* Horse number—the number the jockey will wear on his back. The number in brackets is the stall the horse will start from.

* Owner—the owner's name. Certain owners will have good form.

* Trainer—the trainer will know his horse inside out and monitor their form. Their job is to work with the jockey, gauge the weather and running, and get the horse in top form and condition for the race. Punters should follow the form of the trainer and jockey.

* Name of jockey—often a crucial element in the outcome of a race. Trainers will often stick to a known combination of horse and a rider who knows that horse well.

* Age of horse—flat races are normally run by younger horses. Certain races such as the Derby are only open to three-year-olds. The Grand National is only open to horses over five years old.

* Weight allowance—the weight, including the jockey, which the horse must carry. Jockeys must weigh in before the race and are often on diets to keep their ideal weight. Flat race jockeys are usually much smaller and lighter than jump jockeys.

09.09.09

RACECARD

2.00 Wilkinson Frenchgate Nursery (Class 3)
For 2yo Rated 0-95 Weights highest weight not less than 9st 7lb Weights raised 4lb Minimum weight 7-12 Penalties after August 29th, each race won 6lb Penalty
£15,000 guaranteed
value 1st £9,714 2nd £2,890.50 3rd £1,444.50 4th £721.50

71
GD-FM

No.	Form	Horse, breeding, owner	Wgt	Jockey/trainer	OR	TS	RPR
1 (9)	11	**MR GRINCH** 12 b g Green Tune - Flyamore M J K Dods	2 9-7	Phillip Makin M Dods	90	82	97
2 (5)	004016	**DESERT AUCTION** 19 D b c Desert Style - Double Gamble A J Ilsley, K T Ivory & G Battocchi	2 9-6	Steve Drowne R Hannon	89	92	95
3 (1)	34211	**LUCKY RAVE** 13 D b c Lucky Story - Rave On Ron Hull	2 9-5	D Brown	88	79	98
4 (3)	231847	**FARMER GILES** 21 b c Danroad - Demeter R A Green	2 9-2	T P Queally M Bell	85	96	96
5 (12)	219	**ATACAMA CROSSING** 33 b c Footstepsinthesand - Endure Paul Moulton	2 9-0	T P O'Shea B Hills	83	85	91
6 (6)	071	**PLEASANT DAY** 20 D b g Noverre - Sunblush Jaber Abdullah	2 8-13b	L Dettori B Meehan	82	66	94
7 (7)	3128	**AUDACITY OF HOPE** 18 b c Red Ransom - Aliena Four Winds Racing	2 8-13t	K Fallon P McBride	82	93	98
8 (8)	91	**BRICK RED** 16 ch c Dubawi - Duchcov Brick Racing	2 8-11	William Buick A Balding	80	75	98
9 (13)	4616	**JUTLAND** 18 D BF b c Halling - Dramatique Sheikh Hamdan Bin Mohammed Al Maktoum	2 8-8	Greg Fairley M Johnston	77	90	98
10 (10)	533120	**FLANEUR** 22 b c Chineur - Tatanka Jeremy Gompertz	2 8-8b	David Allan T Easterby	77	97	97
11 (4)	415	**MISS SMILLA** 46 b f Red Ransom - Snowing Findlay & Bloom	2 8-8	Tony Culhane K Ryan	77	89	97
12 (2)	233012	**TRANSFIXED** 19 D b f Trans Island - Rectify Mrs I M Folkes	2 8-7	John Egan P Evans	76	94	96
13 (11)	01	**RANSOM NOTE** 18 D b c Red Ransom - Zacheta H R Mould	2 8-6	Michael Hills B Hills	75	87	97

Jamie Spencer OR83

2008 (16 ran) **Ballantrae** (16) M L W Bell 2 9-3 12/1

Betting forecast: 7/2 Ransom Note,6/1 Mr Grinch,7/1 Pleasant Day,15/2 Audacity Of Hope,9/1 Jutland,10/1 Brick Red,12/1 Atacama Crossing,12/1 Desert Auction,12/1 Farmer Giles,12/1 Transfixed, 16/1 Flaneur,20/1 Miss Smilla.

SPOTLIGHT VERDICT A case can be made for several, with **RANSOM NOTE** perhaps the most interesting off bottom weight having shown the right sort of progress to win at Chester and promising better to come. **Atacama Crossing** could make it a 1-2 for the stable.[Frank Carter]

* Jockey's colors—the rider's silks, or the colored top he wears, are crucial when following the race. Outlandish silk shirts include spots, stripes, diamonds and stars.

* Number of days since the horse last ran a competitive race—indicated by the number after the horse's name. The higher the number the lower the race fitness of the horse.

Reading the form:

/	the horse did not run in the last season
–	the dash separates the current season from the last
	the position form is read from right to left, e.g. 0–135—horse finished 5th in last race, 3rd in race before that, 1st in one before that, and the previous season placed outside the top nine.
P or PU	horse pulled up and didn't finish race
F	fallen
B or BD	brought down
U	unseated rider
RTR	refused to race
RO	ran out
C	won on today's course
D	won on today's distance
CD	won on both course and distance
BF	in last race this horse was the beaten favorite
RPR	Racing Post rating
TS	top speed
OR	official rating

Types of bet:

Simple odds. 6/1 said "six to one" means you'll make a profit of six dollars for every dollar you bet. You also get back your stake so you'd win $7 for every dollar bet. Betting will change throughout a race and the final bet is the bet you win on. Bets can be locked if you tell the bookie you'll have the current price when you place your bet.

To win. Also referred to as "on the nose"—means a bet on a selected horse to win overall.

The place. Only available at the racecourse, these winnings are only a fraction of the win price. You can choose a horse place and win if your horse finishes first or second. Likewise, if you choose your horse to show, you win if it comes in first, second, or third.

Each way bet. Two bets in one; a win bet and a place bet. If your horse wins you get both bets back but if it only places you receive the return from only the place bet. For example, if you put $2,—which would actually cost you $4 because it's a two-bets-in-one deal—on each way for a horse at 4-1 and your horse wins you'll get back $8 in return plus your $2 original stake, $2 for a quarter of the odds and $2 for the place bet stake.

Straight forecast. You must select the first and second places in a series of races. Also called an Exacta bet. More common in greyhound racing.

The place pot. UK tote bet in which you must bet on a horse being placed in the first six races of any meet.

Accumulator. Also known as a "roll-up"—is one bet with four or more selections from different races. All your selected horses must win in order to make a return. Wins from each selection are accumulated or reinvested on the successive races.

Each-way accumulator. As above but with two bets on four or more selections in different races. The first bet is on horses to win, and the second bet on horses to be placed.

How to place a bet at the bookie's

Entering a bookie's for the first time can be a potentially embarrassing experience if you don't have a clue what you are doing and it's full of hardened punters shouting at the screens. So here's a quick idiot's guide.

* Pick up a slip and look at the screens. All the information you need is shown on them—from events to odds.

* The betting odds represent the probability of the outcome of the event if the event was repeated over and over. Write in your stake, for example, $3. Your selection (or horse's name), the time of race, e.g. 3:15. And finally the course, for example, Ascot.

* Take the slip to the counter. Your details will be processed and you will be given a receipt.

* Make sure you say, "I'll take the price please" as this will guarantee you receive the odds on your slip. They will confirm this by writing it on the slip. Until you get the hang of the betting lark, always take the current price as the odds normally shorten throughout the day.

* Now all you have to do is to wait for your horse to come in and book a flight to Las Vegas. Where you can lose it all at leisure...

Further hints and tips for the novice:

---

*   Avoid apprentice and maiden races—quite simply they're harder to predict because if a horse has never won a race before, it makes it harder to judge the odds.

---

*   All-weather races should be avoided until you know several horses and jockeys well enough to gauge a win or a place.

---

*   A long gap since the horse's last outing could mean it isn't fit or it's been held back for a possible win in a major race.

---

*   Study the form. Learn everything you can about the horse, jockey, and trainer you want to back.

---

*   The draw, or the horse's placing in the starting stalls in flat races, can effect how a horse runs. Find out what different courses' draws mean to the outcome

---

*   How your horse reacts to jumps over different heights is important when choosing who to back in a National Hunt. Again, try to find out more about its form over jumps; some courses are more difficult so horses need to be experienced.

---

*   Balance youth and experience when picking a horse to bet on.

---

*   *The Racing Post* is a good place to begin when trying to understand the complex language of horse racing. And even if you can't read a word of it at first, waltzing around the track with a copy under your arm will make you look like a true punter.

How to moonwalk like Michael Jackson

When you add up all of Michael Jackson's hit songs from "ABC" to "Billie Jean"—let's forget "Heal the World" for now—not to mention all his groundbreaking albums—it's quite easy to forget the dancing legacy he also left behind.

In honor of the late and great Jacko here's how to pay homage to a musical legend:

Step 1. Slide your feet into some slip-ons without much grip on the sole; a pair of your dad's slippers will do the trick.

Step 2. Pull on one white glove.

Step 3. Find a shiny wooden or tile floor on an even surface.

Step 4. Place your feet about a foot apart with your left foot at the front.

Step 5. Lift your right heel and place your weight on your right toes. Bend your right knee slightly to help with balance. Your sole should be at a right angle to the floor.

Step 6. Keeping your left foot flat and your leg straight, slide it back across the floor.

Step 7. Once your left foot is a foot behind your right foot, straighten your right leg and snap your right heel down. Simultaneously raise your left heel, by bending your knee, and shift your weight over to your left toe. Important: both toes never leave the floor.

Step 8. Slide your right foot back and keep it flat to the floor. If you want to add another layer of coolness, as you slide your left foot back move your right arm forward and vice versa.

Step 9. Repeat the movements.

Step 10. Show off your moonwalking skills during drunken nights out, children's parties and weddings.

How to behave immediately after sex

Porsche Carrera GT, 0–60 in 3.9 seconds. McLaren F1, 0–60 in 3.2 seconds. Bugatti Veyron, 0–60 in 2.5 seconds. Man Post-Sex C21 Model, 0–sleep in 2 seconds flat.

Here's how to make sure you don't pass out before your after-sex duty of care is complete:

Cuddling. The most important part of the post-coitus ritual. When a woman gives herself to a man, regardless of whether you only met each other that night or have been married for twenty years, she wants to feel loved and appreciated. Hold her, give her a squeeze, kiss her forehead, compliment her, tell her how good it was or simply call her beautiful. Nonchalance isn't cool in these instances; it's up to the man to make sure the woman doesn't feel used.

Pillow talk. While endorphins and adrenaline are surging through your virile veins, for a woman, the immediate post-sex period is one of high emotion and openness. Never one to pass up the chance for a good chat, she likes to get her problems off her chest right after you've got your rocks off. Yes, she'll want to "talk," when all you want to do is snore. If you don't want to leave her feeling used and wounded, don't shirk the post-sex pillow talk. Embrace the opportunity and try to stay awake.

Stay awake. If you feel the urge to sleep is overwhelming, take precautions. Sit up with your back firmly against the headboard or simply prop your head up on one hand. With the odd perfectly placed "uh-ha" she'll think you're listening attentively—as long as you don't doze and drool. Spooning is a good position for chitchat as while she witters on you can pepper her neck with kisses. After ten minutes or so she'll begin to relax and you can both ease into blissful after-sex slumber.

Beyond the bed. Just because the deed took place in the bedroom doesn't mean you have to stay there. The post-sex section of the Kama Sutra says washing each other's bodies, eating fruit and cold meats—ah, the romance of corned beef— massaging, tickling, pillow fights and even sitting naked outside under the moonlight are all viable and romantic options after sex; not to mention ways to get the neighbors' tongues wagging.

One night stands. How to survive the walk of shame:

*   At the moment of climax do not zip up, slip your socks back on—if you bothered to take them off in the first place—and make a break for the door.

*   If you don't plan on staying, do the decent thing and wait until she's fast asleep before you make a run for it. Do not take a picture of her with your phone.

*   Leave a note thanking her for a great night and initial it if you don't want her to have a record of your name. Phone number and kisses are optional.

*   If you stay, when you wake up gather your things quietly, get dressed in a jiffy, don't worry about your teeth or shoelaces, and slide out the front door.

*   Do not leave any belongings in the room, especially the boxers dangling from the lampshade, your wallet, or anything you'll have to go back for.

* When you can't remember her name simply nod and smile, say you've got to get to work, and leave the room before she has a chance to get out of bed.

* Once outside it will be about 6 a.m.—the obligatory hour for walkers of shame. Head for the nearest bus stop, peruse the map, and locate your position. Make a note to self not to end up in this situation again.

Anti-dating rules: how to turn a girl off if you don't like her

Designed to take the excruciating emotional turmoil out of meeting a stranger (by skipping straight to the excruciating emotional turmoil of dating a stranger), blind dates often result in at least one person wishing they were actually blind. And when you end up on a date with a girl you wouldn't share public transport with, let alone your bed, it's time to rid yourself of the dating dead wood.

Be as elusive as Lord Lucan. Tell her you're busy all the time or never return her texts, emails or phone calls and pray to God she doesn't pop round your apartment stating she was "just passing." Even if you hang out in the same places, the Houdini trick can still work wonders. Be awkward, bar anything but small talk, and reduce conversations to the length of a Twitter post.

Drop hints like a demented and corrupt bar trivia host.
Tell her you're now in a relationship with someone else who's very insecure and struggles with your platonic female friends.

Be a gentleman. Call her or arrange a meeting. Tell her straight that you don't want to mislead her and you don't have any romantic feeling for her and/or you're not looking for a relationship with her right now. Don't say you'd like to stay friends as that means she can still contact you. Unless she's a stalker, she'll respect your wishes.

Disgust her. For most men this won't be any trouble at all. Put the nice version of you to one side and kick back as though you're watching football with your best friends. Wear really old dirty clothes, maybe some trousers with a nasty stain at the crotch, and make sure you smell really bad. Don't clean your teeth for a week before the date, and have a really strong, garlicky lunch. Then right at the beginning of the date, grab her and give her a really bad kiss, sticking your tongue right in her mouth. Belch, pick your nose, pick your feet, stick your finger in your ear then smell it, be perverse, cup a fart and throw it in her face. Talk about yourself all night, bitch and moan the whole time and act really depressed. Drink too much, then throw up outside the bar or restaurant. And so on. If she still pursues you after this, it must be love.

Shift her affections. Every man has a friend who is still a virgin at the age of 27 and this is the moment you'll be thankful you stuck by him through all those years in nookie no-man's-land. Set up a date for all three of you, then get another friend to call you at a set time and scarper using some pretext. With any luck, she and Mr. No-Nookie will hit it off, leaving you off the hook.

The rules of going commando

California casual. Dingle dangling. Alfresco. Free-balling. Whatever you call it, walking around with no underwear, even if you're just running to the corner shop to buy a paper, can have its pitfalls. So here's the ultimate guide to going commando in style.

When walking for miles in tropical climes and humid conditions, the tough military men supposedly ditched their pants because they caused uncomfortable chafing and crotch rot—soreness and redness after your underwear soaks up sweat, remains moist and chafes against your skin. Driving for long hours and wet and sandy settings also call for a commando approach to your downstairs pair. Stagnant sitting can cause stickiness and sweat and sand creates a sandpaper reaction on your privates—a sensation even the most ardent sadomasochist would struggle to find pleasurable.

Now for the pitfalls. These are few things you have to keep an eye on when stepping out alfresco:

*   Your package becomes a little more visible through only one layer of protection so prepare yourself for some smiles or smirks depending on what end of the length spectrum you stand at, especially if you're wearing light linen or cotton trousers and shorts.

*   Take extra care when shaking after a trip to the urinal; the damp wee-wee spot has led to many a free-balling man's misery.

* Circumcised men may find the abrasion a little too much.

* Avoid trousers with a zipper.

* When wearing shorts don't lift your legs up, particularly while on crowded public transport.

* Kilt wearers on the other hand shouldn't be tempted to cover up; the true Scotsman will always make his little Scotsman brave the blizzardy highlands.

* Builder's bum is a hazard to be avoided.

* Check your fly at regular intervals.

How to get off the phone from a cold caller

The Four Horsemen of the Apocalypse. War, Famine, Death, and Cold Callers. Drastic telecom times call for drastic telecom measures.

The softly softly approach. Wait for the salesperson to finish and then calmly tell them you're sorry but you're not interested. If they keep on at you—which they usually do—tell them you've complained to the police regarding cold caller harassment. Ask for their company number and individual name and once they freak out they'll say their goodbyes and leave you in peace.

Time on your side? Pretend to listen attentively to what they're telling you and feign an interest in their product. Answer all their questions and then at the all-important moment of payment inform them you don't a) have the money, b) have any means of paying over the phone, and c) understand the payment system.

Reverse the roles. Ask the cold caller to participate in your very own Cold Caller Questionnaire. "It should only take about an hour, are you interested?" The chances are they won't be.

Bamboozle them to death. No matter what they're selling, ask intricate and incredibly specific questions. This can cause havoc for the script-reading slaves. If they're selling you a washing machine ask them if it can get bloodstains out or if the outlet tube will take a Q46 tubular bell designed by Mike Oldfield in 1846. Bamboozle and mess around with them. They'll eventually admit defeat. After all, time is money and money is what makes the telecom occult tick.

Play with their heads. A cruel option but an option none-the-less. On answering say you're not the right person to talk to and place the receiver on the worktop. Once the muffled "Hellos" die down they'll have finally got the hint and hung up. Alternatively, pick up the phone and say, "Hello." When they begin to speak say, "Hello? Is anyone there? Hello?" Wait a few more minutes and repeat. Soon enough you'll hear the sweet sound of a cold caller flat-lining.

How to get served at a busy bar

The standard rules of human interaction are immediately thrown away when men find themselves faced with an overcrowded bar. Ignore your tendencies towards politeness and be prepared to throw elbows. If you don't, it could be hours before you see your next drink. The rewards for your aggressive play couldn't be better—an ice cold beer as well as a chance to hit on the lovely young ladies taking tequila shots at the front of the bar.

The first thing to do is find the least busy part of the bar away from the taps. Situate yourself behind someone who's being served and as they turn and leave, shoot your arm through, grab onto the bar counter, and pull yourself through the gap. Next, gently ease your shoulders into the gap, squeezing any others out of the way, so you are standing facing the bar. Now, get the bartender's attention. Don't shout like you're head's on fire, just be patient and concentrate. Don't get distracted in conversation with the friend who is helping you carry the drinks—stay focused or you may miss your chance. A moment will arise when the bartender finishes serving someone and looks up for his next customer, that's the moment you strike. Even if you know that the person next to you has been waiting for ages, when the bartender asks "Who's next," never hesitate. Get in there and take no prisoners! With a big smile on your face, raise your eyebrows and make eye contact. Once you have their precious attention, give him or her your order in a clear and friendly voice. Soon enough you'll be supping your nice cold beer safe in the knowledge you didn't have to kill anyone to get it.

Advanced tips:

Shorten the odds. Work in pairs. If two of you go to different areas of the bar, you double your chances of being served. Stay in constant eye contact. The first one to get to the bartender orders for both of you. Use your charm. If there is a female bartender, a surefire tip is to say loudly to a female customer near you that she is next. You will be served immediately after.

How to talk yourself out of a fight

Whether it was the cold smack of a slipper on a bare buttock or a rolled-up newspaper clashing against the coarse palm of a shaking hand, the consequences of stepping out of line as a child were usually bearable. Hotheaded situations involving a burly brute with "Love" and "Hate" tattooed across his fingers are a different kettle of fish altogether.

Here's how to use your brains instead of your brawn:

* Sometimes saying, "I'm not looking for any trouble" and offering to buy them a drink can defuse smaller confrontations such as spilling someone's pint or bumping into someone. However, don't give them your credit card and tell them to set up a tab, no matter how much they might remind you of the Incredible Hulk.

* If some bloke is giving you the evil eye for no apparent reason, show him you're not intimidated. Don't give a hint of weakness or aggression.

* If he squares up to you, stand your ground with confidence. Stand with your feet a good distance apart and keep still. Don't shuffle, slouch or put your hands in your pockets. Keep your arms by your sides not clenched into fists. Never step up to someone, toe to toe. Nor give in to temptation, grab a pool cue and shout, "Let's be having you." This will only make matters worse.

* Don't fidget. Don't nod aggressively as if to say, "Yeah, I'm up for it!" Don't shrug. Don't smile weakly. All these things lessen his opinion of you and give him more reason to slap you in the mouth. Never interrupt him and keep eye contact at all times.

* Speak calmly and don't shout in his face. Command respect with a consistent tone of voice. Be clear, calm and concise. **Don't crack jokes.**

* If he doesn't back down, don't panic. Reason with him some more by pointing out what the endgame will be. "I'm pretty sure we both don't want this situation to turn into a violent one. I'm not too keen on black eyes and broken bones. Are you? Why don't we both take a step back?" By scattering a few questions here and there he has to think about the situation once more and confront what he really wants.

* If you've used all reasoning and he still wants a fight, the chances are he'd want a fisticuffs even if Gandhi and Nelson Mandela were doing the talking.

* When this occurs the only option is to ignore what's being said and leave the confrontation, stating, "I'm going to go now," as you back away. Countless men have got off at an earlier bus stop or left half of their pint due to bullies. Don't think this is cowardice; some people will pick a fight with you no matter what. Walking away is often the bravest option of all.

How to put up shelves like a superhero

You will need:
- brackets
- an AC electrical detector
- a pipe detector
- screwdriver
- electric drill with masonry bit
- hammer
- screws (2" or longer)
- Rawlplugs (at least 1")
- pencil
- spirit level

We men prefer a little dirt to a little shine. That's why we don't buy into that preassembled furniture nonsense. Real home furnishings aren't delivered by big burly men; real home furnishings come in eight thousand different pieces and require a little sweat and a ridiculously large toolbox. So next time you're in an IKEA, laugh in the face of those flimsy shelves, knowing that while most will be brought to tears by their idiotic instructions, you can conquer them like a superhero.

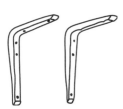

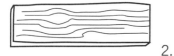

After the midday match and before the Saturday night steak, the quest for the Excalibur of the toolbox must begin. We wade into the treacherous garage, plunge our hand into the sea of dust, clutch the handle and pull, as if from stone, the drill which will lead the way in the almighty quest of putting up the shelves.

1. First, run your AC electrical and pipe detector along the chosen wall. Depending on the model, it will flash or beep if there are any electrical cables or gas or water pipes behind the scenes. Once you've got the all clear, place the shelf against the wall and mark its edges with your pencil. Don't stretch, use a ladder if need be.

2. Hold one bracket up, a few inches in from your original mark, and place the spirit level on top of the bracket. Make sure the spirit bubble is roughly centered on the level and mark the position of the bracket's holes. If you're putting up a floating shelf, the bracket will be one long frame the width of the shelf as opposed to two separate brackets placed at either end.

3. If there is a lady in the house, it is worth asking her if she is entirely happy with the positioning of the shelf. She may have wanted it in the alcove, not above the fireplace, so consult at this point.

4. Take the bracket away and use the electrical drill to make two pilot holes in the wall, using a masonry drill bit with a diameter slightly less than that of the holes in your bracket, but corresponding to the size of your Rawlplugs. Drill all the holes to the depth of the Rawlplug by marking the drill bit at the correct depth with a felt pen. A great way to save on mess at this point is to Blu Tac an envelope on the base board under each hole—this will collect the crumbs of plaster and paint and reduce the clean-up time once you've finished.

5. Next, tap a Rawlplug into each hole using the hammer.

6. Place the bracket back over and screw the screws in until it is secure. But don't screw too tightly.

7. Hold the other bracket in place and rest the shelf across both brackets.

8. Place the spirit level on the shelf and adjust the trajectory of the left-hand bracket until the bubble is in the middle of the level.

9. Once you're happy, dot a mark in the holes of the other bracket with your pencil.

10. Take the shelf and level away and screw in the other bracket as before, not forgetting the Rawlplugs and starting with the lower hole.

11. Check the spirit level again, and step back to see if the symmetry is correct. Tighten all four screws flush with the wall.

12. Last but not least, vertically screw the shelf into the brackets—make sure your screws are no longer than the width of your shelf. Put a weight on top of the shelf so it stays put, and tighten the screws in underneath through the holes at the front and back of the bracket.

Your new display area is now ready to hold your prized Disney films and *Die Hard* box set.

How to act when you're in a posh restaurant for the first time

Eating together has always been important to society. The word companion comes from Latin. "Com" means "with" or "together" and "panis" means "food" or "bread." So we have always correlated eating with togetherness and companionship, a time to share ideas and thoughts.

But, if "eating out" normally means a quickie kebab or a KFC, dining in a posh restaurant for the first time is likely to pose a few challenges. You want to be judged on your personality, not your manners, so don't let them let you down.

The Basics:

* A good way to avoid committing a humiliating faux pas is to take an elongated sip of water at the start of each phase of the meal and watch what someone else does first. Peeling prawns, tackling a greasy snail or supping soup is a lot easier to do when you've had your own private demonstration. (If your fellow diners are chugging the water too, dig in before the food gets cold. They can only copy your mistakes!)

* In certain company be careful of what you say. Don't get too involved or heated (so watch your drink).

* Wait for your guest and others to tuck in before you do.

* Never answer your phone or start texting while you're dining.

* If you pour yourself a glass of water or wine, offer those within your reach some and pour it twisting the bottle up and away when the glass is half full. Swallow your food before drinking (and your drink before eating) and hold your wine glass at the stem.

* Never lift your bowl or plate to your mouth to lick it, or sup the contents.

* If you are having shellfish such as oysters, mussels, prawns or lobster, you will probably be given a small bowl of water with a slice of lemon in it. This is not for drinking. It is for rinsing your fingers, so don't slurp it.

* **Never whistle at a waiter or click your fingers to gain their attention.** Simply make eye contact with a passing waiter and raise your hand slightly or simply say "Excuse me." No matter how you long you are ignored for, resist the temptation to stick out your foot and trip up the waiter. Unless you are dining alone.

* If you run out of wine feel free to turn the bottle upside down in the cooler, ensuring it's completely empty first of course.

* Your napkin will be within your place setting so don't pinch your neighbor's. Never tuck it into your collar. Place it on your lap and don't blow your nose with it or crumple it up and put it on the plate at the end of the meal. Fold it loosely and place it back on the table.

* Order extras like water or a basket of bread first, then your starter and your main. It is polite to let a lady order first and the person who is paying should go last. In most high-end establishments the waiter will go round the table once and take your starter and main at the same time. He will return to take your dessert and coffee or cheese orders.

* Tear your bread, don't cut it and transfer butter onto your bread plate, not directly from dish to dough. Don't spread butter on your bread all at once. Tear a small piece off, add butter, and then eat.

* When you've finished eating, place your knife and fork close together on your plate—not on top of one another—and rotate them so their points face roughly at 10 o'clock. Never push your plate away from you.

THE ENGLISH GUIDE TO AN ITALIAN MENU:

L'antipasto—"before the meal" nibbles such as bread or olives

Il primo—"first course" or starter

Il secondo—"second course" or main meal

Il contorno—side dish, in Italy this will normally be a salad

Il dolce—dessert

Il conto—the bill

Il servizio—service charge or suggested tip

Il coperto—cover charge

THE ENGLISH GUIDE TO A FRENCH MENU:

Le menu—set menu with a fixed price and three or five courses
depending on how much you pay

A la carte—dishes ordered independently from the main menu

La Carte des vins—wine list

Une dégustation—nope, not disgusting. This is the tasting menu;
multiple dishes of bite-size meals

Apéritif—pre-dinner drink

Hors d'oeuvres—appetizers such as olives or canapés

Entrée—starter

Plat principal—main course

Digestif—after-dinner drink. Those French love a tipple

Le plat du jour—daily special

L'ardoise—the specials board

Gratuit or offert—indicates these tidbits are free

Des cuisses de grenouille—should you wish to brave it, frog's legs

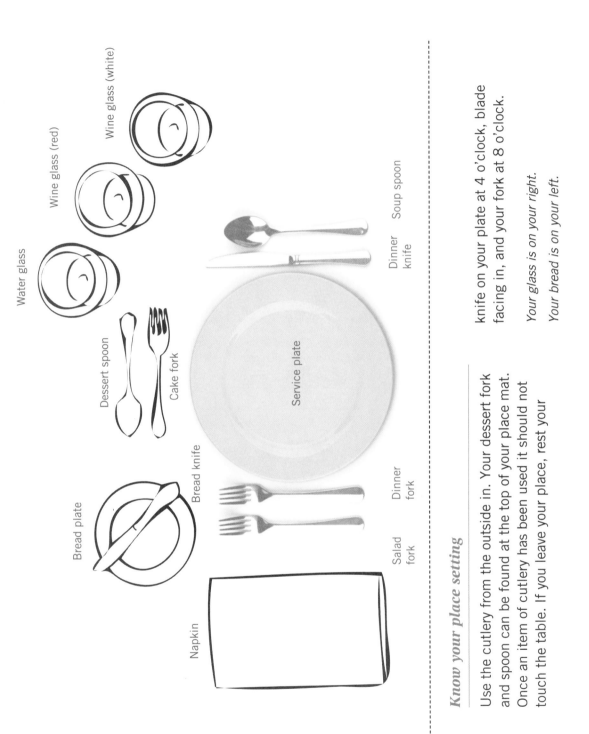

Wine glass (white)

Wine glass (red)

Water glass

Dessert spoon

Cake fork

Bread knife

Bread plate

Napkin

Service plate

Soup spoon

Dinner knife

Dinner fork

Salad fork

Know your place setting

Use the cutlery from the outside in. Your dessert fork and spoon can be found at the top of your place mat. Once an item of cutlery has been used it should not touch the table. If you leave your place, rest your knife on your plate at 4 o'clock, blade facing in, and your fork at 8 o'clock.

Your glass is on your right.
Your bread is on your left.

An introduction to wine

Between the ages of sixteen and twenty-one, drinking alcohol usually involves dabbling in your parents' drinks cabinet and sneaking down to the basement to drink with some friends while playing Xbox. Once you're of legal drinking age and it's crucial to impress girls when you're out at a fancy restaurant, it's learn-your-wine time.

Match your food with a wine:

FOOD	RED	WHITE
Red Meat (beef, lamb, veal)	Cabernet Sauvignon	White Zinfandel (Rose)
	Rioja	
	Chianti	
	Shiraz	
	Pinot Noir	
	Zinfandel	
White Meat (chicken, pork)	Pinot Noir	Pinot Grigio
	Merlot	Sauvignon Blanc
		Chardonnay
		White Zinfandel
		Riesling
Seafood	Merlot	Chardonnay
		Sauvignon Blanc
		Pinot Grigio
Pasta or vegetarian meals	Merlot	Chardonnay
	Valpolicella	Soave
Hot and spicy	Zinfandel	Gewurtztraminer
		White Zinfandel
		Riesling
		Sauvignon Blanc

The most respected regional wines:

REGION	RED	WHITE
France	Cabernet Sauvignon	Pinot Grigio
	Merlot	Sauvignon Blanc
	Pinot Noir	Chardonnay
		Riesling
		Gewurtstraminer
Germany		Riesling
Italy	Chianti	Soave
	Valpolicella	
Spain	Rioja	
Australia	Shiraz	Chardonnay
	Merlot	Riesling
	Cabernet Sauvignon	
New Zealand	Pinot Noir	Chardonnay
	Merlot	Sauvignon Blanc
South Africa		Chardonnay
		Sauvignon Blanc
Chile	Cabernet Sauvignon	Chardonnay
	Shiraz	Sauvignon Blanc
	Merlot	
Argentina	Cabernet Sauvignon	
California	Zinfandel	White Zinfandel
	Pinot Noir	
	Merlot	
	Cabernet Sauvignon	

How to appease the pub locals

The local pub has been offering man a sanctuary from home and work since the first pint was poured. Whether a spit and sawdust boozer with complimentary peanuts, or a gastropub offering moules marinières with your Chardonnay, a pub is defined by one thing: its regulars. Braving an unfamiliar establishment and standing out like a nipple in a cold breeze can result in the locals sharpening their pitchforks and stoking the coals under the wicker man to make you feel really at home. However, follow these almost religious procedures to appease the regulars, and you'll slot in like you've been drinking there your whole life.

Upon entering. Opt for the public bar as opposed to the lounge as this is where the tourists go for a bite to eat. The last thing you want to do is give the impression you're a tourist so public bar it is. Offer a good evening or afternoon, accompanied by a smile and a nod in the general direction of the bar. This will probably earn you one in reply from the staff and perhaps a nod or two from the locals sitting on the bar stools. Later attempts at conversation will be easier if you execute this greeting with aplomb. But don't follow that up with a gutsy comment about the bad harvest, especially if you are in fact a systems analyst from a Fortune 500 company.

Local stare factor. This is determined by the amount of people who stop and stare at you when you enter. A pub with a 75% plus stare factor: turn around and drink somewhere else. It might just save your life.

Drinks. Stick to a pint of beer; ordering a fancy cocktail with a sparkler on top will earn you a beating with the belt hung above the door. Swirling a glass of red wine, filling your nostrils and declaring the bottle "corked" is also ill-advised. Chugging a whisky without grimacing like someone's just pissed in your pocket, however, will earn you local kudos. If the pub has a wide range of ales and guest beers ask for a recommendation from the staff or the locals.

The bar staff and landlord. When ordering, don't misconstrue yells from the locals of "Come on!" or, "I've been standing here all night," for a public house mutiny. It is a God-given right for locals to banter with the bar staff. A stranger waltzing in and attempting to do the same is a local pub felony punishable with death. Well, barring at least. Manners maketh man, and get him served too.

Converse. Locals sitting at the bar are usually willing to engage in conversation. Open body language, such as boots facing out from the bar and staff taking part in the discussion, is a sign for you to chip in. Offer a few conversational gambits first, and see how they go down. Don't kick off with, "The death penalty for sex offenders. Discuss."

Pub arguments. Follow one strict rule—don't take them too seriously. Never be aggressive and be aware that these discussions are a form of social bonding and, bizarre as it may seem, endearment. If you get yourself into hot water you can cool everything down by saying, "I think it must be my round," with a big grin. Irony, sarcasm, puns, banter, backchat, teasing, faux chauvinism and witticisms are all run of the mill. If the regulars pick up on your personal habits or features it means you're being accepted into the fold; if they don't like you they'll simply ignore you. Or burn you at the stake.

How to buy your girlfriend lingerie without looking like a pervert

When you commit to buying your girlfriend lingerie understand this: you might also be committing yourself to life as a bachelor. Navigating your way through the lingerie section of a clothes shop is like walking into a minefield. If you buy her something her grandma might wear, she'll accuse you of thinking that she's frumpy. If you buy her a black and red lace-up basque, crotchless panties, and suspenders, you'll be accused of thinking she's a tart. But play your cards right, and you can make it a win-win purchase.

Step 1. Reconnaissance. Get into her underwear drawer and have a good root around. You're looking for her bra size, e.g. 34B, and pant size, e.g. 14. While you're in the underwear drawer also note any colors, patterns or fabrics she likes, but

French Underwear

Nylon bodice
with panties

Silk bra and
panties

8.5 / 10

6.5 / 10

4 / 10

don't overstay your welcome—explaining to your girlfriend that you're not a cross-dresser is something no man should ever have to do…more than once.

Step 2. Research. Get on the Internet and find the best price for you. Remember that, if you are using your work computer, you may be contravening the company Internet protocols, not to mention confusing the IT administrator, so be discreet. There are all sorts of lingerie: French underwear, push-up bras, suspender belts, stockings, bustiers and basques. All very exciting, for sure, but soon enough you'll need to stop drooling and start thinking.

Step 3. Buying. Find a female assistant and ask for help. Tell her what your girlfriend doesn't like about her body, and she'll be able to help you pick out something sexy and thoughtful that isn't slutty and offensive. No matter what you might be swayed by, crotchless panties are a no-no. Pure silk is the classiest option, and fine cotton can be lovely too. If you can afford it, avoid cheap nylons and synthetics. Flesh colors and ointment pinks ARE NOT sexy. Black or white is your safest bet.

Finally, get it gift-wrapped to add a touch of class. And keep the receipt—women are notoriously hard to please and she might want to exercise her right to exchange, especially if you bought her a leopard-print G-string.

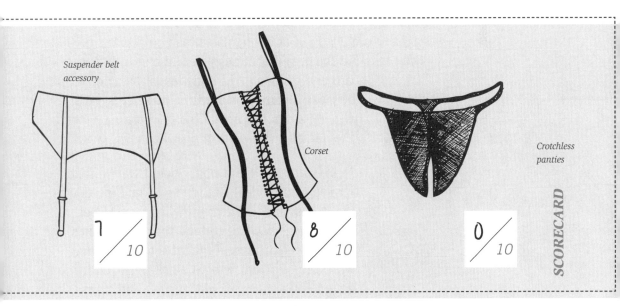

Suspender belt accessory

Corset

Crotchless panties

7/10   8/10   0/10

SCORECARD

Walk-through guide to speed dating

Speed dating—the fast track to happiness. Or hell, depending on the percentage of women present old enough to be your mom. Worse, are your mom. Here's how to have an experience you won't forget in a hurry.

Find a speed-dating company on the Internet. Sign up and pay by card to confirm the booking. You will receive your login details to the site as well as directions to the venue.

Dress for the evening as though you were going on a real date. Looking good will give you confidence—but don't overdo it. You don't want to look like an overdressed jerk. A modestly dressed jerk is far more likely to pull.

When you arrive, saunter over to the bar and throw a whisky down your throat Wild West style before making your way over to the function room; you'll recognize it immediately as it will resemble a mature version of the Junior High dance—men floating around, biting their thumbs as the women, standing in little clusters, giggle and timidly point at the hunkiest man on display. Give your name to the organizer. She or he will be the one with a clipboard and a smile like a cheerleader on acid. You will be given a name badge with a number on it, a pen, and a piece of card. This is where you write the names and details of the people you meet.

Next, stand back and wait. Soon it will be time for you to take your seat. The girls go first, don't barge past and knock them flying like skittles at a teenage bowling party. Once all the ladies are seated, sit down at the table corresponding with your number. When the bell rings you'll have three minutes to sell yourself and assess the talent.

Make eye contact with your speed date, and if you are attracted to her use body language to your advantage. No, that doesn't mean licking your lips while staring at her cleavage. Simply hold eye contact, and smile as you talk. Ask witty and open questions, i.e., ones that require more than "yes" or "no" for an answer. Something like, "If you were a biscuit, which sort of biscuit would you be?" If the answer is Cream Cracker, you've been warned.

Don't try too hard, but let your personality shine through. Be honest—don't give her a pack of lies about running a multi-national record company when you actually work in the local used record shop.

Mumbling into the table while shiftily looking over your shoulder is not going to seduce anyone, but don't talk about yourself too much or spill out your entire life story. Speed dating doesn't mean speed talking. Allow the woman space to talk, to answer your questions and to ask you questions in return.

When the bell rings again you'll have about twenty seconds to shuffle to the next table. Say goodbye and shake hands before you leave the table, and don't sprint off, even if it was the worst three minutes of your entire life. Fill out your card while you move to the next table. Some people write down everything, others just write down pointers to remind themselves later on.

There will be a break halfway through and this is a good time to nip to the loo or get another drink—you'll probably need a stiff one by this point. If the first half has gone disastrously, reflect on where you might be going wrong. If you suspect you've barely got any ticks, perhaps you should be more smiley and open?

When the night is over the last bell will toll and the organizers will thank you all for coming. Stay behind and talk to the others if you're having a good time, or simply run. The choice is yours and it will not really affect how many ticks you'll earn.

Once home, log on to the site and add your ticks. Ticks imply that you would "consider" meeting that person again. They are not, thank God, legally binding. Over the next week or so, the girls will add their ticks and you will be informed via email or by logging in every day—you know you will, you desperado!—if you've got a match.

If someone wants another dose of your witty repartee, you will receive the phone number or email of your speed dating match and you can start dating the lucky lady for real.

Speed dating topics to avoid:

* Don't moan about how terrible your day or life has been. Save that for when she's officially your girlfriend.

* Computer game "chat" and *Dungeons and Dragons* references are best avoided at all costs.

* Don't mention how goddamn lonely you are.

* Never, ever, ever say, "You're the girl of my dreams and if you leave with me right now, you'll never regret it." Or try the same line minus the word "never." That should get you a laugh, at the very least.

Killer questions to get the conversation flowing:

* What did you want to be when you were a kid? (Don't ask where it all went wrong.)

* What is your greatest achievement? (If she pauses for more than 10 seconds, move on.)

* What's the best experience you've ever had? (Ditto, and move on to worst experiences.)

* If you could live in any time any place where would it be?

* What animal/historical figure/celebrity would you like to be for a day?

How to make a bed like a nurse

Remember when your grandma tucked you into bed and it felt as though you were wearing a straight-jacket; your breath constricted, your arms pinned close to your sides...Blankets and eiderdowns may be a thing of the past, but a nicely made bed is a welcome retreat at the end of a hard day. Here's how to do it in less than five minutes.

Change your sheets and duvet cover every two weeks.

Spread the new bottom sheet over the bed and pull the corners so they overhang the mattress evenly. Smooth out the center and tuck any spare sheet tightly under the side of the mattress. Don't worry about hospital corners.

Pillows and duvets should be plumped and aired every two weeks. If possible leave them out in the sunshine for the day to give them a good airing. Sunshine will also help kill any germs. Stuff your pillows in pillowcases and place at the head of the bed. The open side of the pillows should face the edge.

Turn your duvet cover inside out. To save time, you should also remember to simply wash and dry it inside out. Reach inside the inside out cover—as though you're going to pull it over your head—and grasp the two corners of the opposite end. Still clutching the cover, through the fabric, grab the two end corners of the duvet. Flick the cover over the duvet and lifting your hands as high as possible—stand on the bed if you like—shake like mad until the cover falls down to the bottom of the duvet. Clip the buttons or toggles at the bottom, shake out at either end, and lay over the bed. Goodnight, Goldilocks.

How to beat BO

Returning to the gym's changing room to discover a man in a radioactive suit brandishing a pair of your glowing tighty-whities and T-shirt is not a joyous experience, even if your favorite TV show is Doctor Who. *Like all your enemies, you have to know what makes BO tick to defeat it.*

Body odor comes from friendly bacteria munching on sweat and natural body oils. The bacteria has to stay because it's reducing the chances of infections taking hold all over our bodies, but we do want to limit the amount of lunch it has. In other words we want to limit what's on the menu. So, from head to toe, this is what you do to reduce the amount of sweat and oil we produce and keep bad odors at bay.

Head. Wash your hair at the roots at least every other day and more frequently when Mr. Sun's out as this will remove dead skin and grease.

Bad Breath. Test your breath by licking the back of your hand and smelling the result, as this is far more effective than breathing into a cupped hand. Brush your teeth and your tongue at least twice a day, floss, and drink lots of water as saliva trumps bacteria. Chewing on parsley can also sweeten bad breath, pineapple cleans the mouth with a friendly enzyme, and a spoonful or two of unsweetened natural yogurt will also reduce the bacteria. See your dentist for a check-up and visit the hygienist every six months.

Armpits. Deodorant will downplay odor, antiperspirants jam up your sweat glands, and cotton clothes will absorb moisture and reduce sweat. If you're ever caught short with no deodorant, a good trick is to nab some baking soda from the kitchen—pat it under your arms just like talcum powder to combat the pong.

A splash of cider vinegar also does the trick. Don't wear the same shirt two days running. If you can't afford to buy a new wardrobe, wash your clothes on a hot cycle and this will help get rid of the smell better than washing on an eco-friendly cycle at 86°F.

Feet. Wash them daily, all over, and between the toes. If the problem persists, and you have unusually malodorous feet, try soaking your feet in a bowl of warm water with a couple of tablespoons of white vinegar. Do this for 10 to 15 minutes each morning before leaving the house. Dry feet thoroughly, and air them by wearing sandals and cotton socks; you never know—they might look nice with your tighty-whities and T-shirt.

How to survive sleeping rough for a night

49

For some people bus stops and bushes are more than just street furniture, they're a makeshift bed. Sleeping with only the twinkling of the stars for company is thought to be endured by up to as many as 1.6 million young people every night in the U.S., and if you're careless with your house keys, fall foul of your backdoor latch, or miss the last train home you'll be living in their street under their rules.

Think of safety first. Find somewhere sheltered from the wind and rain; preferably somewhere you won't be spotted but not too far from civilization. Don't trust anyone you don't know and keep any items you own in your pockets.

Keeping warm is the next most important thing, so avoid sleeping directly on the ground with a hubcap for a pillow and bed down with some cardboard or newspapers. There are usually lots of unwanted newspapers in bins and cardboard outside shops. Try to cover your hands, feet, and head as body heat escapes from these places first. Take a newspaper and wrap it round your midriff and back, against your skin, then pull your top down over it. Newspaper is extremely insulating and will help you retain body heat.

Snow is also a superb insulator if you happen to live in Alaska or get caught out at night in the Rockies—it takes five minutes to build a snow hole and it is a lifesaver.

Once morning breaks, you'll return home covered in grime and dopey-eyed but the next time you pass someone on the streets you'll be able to empathize with their plight and flip them a thought, or even a coin.

How to fart in front of your girlfriend

Read any relationship's small print and you'll find the unwritten rule declaring the right to fart once the honeymoon's over. Anyone who argues differently has never truly been in love.

However, two whole months of excessive clenching can be detrimental to any young man's health, and result in a *Riverdance* leg movement resembling a seizure of some kind. Here's how to break wind without breaking the rules of relationship harmony.

Outside. Secure separation from your loved one and let the bountiful British breeze do the rest. Don't, no matter how tempting, cock your leg like a Jack Russell under his favorite tree, and trumpet the first verse of the "Last Post."

Indoors. Go covert. Excuse yourself, go to the room furthest away from you, open a window and relax. Don't drop your trousers, squeeze your buttocks between the frame and announce yourself loudly to the neighbors, and, if you choose the toilet, be warned. A silent squeaker can often sound like a bomb blast when amplified in the toilet bowl, reddening your cheeks and ruining your chances.

Watch what you eat. Scoffing a three-bean burrito and expecting the jungle to be free of rumble is noxious naivety. We all know what beanz meanz.

Get a dog. Book-ending every sulphuric stencher with a lift of the T-shirt and a muffled "Busterrrrrrr!" like a highwayman with a speech impediment will completely absolve you of responsibility.

Last but not least. Embrace your bowel movements and introduce a "Dutch Oven" into your midnight playground. Fart, lift the bed covers over her head and, at the top of your voice, yell "Death to the honeymoon." Not even a pack of flatulent wolves could get you out of that one.

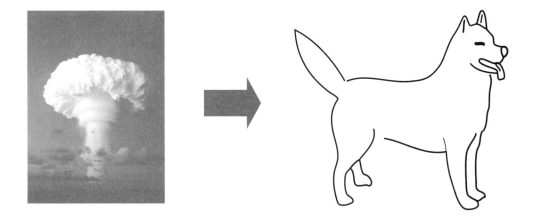

How to impress your girlfriend's parents

"Deceased, the day he met my parents." So reads the epitaph to many a relationship's tombstone. Here's a way to put a stop to one of love's most common killers.

Preparation. Do some research about her parents' interests and lives so you can tailor your conversation winningly when you meet them. That way they'll see you as an intelligent lively person, not just some lowlife Lothario desperate to get into their daughter's underwear.

First impressions. Dress smart. We're not talking necktie and suspenders, but shirt and jeans is a good start.

The greeting. A warm smile and a kind "nice to meet you" will suffice for Mom, but only a strong handshake will do for Dad. He's going to try to break your hand, so you better be ready and give as good as you get in return.

General rules. Don't swear, address them as Mr. and Mrs., not Mom and Dad (unless they tell you otherwise), and don't make sexual comments to the daughter or the mother—it has happened. Be polite, but speak your mind, smile a lot, and don't, whatever happens, lose confidence. Also, remember to butter them up and tell them what a witty, intelligent, and lovely daughter they have. But don't overdo it; you don't want to give the impression you'd go on a killing spree if she dumped you the following evening. Don't be afraid to show your belle a bit of affection, but a full-on makeout while Dad is saying grace is beyond the pale.

Table manners. Compliment the cooking with enthusiasm and accept a plate of seconds no matter how unspeakable it is. Don't drink too much alcohol—throwing up in their toilet and urinating in the cat's litter tray won't win any Brownie (or Scout) points.

The departure. If it looks like Mom wants a hug, don't disappoint. Doing the same to Dad might be overstepping the mark. If either want a kiss, keep your tongue in your mouth.

Gareth May

How to get a spider out of the bath without having a panic attack

Arachnophobia: the fear of spiders and a 1990s B-movie staring John Goodman and a papier-mâché tarantula even a tripped-out Damien Hirst couldn't cook up. Spiders are one of the few creatures that make grown men turn into little girls. Here's how to deal with the little bastards.

If time is on your side, simply avoid all contact. Tear off a lengthy piece of toilet paper and drape it over the edge of the bath to create a makeshift ladder. Leave the bathroom and the next time you enter he'll have done a runner.

If immediate action is required—your lady wants a bath, now— grab a jam jar or mug and place it over the spider. He'll start scuttling around, so quickly slide a piece of hard cardboard under your receptacle and flick it upright, trapping the spider inside. Trek out to the garden, find a patch of grass, remove the cardboard lid, invert the jar and tap the lid until the spider topples out, bleary-eyed and befuddled. When you return to the house, it is of paramount importance that you throw the contents of the empty jar over your girlfriend, who will respond by searching for the phantom spider down her top for the rest of the night. Either that or she'll dump you. If you're just going to fling the poor soul out of the nearest window, flick the jam jar several times until he's gone.

Feel like being a knight in shining armor? Use your hands. Cup them like you're drinking from a stream, leaving a gap at the fingers. Move towards the spider and surround him. Once he's in your finger cage close the gap. This will make him panic and leap about so resist the temptation to fling him into the corner, and run from the room like you've just walked in on your mom in the shower, but keep your hands closed until you're outside.

Dispatching cobwebs is also easy. Bend a clothes hanger over into a smaller triangle and scoop the whole web up. Carefully place it outside in the bushes and you have reclaimed your home, masculinity intact.

Contrary to household myths spiders don't come out of the drain. The U-bend, which is designed to stop things clogging up the drain and halt the foul stench of the sewers, contains a couple of inches of water. So unless the spider is a keen scuba diver he's not coming through. Where they do come from is anyone's guess. What we do know is that they never knock at the front door.

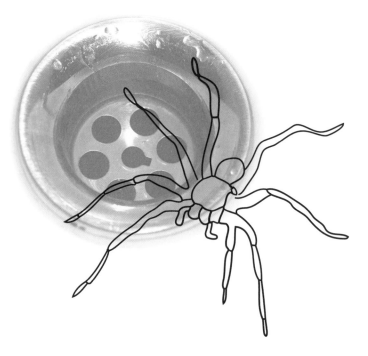

Spa etiquette

Latvians and Estonians beat one another with wet birch branches. Finns cool themselves down by running outside, diving into the snow, and rolling about—all completely naked. Germans and Austrians demand all visitors strip. While we fall over ourselves apologizing if our private parts accidentally go public.

Follow these guidelines and make sure you don't pull a spa faux pas:

* Switch your phone off and talk like you're in a library or you'll be greeted with copious amounts of annoyed people putting their fingers to the lips and saying, "Shuuuuuush."

* Use the robes and towels provided; tying a makeshift toga made of shower curtain around your waist isn't recommended.

* If you're in Latvia, there's no need to tear down a birch tree on your way. All thrashing equipment will be provided.

* Wear flip-flops. You might be sharing a sauna with an athlete, but you don't want to go home with his or her foot.

* Don't eat a heavy meal before entering the spa and don't take your egg salad sandwiches in with you either. If you need to eat while you are there, stick to a healthy and inoffensive fruit salad or yogurt.

* If you're booked in for a facial, have a shave two hours prior to the treatment.

* If you're worried about getting naked—don't. It's perfectly acceptable to wear swimming trunks. Graying old tighty-whities are less welcome.

* Use all the amenities on offer; if you've spent a lot of money, take your time and make the most of it.

Massage Tips:

* Take a warm shower before the massage.

* Drink plenty of water before and after.

* You can request to keep your underpants or swimmers on if you'd rather not go commando.

* Never drink alcohol before a massage—however, a massage is just the thing if you have a hangover.

* If you want a male—God knows why—masseur feel free to ask.

* If the New-Agey music is too loud, the lights too low, or the temperature too hot—speak up.

* Likewise, if you prefer a stronger touch—if she thinks she's being too rough, inform her you're enjoying it.

* Take your time to leave the treatment room after the massage—but don't snuggle up and start to snore.

* You are not expected to talk—you're having a massage, not taking a taxi.

* It's quite common to get an erection mid-massage and very uncouth to do anything with it. Say no more.

Steam room and sauna rules:

* Don't wear swimming shorts with bits of metal on them or you'll be hopping like Tigger when they get hot and burn your bits.

* Remove glasses or contact lenses before a steam or sauna.

* Sit on your towel.

* Roughly fifteen minutes is about right for a sauna, six minutes for steam.

* Have a cold shower or a dip in the plunge pool between sessions to get the circulation going and cool you down.

* If you begin to feel dizzy or out of sorts leave straight away.

* The higher up you sit the hotter it will be in the sauna or steam room.

* Drink plenty of water.

Quick guide to shaving brushes

Invest in a badger-hair brush, not a cheap imitation. Badger hair is used due to its natural strength, enduring qualities, its ability to retain water, and overall softness. Note: no badgers were harmed in the making of this tip.

A brush's quality and price depends on the size of the handle and the quality and density of the hair. The best brushes are handmade from the hair from a badger's neck—the best hair for water retention on the planet. They can cost from $40 to $800 but if you apply the foam properly a cheaper brush will work fine.

There are three types of brush:

Pure. Dark hair with a coarser feel. *Short to medium length.*

Best. Grayish tip with a softer touch. *Medium to long length.*

Super. Cream-white tip, super-soft touch. *Longest length.*

* Always store the brush upright on its handle; you will damage the bristles if you rest it on its side.

* Look after your brush properly and it will serve you well for three years at least.

STI breakdown: symptoms and treatments

Presenting Complaint

You order every innuendo-named cocktail on the menu, stand in the pouring rain while she searches for her house keys, before swinging your trousers around like a Chippendale and smashing the bedside lamp. You suffer a major malfunction at the most inappropriate time. Wake up and accidentally wander into her roommate's bedroom naked looking for the toilet, then grab your clothes and run to the nearest bus stop while cradling your testicles.

Drunken one-night stands can be good, bad, or downright ugly, but we've all had one. Trouble is, you can end up with more than you bargained for in the form of an STI. Here's a guide to what to look for and how to deal with the problem:

SECTION A: CHLAMYDIA

Symptoms	Treatment
Known as the silent disease because there are often no symptoms. A watery and gray discharge from the penis, which can mark your underwear, inflamed and swollen testicles, irritation at the end of the penis which will disappear after 2–3 days, swelling and irritation of the eyes.	Several checks are administrated including urine test, swabs, and testicle examination. A course of antibiotics is prescribed. Chlamydia is best treated early on; if it is left untreated for longer it can be a lot harder to cure and can cause infertility.

Examination notes:

Onset of symptoms: 1–3 weeks

SECTION B: CRABS OR PUBIC LICE

Symptoms	Treatment
Itchy skin at night, red pimply rash, visible tiny white eggs like head nits and/or yellow-gray crab-like lice in your pubic hair, armpits or eyebrows, bites on thighs forming blue spots on skin.	Wash all your clothes and bedding on a 125°F wash to kill all the lice. Malathion lotion can be bought over the counter, but see your GP for a prescription and advice on special shampoos, creams, or lotions to banish the critters for good.

Examination notes:

Onset of symptoms: 1–3 weeks

SECTION C: GENITAL WARTS

Symptoms	Treatment
White or flesh-colored singular bumps or cauliflower clusters anywhere on the penis and urinary tract. Itchy and difficult to spot.	There is no guaranteed way to completely cure genital warts, which may return after treatment. Various courses of treatment are available including application of a resin by a nurse, a gel, freezing with liquid nitrogen, laser treatment, and minor surgery.

Examination notes:

Onset of symptoms: 1–3 months

SECTION D: GONORRHOEA

Symptoms	Treatment
Burning sensation when peeing, a thick yellow, green, or white discharge from the penis or bottom, inflamed testes or prostate gland. Increased urination.	A swab at the sexual health clinic will confirm the infection, followed by a course of antibiotics in tablet, liquid, or injection form.

Examination notes:

Onset of symptoms: 1–14 days

SECTION E: SYPHILIS

Symptoms	Treatment
Small painless ulcers on the penis, bottom, and lips, swollen lumps on groin, neck, or armpit, a rash that doesn't itch and fever. When left untreated syphilis can be fatal.	After diagnosis syphilis is easily treated with a 1–14 day course of antibiotics. Check-up needed before you can resume normal sexual contact.

Examination notes:

Onset of symptoms: 10 days–3 months

SECTION F: HEPATITIS A OR B

Symptoms

Yellowing of the whites of your eyes and skin, vomiting, flu, no appetite, joint ache, weight loss, abdominal pain.

Treatment

A blood test is needed to confirm the infection which is difficult to treat. May clear up by itself within two months but may recur. Avoid fatty foods and alcohol as hepatitis can lead to more serious liver disease.

Examination notes:

Onset of symptoms: 1–3 weeks

SECTION G: HERPES

Symptoms

Itchy and tingling sensation in the genital area, small painful blisters which leave painful sores when burst, headaches, pain when urinating, backache, swollen glands, and fever. Sometimes symptoms do not occur for several years while the virus remains dormant. Outbreaks can last for up to 20 days before becoming dormant once more.

Examination notes:

Onset of symptoms: 2–7 days

Treatment

Several checks are administrated including urine test, swabs, and a blood test. There is no effective treatment that will cure genital herpes, as the virus remains in the body once it is infected, but anti-viral drugs can be diagnosed which will lessen the symptoms over time. To deal with an outbreak when it occurs, take painkillers, wash your genitals with salty warm water, wear loose clothing, pee in the bath to reduce pain when urinating, drinks lots of water, get lots of rest, and avoid sexual contact from the onset of symptoms until the sores have completely healed.

A breakdown of golf scoring

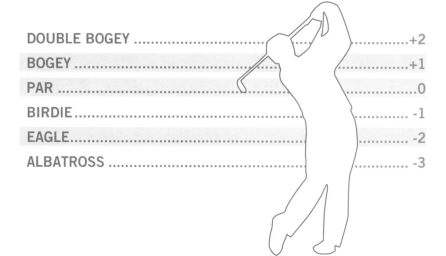

DOUBLE BOGEY .... +2

BOGEY .... +1

PAR 0

BIRDIE .... -1

EAGLE .... -2

ALBATROSS .... -3

The quick metric to imperial conversion guide

INCHES TO CENTIMETERS ... *Multiply by 2.5*

YARD TO METERS .... *Subtract 10% (1m = 3.3 yards)*

MILES TO KILOMETERS .... *Multiply by 1.6 (or 8/5)*

FAHRENHEIT TO CELSIUS .... *Multiply by 5, and divide by 9 (roughly, take away 30, divide by 2)*

PINTS TO LITERS .... *Halve (1l = 1 ¾ pints)*

GALLONS TO LITERS .... *Multiply by 4.5*

POUNDS TO KILOS .... *Halve (1kg = 2¼lb)*

How to change a tire like an AAA man

Underworld. Netherworld. Inferno. Abode of the Damned. Hell has many names yet one true definition: finding yourself stranded on a country lane that looks like the film set of Deliverance *with a shrieking girlfriend, pouring rain, no battery on your phone, a punctured tire, and no idea how to change it.*

Tip: If you are nervous about changing a tire, it might be a good idea to have a trial run at home in good weather and in daylight. Then you'll be more confident when you have to do it in an emergency situation.

Here's how to deal with the situation like a seasoned AAA man.

Be prepared. As a driver it's up to you to make sure that your car is properly equipped for emergency breakdowns.

IN YOUR GLOVE COMPARTMENT, YOU SHOULD HAVE:

- *Vehicle handbook* which you should have read thoroughly and be able to recite on demand

- *Flashlight and spare batteries*

IN YOUR TRUNK:

- *Hazard triangle*

- *Spare tire* with adequate tread. If, like most men, you have never looked at your spare tire, check it. In the worse case scenario it could be one of those weedy "training" wheels that looks more at home on a child's pedal car. And unless you drive a child's pedal car, it's not really going to help you out in a crisis.

- *A jack* suitable for your type of car

- *Lug wrench*
- *Wheel chock*

LUXURIES:

- *Something to kneel on*—not your girlfriend's coat, or her dog
- *Gloves*
- *Reflective jacket* for safety

WHAT TO DO:

1. When you get a puncture, slow down and drive at no more than 5mph until you are at a lay-by or a side turning with a hard, smooth, level surface. Pull on the handbrake and put the car into either first gear (if pointing up a hill) or reverse (if pointing down one). If it's an automatic, select "park."

2. Turn off the engine and turn on your hazard lights.

3. Get all passengers out of the car, for their safety. Yes, your girlfriend can suffer in the freezing cold with you. All passengers should move away from the car and well out of the road.

4. Place the hazard triangle at the side of the road to alert other drivers.

5. Chock the wheel diagonally opposite the flat tire—a piece of wood or a brick will do.

6. Take out the spare tire, the jack and the lug wrench from the trunk.

7. Now remove the hubcap with the end of the jack handle.

8. Next, position the jack as indicated in your owner's handbook—this is important as the jack will pierce the car's underside if it isn't placed beneath a strengthened area.

9. Then, without having jacked up the car, and using the lug wrench, loosen the nuts on the wheel you intend to change by half a turn, but do not remove them. Turn counter-clockwise to loosen and try to loosen all the nuts equally.

10. Start pumping the jack; keep going until the flat tire lifts off the ground by about 2–3 inches. Once the car body is raised sufficiently, push the spare wheel under the body; this will act as a safety cushion should the car slip off the jack. Unscrew the nuts in diagonal pairs, remove, and place together in the upturned hubcap.

11. After having taken off the nuts, remove the wheel with your weight forward to stop you from falling backward. Fit the spare, ensuring the valve stem is on the outside.

12. Fit wheel nuts in diagonal pairs and turn until finger-tight, but don't tighten them all the way.

13. Using the jack, lower the car until the tire just kisses the road. Then, using the lug wrench, lightly tighten the wheel nuts.

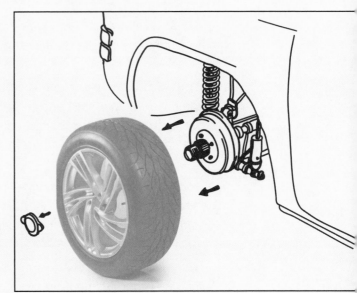

14. Remove the punctured wheel from under the car, finish lowering the vehicle and remove the jack.

15. Finally, fully tighten the wheel nuts and get back on the road from hell. Don't forget to get the damaged tire replaced or repaired as soon as possible—you never know when there'll be a next time.

How to tie the perfect full Windsor knot

For some modern males, the rule of thumb is the bigger the knot, the bigger the impact. Step up, the Windsor knot. This wide and triangular knot, the fat man of the tie world, is worn by most respectable men.

Stand in front of the mirror; this makes sure you get all the crossovers correct and reduces the risk of auto-strangulation.

Lift up your shirt collar and place the tie around your neck.

Step 1. The fat end, **F**, should hang about twice the distance, a foot or so, below the thinner end, **T**.

Step 2. Cross **F** over **T** and then bring **F up through the gap** between the collar of your shirt and tie as close to your neck as you can go without fainting. You've got to do this three times so don't allow the knot to get fat from the off.

Step 3. Pull **F back down, underneath T** and to the right and back through the loop to your right. By this point **F** will be inside out and the knot around your neck will be fairly fat.

Step 4. Bring **F across the front to the left**, pull it up through the loop and then, using a finger to widen the gap, push back down through the outer part of the loop you just made.

Step 5. Finally, tighten the knot carefully, adjust and straighten out. It should be tight to your neck, just below your Adam's apple, and there should be what's called a "Vicious V" where the tie leaves the knot.

The fat part of the tie should hang about an inch above your belt buckle, two shirt buttons up from your waist, so if the thinner end hangs below try again with the fat end hanging lower down.

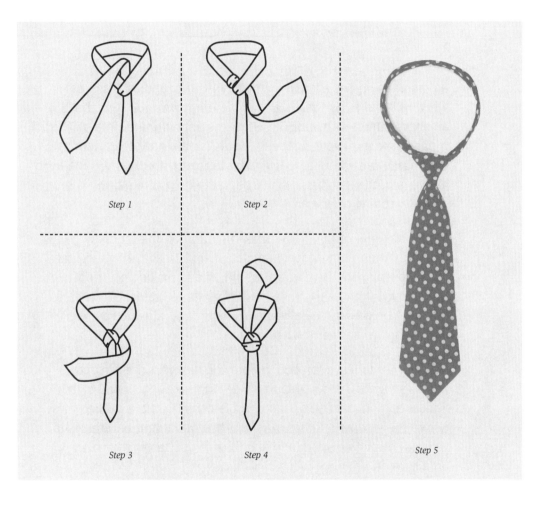

Step 1

Step 2

Step 3

Step 4

Step 5

In a professional setting, ties say a lot about our character so resist the temptation to take a school compass to it. Just take your time and you'll get it right.

How to convince your girlfriend it's NOT man-flu

Mocking men for suffering from a hypochondriac's dose of man-flu has become a popular female winter sport. Here's how to reclaim a man's right to be ill too.

As much as it goes against your every instinct and as much as you'd rather die than make an appointment with your GP, make an appointment with your GP. Stick the appointment time on the fridge; write it on your forehead, whatever you have to do to make the missus see you're actually going to the doctor. By the time her gaping mouth has closed, you'll be in the drugstore getting your mitts on some antibiotics.

In the first days of the illness make an effort to do everything yourself. When the first few barrages of snide man-flu remarks let fly, keep your cool. By getting out of bed and making an effort to go to work, you'll probably make her feel guilty as hell for all the jibes the night before—especially when she finds an anemic zombie sobbing in the shower the next morning.

Wait for her to leave for work before you don your dressing gown and swan around the house like Hugh Hefner with a head cold. Ensure all comics, DVDs, and console controllers are packed away before the mocker's return. Any hint that you might have enjoyed your day away from work and she'll be on you faster than a fly on a cowpat.

Feel free to milk the malady and add an extra day of loafing to polish off the *Die Hard* quadrilogy. Stay in bed until she's out the door on this day and by the time she's home make sure you're up, changed, and showered. Be warned, bluffing any more than one extra day is man-flu madness and any subsequent illness will be met with suspicion and so much lentil soup you'll wish you'd gone to work instead.

You will need:

Hot water bottle

Man-size tissues

Cup of tea

DVDs

Lots of sympathy

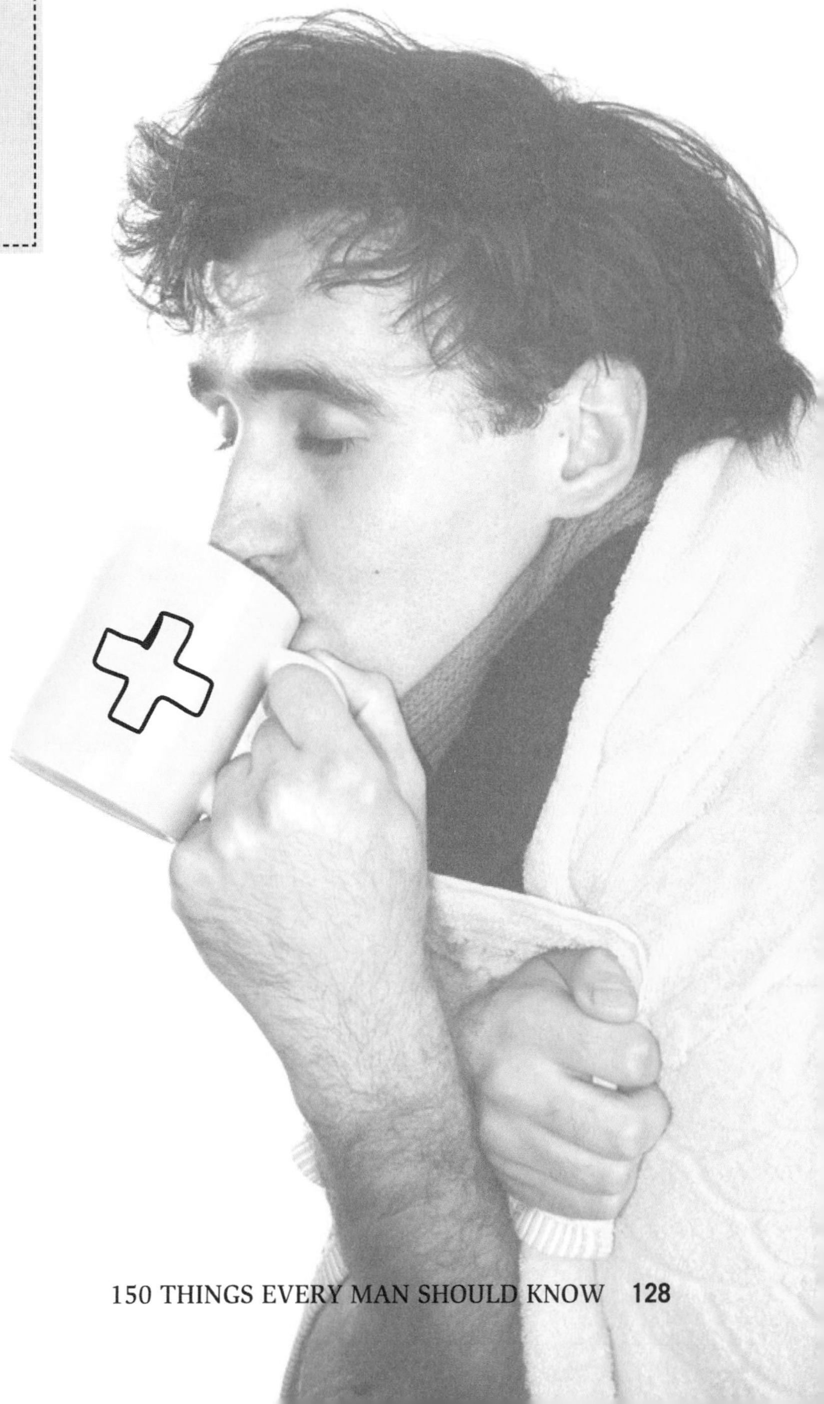

How to wolf whistle

Impress the foreman, stagger the lead singer, and hail that cabbie with this blow-by-blow guide to the wolf whistle.

Stand in front of the mirror while you practice.

1. Pull your lips back, so that they are tightly pulled in over your teeth. You should now resemble a gummy old man. The outer edges of your lips might still be visible—this is fine.

2. Put your fingers in your mouth to pull your lower lip taut over your teeth. The fingers you choose depend on whether you have fat or thin fingers; a big or tiny mouth.

The choices are as follows:

* *U-shape with thumb and middle finger or index finger of one hand*
* *Right-hand and left-hand index fingers*
* *Right-hand and left-hand middle fingers*
* *Right-hand and left-hand little fingers*

3. Place each finger halfway between the corners and center of your lips, to the first knuckle. Angle your fingernails inwards, toward the center of your tongue.

4. Draw your tongue back so the tip touches the bottom of your mouth at the lower gums. Broaden and flatten it over your lower back teeth.

5. Inhale deeply and then exhale quickly, forcing your breath out over the top of your tongue and your lower lip. Experiment with your tongue position, the lips and finger positioning and the power of your blow, until you can hear a resemblance of a whistle. Blow gently at first and adjust until the pitch increases.

6. Once you have a weak-sounding whistle, you can perfect your technique to hone it to a strong, high-pitched and clear sound—which might come in handy if your parents' collie is running towards the interstate. To do this you need to form a "bevel." This is an angled edge that, when air flows through it, creates a strong tone. You've found the "sweet spot" when air is blown directly over the sharpest part of the bevel, maximizing the volume and tone of your whistle. You'll find the bevel and sweet spot by trial and error, varying your fingers and lip position.

7. Practice in front of a mirror when the mood takes you—it might take a week or two, but don't despair. When you hear that ear-piercing clear high-pitch, you're on the money and an official member of the builders' union.

How to carve a chicken like your dad

Sunday. You've slept in, taken a bath, and read the papers. Weekend sports are on and the smell of a roast fills the house. Soon it will be time to carve the chicken. Here's how to show your dad how it's done.

Remove the chicken from the oven, loosely cover with foil and leave to rest for fifteen minutes. This makes it easier to carve.

Lift the bird on to a chopping board and remove any string.

Use a very sharp carving knife and a fork to steady the bird.

Slide the knife down through the skin, between the body and the leg. Pull the thigh meat away from the bird, by wiggling the knife, until the joint is exposed. Chop down through the ball and socket joint to remove the drumstick and thigh. Divide the drumstick and thigh cutting at the joint. Remove the wings with a knife or by twisting them away by hand.

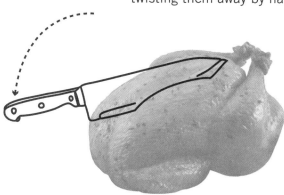

Push the knife carefully down one side of the breastbone and cut the whole breast away from the carcass. Slice the breast into portions.

Spin the chicken round and repeat on the other side.

Drop any scraps of meat to the baying crowd of cats, dogs and grandparents.

Present all the chicken pieces along with any stuffing or trimmings on a serving dish and watch as the family or guests devour it without any acknowledgement of your artistry.

Sports injuries breakdown

Like David Beckham in the 2002 World Cup and Wayne Rooney in the 2004 Euros, many a man's summer has been ruined by the dreaded metatarsal. The soccer player's Achilles's heel, this seemingly insignificant little bone in the foot has plagued fans and players for thousands of years.

Here's a list of other sporting ailments to be on the lookout for and how to treat them.

Runner's knee.

Symptoms. A swelling at the back of your knee and a grating sensation as you walk. Caused by running on hard surfaces such as pavements and roads.

Healing. Apply the PRICE regimen and when you return to running, stick to grass surfaces.

Tennis elbow.

Symptoms. Swelling on the outer edge of the elbow, caused by an inflamed tendon. Your elbow will be tender to the touch and painful during movement, particularly pouring, gripping, lifting, and opening doors. Can remain painful for up to 12 weeks.

Healing. Limit movement of your elbow for 2–3 weeks—so you'll have to use the other hand if indulging in self-pleasure. Anti-inflammatory tablets, an elbow support or, if you're gearing up for the Wimbledon semi-final, a cortisone injection are also options.

Golfer's elbow.

Symptoms. As for tennis elbow, but affects the underside of the elbow.

Healing. The PRICE regimen, limit movement, anti-inflammatory tablets and avoid the driving range for a few weeks.

Jogger's nipple.

Symptoms. Itchy and inflamed nipples caused by excessive chafing during running, especially in wintery climes.

Healing. Liberally apply petroleum jelly before your brisk jaunt round the park to relieve pain and, in future, as a preventative measure.

Pulled muscles and strains.

Symptoms. Pulled and strained muscles cause pain, muscle spasms, loss of strength, and possibly swelling.

Healing. Stick to PRICE regimen, try a hot soak with Epsom Salts and for minor sprains and muscle strain apply Tiger Balm.

PRICE *is a healing regimen used mostly for sprains and strains, however the principles apply for pretty much any sports injury:*

P—Protect the area with support such as a sling, if necessary.

R—Rest for at least 48–72 hours.

I—Ice. Use an ice pack or a bag of frozen peas on the affected area for 10 minutes every 2 hours.

C—Compress the injury with bandages to reduce movement and swelling.

E—Elevate the body part on a pillow and get your mom to bring you tea.

How to overtake like Jeff Gordon

When you're in a rush all the traffic lights turn red. Roadwork pops up out of nowhere. Normally bare pedestrian crossings become teeming with annoying people sauntering to the other side. And to cap it all you get stuck behind someone doing their best impression of Morgan Freeman in Driving Miss Daisy.

Here's how to overtake so Morgan won't see you for dust:

1. Even Galileo, Isambard Kingdom Brunel, and Judith Chalmers rolled into one couldn't judge the speed of oncoming traffic. If in doubt pull back in.

2. Always indicate well in advance when waiting to overtake.

3. If you want to overtake more than one vehicle, make sure the road is well clear ahead and that there is a sizeable gap before each car should you need to pull in sharply.

4. If you're tired, do not overtake. You might be desperate for a bed but a hospital bed shouldn't be considered an option.

5. Ask yourself at least three times if it's really essential to overtake the car in front.

6. When overtaking at night look for signs of oncoming headlights in the distance or around corners.

7. Give yourself extra distance when overtaking a truck, both when behind and alongside.

8. Never overtake on corners, a brow of a hill, a bendy windy road, or before a humpback bridge. If the road ahead isn't straight don't even think about it.

9. Never attempt to overtake when there are turnings ahead as a car may pop up from nowhere.

10. After overtaking, pull in at a safe distance (at least a car length) and indicate back in.

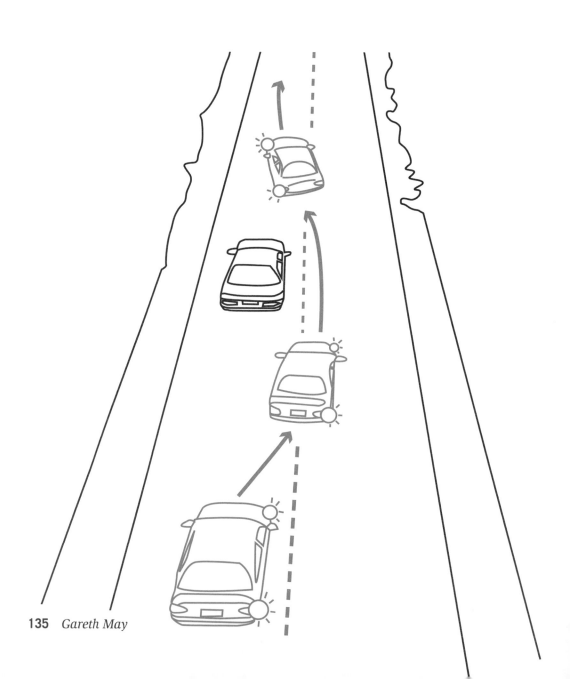

How to tell if your pint of real ale has gone bad

Underage drinking followed a strict regime. Shuffle into the bar in a huddle. Brave the bar with hands wrist-deep in pockets. Order in the most inarticulate, inexpressive manner possible, attempting to lower your voice so that any dogs in the vicinity don't start running for you. Cry at the sound of four half-pint glasses being filled with ice and Diet Coke.

But times move on and the true man will soon enough need to know how to spot a dodgy brew and when to return it. You wouldn't want to reject a perfectly poured pint, would you?

What to look out for:

Pipe cleaner still in pipes. A distinct taste of bleach should make the landlord take note and offer a fresh pint. A watery pint may well mean the pipes have been cleaned but the old beer hasn't been flushed through properly.

Premature pouring. A cloudy pint, sulphurous smell and metallic taste indicate inadequate resting time. Barrels of ale should be left to rest—"laid to clear" in brewery speak—for at least a day.

Bacteria or yeast infection. A smell of sweat or sewage means the pub's pipes have a yeast infection. Or your friend needs a bath. Hazy beer is another indicator. If everything looks hazy, the beer's fine and it's you with the problem.

Dirty pipes. If your beer isn't as clear and shiny as a Crufts winner's coat, look for little globules floating about in the liquid—reminiscent of the spaceship in *Inner Space*, without Dennis Quaid of course. Dip your finger into the head. If you pull it out and no amount of head sticks, you might be the victim of dirty pipes.

Keg laid too long. Old barrels produce beer with an insipid and flat taste. A lingering TCP tang, or vinegar flavor also indicate your beer is off.

Sunlight damage. The smell of cabbage or rotten eggs means the kegs have been left in the sunlight and earned more that a good tan.

Watered down. A watery taste may be caused by a lack of carbonation, or an over-chilled glass, as the icy condensation has "watered" down the beer. Don't hesitate to ask for another.

Oxidization. Look out for how the bartender pulls your pint. Smooth plunging motions ensure the beer isn't filled with oxygen. If the bartender rushed the pouring and you end up with a beer smelling of wet paper, feel free to return it.

Problem with the glass. If the glass is too warm your beer will lose flavor. If the head is non-existent or quickly fading, the glass may be dirty.

Advanced tips:

Always compare your pint with one of your friends' before complaining.

Let the beer rest at room temperature before judging its cloudiness. A "chilled haze" forms when the beer is still cold and won't dissipate until it warms up.

Real ales and lagers range from pitch black to light blonde, so know what your beer should look like before complaining.

Wheat beer will often be cloudy.

Be guaranteed a fresher pint by asking for popular ale—active lines mean a better pint.

Hop beer smells fruity and flowery. Malt beer will smell nutty with hints of caramel.

Some beers do have a strong yeasty aftertaste. Don't confuse a fault with your taste buds with a fault with the pub.

A good lasting head equals a good beer. No oral sex jokes please.

No matter how desperate you are, never drink out-of-date beer in cans or bottles.

How to clean borrowed CDs and DVDs in an emergency

Losing a best friend over a mistake is a hard pill to swallow. Sleeping with his girlfriend, his sister, his mom, or even trying to get into bed with him can, and will, result in the two of you never speaking again. However, scratch his favorite CD and the police might have a homicide on their hands. Here's how to clean the evidence before your treachery is revealed to all.

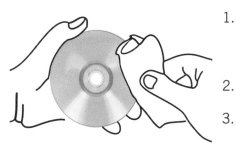

1. Delicately hold the CD by inserting a finger through the middle or by holding it at the edges. Don't touch the shiny bit you're trying to clean.

2. Use a soft clean cloth to wipe off any dust.

3. Greasy or sticky surface—mix some shampoo or dishwasher liquid with warm water and wipe over the surface with the cloth. Wipe back and forth very softly from the center. Don't follow the circles in a circular motion.

4. Fingerprints—after they've been dusted and sent to NCIS, fingerprints should be treated in the same manner as above but with ethanol or methanol. If neither of these are at hand, stick with dishwasher liquid.

5. Never use petroleum-based liquids, as this will ruin the CD.

6. Deep scratches—use car polish but don't polish it all at once. Do it slowly over a day or you risk making matters worse.

7. Small scratches—coat in toothpaste, literally as though you're icing a cake. Leave for a minute or two, then wash off completely under a running tap with warm water.

8. Tiny scratches can be removed with a pencil eraser.

9. Dry completely with a soft clean absorbent cloth before putting the CD back in its case. Don't use a towel, toilet paper, paper tissue or the shirt you're wearing, as they are too abrasive. Cloths specially designed for cleaning your sunglasses or camera lens are ideal.

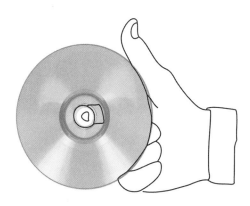

How to remove lipstick from your collar

If you can't wash the shirt right away, blot the lipstick with cold water. Don't saturate it or you will spread the stain. When you're ready to wash, coat the stain in baking soda and wet it with a sponge. Leave to stand for five minutes. Use a dishwashing liquid and soak the shirt in warm soapy water overnight. Wash the shirt like you normally would. Air-dry.

Blot the stain with household ammonia using a cotton ball or Q-tip, then wash the shirt normally.

Hair spray can also do wonders; spray, leave for a couple of minutes, wipe clean, and rinse the stain with warm water.

How to give a massage like a trained masseur

Portuguese personal trainers called Antonio. Antiquarian bookdealers named Ray. Skinny tight-jeaned plumbers called Paul. Men out for your girlfriend come in many shapes and sizes. And none are more feared by men and revered by women than the trained masseur. Strolling into the room with a torso like a porcelain sculpture, swept-back black hair and a family heirloom hidden in his underpants. There's only one way to outdo the mighty masseur: become one yourself.

Setting the scene is your first task. Cracking open a can of Bud Light and mounting your girlfriend like she's Red Rum is not conducive to romance. Preparing a roaring log fire, lighting a few scented candles, placing a blanket on the floor and putting on her favorite mellow or soft music is.

A few pointers first:

The room must be comfortably warm—warm enough to be naked. Massage brings the blood to the surface of the skin and can cool the recipient.

A part of your skin should always be touching hers.

Never ever apply pressure directly on to the spine or neck, you are not a chiropractor and will break her back.

Use scented massage oil but don't grease up like a mechanic— you're rubbing someone's back, not removing an engine. Different scented oils have different effects—lavender is relaxing, ylang ylang and rose are sensuous.

Close your eyes and relax—unless you suddenly smell burning, in which case you'd better hope you don't open them to a reimagining of *The Towering Inferno* starring you, your girlfriend and a rather guilty-looking scented candle.

Once the mood is set you can begin:

Fan stroke. Relaxes and warms the muscles. Place your hands just above her hips and either side of her spine, with your palms down and fingers facing towards her neck. Gradually move them slowly up to her shoulders, fan out to the ends and draw them back down along her rib cage, essentially making the shape of a falling teardrop. Do this eight or so times, applying more pressure with each stroke.

Fig. 1. Fan stroke

Kneading. Get the blood flowing. Grip the flesh around her shoulders lightly between your fingers and the heel of your hands and working slowly and rhythmically squeeze the triangular muscle, the trapezius, beneath the skin. If she cries out you're probably pinching her and not, as your testicles are telling your brain, the genetically engineered love child of Daniel Craig and Russell Brand.

Milking. Deep muscle massage. Knead the muscle with one hand, remove it after one or two squeezes and replace with your other hand. Doing this milking relay will probably result in discovering hard "knots" deep down in the muscle. Work these out using your palm and thumb. They'll keep moving about so give chase; ridding your lover of these little critters is where her back really benefits even if your hands don't.

Fig. 2. Kneading

Raking. Increases circulation. Place your fingertips on her shoulders and slowly rake all the way down to the bottom remembering to apply less and less pressure with each movement.

Feather touches. Rounds the massage off sensually. Repeat the raking motion without any pressure whatsoever. After a few downward strokes break off and doodle with your fingertips, draw invisible love hearts or play a solitary game of noughts and crosses until her groans cease and your hands tire.

Finally, kiss her on the neck and remove your hands at the same time. With any luck, and if she hasn't slipped a disc, her trapezius might not be the only muscle to get a squeeze tonight. Although if she hasn't moved after ten minutes expect nothing more than a lawsuit.

How to fake the perfect sick day

TODAY

Forget all those Kung Fu movies you've seen where the master has a long wispy beard and a balding head. The true master of speed and deception wears a suit and tie. Gentlemen, behold the art of the sick day-puller.

Timing your sick day is crucial, as is planning. The day before you plan to pull one, go into work a lot quieter than usual. As the day drags towards lunch begin to act out your chosen illness. Cough, wince when you swallow or visit the toilet every hour, but don't overdo it; spending the whole afternoon in the loo will arouse the wrong kind of suspicion. At the end of the day your colleagues will notice you're "not yourself" and ask how you are. A simple "I don't feel great if I'm honest" will do and when you leave be sure to say, "See you tomorrow" before you go.

The next morning make the phone call to work. Talk directly to your manager and sound like you're ill. Go into detail, "It's coming out both ends and it just won't stop" will do the trick, but make sure it matches the illness you feigned the previous day.

For a really effective and more advanced sick day, take two days off. The phone call to your manager on the second day will be slightly different, but no less convincing, e.g. "I'm still not quite right—I think I should take one more day at home but I'll be all right tomorrow I'm sure."

Offer to have your work sent to you via email. The manager will decline, but he'll think you're a dedicated member of the workforce and not, as is the truth, a lowly skiver. You can spend the rest of the day doing whatever you like. Just don't go anywhere near your place of work; that's pull-a-sick-day-suicide.

The next day act like you did the day you set the sick day up just switch it round. Act ill in the morning and then by the end of the day leave with a spring in your step and a smile on your face.

January 2nd is traditionally the most popular day of all to pull a sick day.

How to clean your bathroom, toilet, and shower in a quarter of an hour

Everyone likes a bath, no one likes cleaning one. But it's a job that must be done, so just do it quickly.

Rubber gloves. The connoisseur's choice and the bathroom cleaners' first line of defense against the evil forces of the porcelain bus. They should be slapped against the wall like an earl's glove to the face of his duelling nemesis. Pulled on like the King's jewel-encrusted gauntlets. Cherished until the war is won and then discarded, removed inside out like a disembowelled Sooty, and never ever used to do the washing-up. The rules of the Marigold are a simple affair and so too are the steps to achieving a showroom bathroom in fifteen minutes.

Step 1. **Assemble your tools.** You need some powerful toilet cleaner with a bent nozzle, toilet brush, sponge or cleaning rag, a roll of toilet paper, bathroom spray, shower cleaner cream, and a washcloth.

Step 2. **Sink.** Clear away toothbrushes, razors, soap, etc. and wipe the sink clean with toilet paper. Spray the basin, tiles and mirror with the bathroom cleaner, leave for a minute or two and wipe clean with the washcloth. Run hot water and wipe once more until glistening pristinely.

Step 3. **Toilet.** Don the Rubber gloves. Squeeze the toilet cleaner around the bowl making sure the nozzle is right up under the rim. The colorful liquid should ooze down into the water like a psychedelic Niagara Falls. Grab the toilet brush and shove it in there too. Scrub vigorously with the toilet brush all around the bowl removing any unsightly stains and clinging matter. Lift toilet seat and use cleaning rag to wipe all around the toilet rim and clean the underside of seat too. Rinse your cloth thoroughly between wipes. Last, lower the seat and wipe it clean. Flush to rinse, making sure the toilet brush gets a good rinse too. Add a dash of bleach or white vinegar to the toilet bowl to sanitize, whiten and add a suitably disinfected smell to your bathroom.

Step 4. **Shower.** Get naked except for the Rubber gloves, make sure the blinds are drawn—unless you're into that kind of thing—and get in with the cream and washcloth. Squirt cream all over the walls of the shower, if it's a walk-in, or all over the bath, if it's a bath, and wipe it all around. Leave for a couple of minutes. Fold your washcloth over and vigorously wipe around the shower, including head, dials, taps, etc. until all the cream is removed. Use a wad of toilet paper to fish out any hair and pubes from the drain. Put in trash or in toilet and flush.

Step 5. **You.** Remove the gloves and throw them over the top along with the washcloth and cream. Turn the shower on, clean your whole body twice with shower gel, grab a towel and step out victorious into your sparkling bathroom.

How to tell if you're falling in love

If you wake up every morning with butterflies in your stomach and a plank of wood in your underpants you're probably in love. Either that or you have some very interesting nocturnal eating habits and have got on the wrong side of a carpenter.

The signs of being truly head over heels include:

1. Spending every waking hour together.

2. Being mesmerized by her presence. Don't confuse this with infatuation; it should be a two-way street.

3. Talking at night for what feels like an eternity—in a good way.

4. You won't want to leave her side but not in an obsessive, possessive stalker way.

5. Making out with her will be better than having full-blown sex with a stranger.

6. Finding different sides to her personality all the time and falling in love with each of them, no matter how grumpy, strange, or childlike they are.

7. You will find yourself mentioning her in every sentence when you're talking to your friends, your colleagues, and even your granny.

8. You tolerate even her worst taste in films and music.

9. You take more care over your appearance and listen to her fashion advice.

10. When you're not with her, you'll find yourself rehearsing stories in your head you'll tell her later about your day, little anecdotes about what happened on the bus, or what the dessert was like in the cafeteria at lunch.

11. Strangely, you like her much more than her pretty friend with the truly magnificent chest.

Ultimately, love is different for everyone but when you meet that special someone it will feel like you're hanging out with all your best friends at once and you'll want to show them everything from your favorite movies to your favorite moves in bed. Fundamentally, thinking about them will make you smile uncontrollably; who knows what you'll do if you receive a text? Curse that carpenter, probably.

How to out-buff a film buff when you know nothing about film

There's nothing more annoying than a film buff chatting up the same girl as you, impressing her with his knowledge of Ingmar Bergman's The Seventh Seal *or the complete works of Kurosawa. So rather than embarrassing yourself and quoting* Police Academy II *here's how to keep up with the conversation and win back her attention.*

The chances are the film buff will mention at least one of the following directors and even if he doesn't you'll blow him away with these cinematic pearls of wisdom.

1. If the conversation strays towards the early days of film simply say: "For me Welles (Orson) reinvented the way stories are told when he made *Citizen Kane.* And to think he was only 26. Unbelievable." Don't say, "The colors are amazing."

2. If horror and suspense crops up try this one: "For me there's no one like Hitchcock. *Vertigo* is out of this world. A detective story about darkness and desire starring James Stewart. Need I say any more?"

3. As far as gangster movies go you can't go wrong with this: "*The Godfather.* Brando, Pacino, Keaton, Duvall, Caan. It really is a who's who of Hollywood."

4. If none of the above fit the bill a mention of Stanley Kubrick or Woody Allen won't go amiss, but you'll often get asked to back up your name-dropping by citing your favorite movie. For Kubrick it's got to be *2001: A Space Odyssey* but, beware, a true fan would just say, "*2001.*" As for Allen it's a toss-up between *Manhattan* and *Annie Hall*; both are romantic and give you the opportunity to say to the girl: "The main character reminds me of you. She is witty and intelligent."

Congratulations—you've out buffed a film buff without resorting to violence. And if you rush, you'll just make it home in time for Police Academy III.

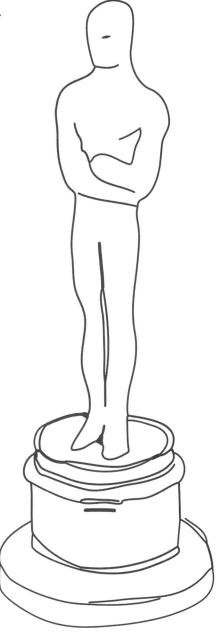

How to wash your clothes like your mom

In your teenage years washing your underwear was part of your mom's job description. Once in your twenties or, heaven forbid, your thirties, you're fast approaching mommy-boy status if your dear old ma is still dealing with your tighty-whities.

Go on. Be a real modern man, and learn how to do your own washing without shrinkage or dying everything pale gray.

Laundry dos and don'ts:

* Divide your clothes into whites, darks and denims, and colors, and wash separately.

* Wash towels separately to keep fluff off your designer T-shirts.

* If your towels or gym socks are smelly and musty, try adding a cupful of white vinegar to the fabric softener compartment.

* Colors that might run—it should warn you on the label— should be washed separately. Be extra wary of new denims and red clothes.

* Avoid high temperatures except for washing white towels and bed linen. If in doubt use 86°F on a normal wash.

* Never put woollens in hot water—only wash in the machine if you have a "Wool Wash" option, otherwise hand wash. Never hang woollens to dry—dry flat to prevent them losing shape

* Silk should only be dry-cleaned or carefully hand washed— remember that when your girlfriend leaves her incredibly expensive one-of-a-kind-underwear lying about the place.

*   Don't overload the washing machine.

*   Liquid or powder detergents should be poured into the dispenser. Tablet detergents should be placed in the net bags (supplied with your pack) at the back of the machine on top of your clothes.

*   Fabric softener should be placed in a separate dispenser and only used if you like the feel of soft fabric on your skin; you big girl.

Guide to washing symbols

 Hand wash only in warm water. Rinse and dry carefully.

Machine wash at the shown temperature in Fahrenheit.

 86°—Colored delicates.

104°—Colored T-shirts and pants.

140°—Very soiled clothes.

 203°—White sheets and towels.

Lines underneath the machine wash symbol inform you of the type of cycle you should use.

 No line—Max speed/cotton cycle.

 One line—Moderate speed/synthetic cycle.

 Two lines—Minimal speed/wool cycle.

△ *OK to bleach.*

◆ *No bleach.*

Drying symbols:

⬜ No dot—No temperature restriction.

⬜ One dot—Maximum temperature of 172°F.

⬜ Two dots—Normal dry.

⬛ Tumble dry at your own risk.

⬜ Hang dry.

⬜ Dry flat.

Ironing symbols:

Ironing allowed.

One dot—Cold iron, 230°F max. Acrylic, nylon and acetate.

Two dots—Hot iron, 300°F max. Polyester and wool.

Three dots—Very hot iron, 392°F. Cotton and linen.

Do not iron.

Dry clean only. The letter and lines indicate special dry cleaning instructions.

Do not dry clean.

There are sometimes other written instructions below the symbols.

Wash like colors together.

Reshape while damp.

Iron on reverse—i.e., iron inside out to preserve logos or printed colors.

Wash inside out.

Guide to NFL postseason division rules

Things can get complicated when teams from the same division have tied records, but don't let those tricky NFL rules leave you tongue-tied. Study up so you can yell your predictions with confidence—preferably through a mouthful of seven-layer dip.

The process to break a tie and determine a division winner:

When two teams have the same won-lost-tied percentages:

1. Head-to-head record.
2. Best won-lost-tied percentage in games played within the division.
3. Best won-lost-tied percentage in common games.
4. Best won-lost-tied percentage in games played within the conference.
5. Strength of victory.
6. Strength of schedule.
7. Best combined ranking among conference teams in points scored and points allowed.
8. Best combined ranking among all teams in points scored and points allowed.
9. Best net points in common games.
10. Best net points in all games.
11. Best net touchdowns in all games.
12. Coin toss.

When three or more teams have the same won-lost-tied percentages:
(Note: If two clubs remain tied after third or other clubs are eliminated during any step, tie breaker reverts to step 1 of the two-club format).

1. Head-to-head record.
2. Best won-lost-tied percentage in games played within the division.
3. Best won-lost-tied percentage in common games.
4. Best won-lost-tied percentage in games played within the conference.
5. Strength of victory.
6. Strength of schedule.
7. Best combined ranking among conference teams in points scored and points allowed.
8. Best combined ranking among all teams in points scored and points allowed.
9. Best net points in common games.
10. Best net points in all games.
11. Best net touchdowns in all games.
12. Coin toss.

What flowers to buy for different occasions

Whether for your mother, sister, or girlfriend, buying a woman flowers can be a minefield. Turn up to a birthday bash with a gas station bouquet of frayed petals and flimsy stalks and you might find yourself wearing the bouquet down the back of your trousers.

Take on board this little lesson in the language of flowers, on the other hand, and you'll be heralded as a model gentleman:

To say "sorry." It may be the hardest word, but so much easier to say with flowers. The rare blue rose symbolizes peace and, being hard to come by, will earn you extra brownie points. Daisies are said to cheer people up and mark new beginnings. Hydrangeas represent understanding, tulips and hyacinths forgiveness, and bluebells suggest sorrowful regret. Alternatively, you could give her a guilt trip with a handful of withered flowers, the symbol of rejected love and gas stations.

Anniversary or Valentine's Day. Forget-me-nots for true love, constancy and memories. Cacti, despite being prickly, symbolize endurance. Red roses are a little passé but if you must go for them buy one or a dozen—eleven red and one white with the white representing your one true love. Just be prepared for the question, "Who do the others represent, you cheating bastard?"

Mother's Day. Yellow flowers are bright and cheery and symbolize adoration, gracefulness and friendship. Dahlias, elegance and dignity, magnolias, magnificence and benevolence, and violets loyalty.

Grandma's birthday. Pink roses sit well with the oldies as they speak of friendship. Purple flowers are often related to royalty and admiration—perfect or the Queen Mom in your life. Irises denote faith and wisdom. A word of warning: don't send Granny orange flowers or chrysanthemums, or worse, orange chrysanthemums (orange symbolizes lust! And, well, chrysanthemums are usually put on graves).

How to take care of a beard

Whether you're going for David Beckham's sexy stubble or Joaquin Phoenix's recluse impression, a beard trimmer with various guard settings is a must-have.

1. Start on a high guard grade and use a range of settings over a few months to find the right look and grade for you.

2. When you trim, don't soak your beard as this could damage the trimmer. Only slightly wet it.

3. Use a normal razor, or unguarded trimmer, to shave on the underside of your chin.

4. Set the trimmer to your usual setting and clip the upper horizontal edges symmetrically.

5. Vertically run your trimmer along the jawline, from ear to chin, in one smooth and steady motion. This will ensure an even clipping. You should be left with a finger's thickness of hair on the underside of your jawline.

6. Run the trimmer over your cheeks, if needed several times, ensuring you are guided by your face's undulations and contours. Wash your beard to remove all clippings.

7. Random gray hairs can be banished with some tweezers—if you're brave.

8. Once you start to trim, your beard will get bushier so be prepared to wield the scythe every other day at least.

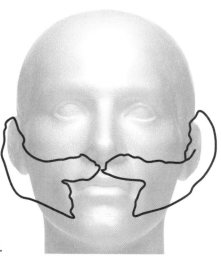

How to take care of a moustache

1. Wet slightly.

2. Comb hair downwards.

3. Use a pair of sharp nail scissors to horizontally cut away any hairs that overhang your top lip.

4. Vertically trim the edges so that they are symmetrical.

5. Push the comb into the body of the mustache and lift it out to the desired depth. Trim down to the teeth of the comb.

6. Comb down once more for a neat finish.

7. Alternatively, look in the mirror, realize that 'staches are for weirdos and shave it all off. Then leave the house in search of a life.

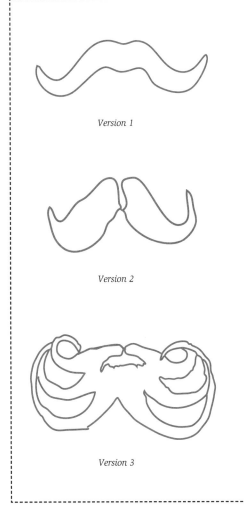

Version 1

Version 2

Version 3

How to survive your first poker night

If you're not careful, the first night you play poker can turn into one long, prolonged wave goodbye to your week's wages. So read carefully because there are certain ways you can reduce the amount you lose and possibly even take home someone else's salary.

 First of all. Watch the other players. Note what hands they win with and what hands they fold on.

 Second. Play a couple of hands yourself, but only bet small amounts of money. It sounds boring and reserved—and it is—but playing safe won't result in you having to choose between telling your dad his Lexus is now owned by Joey "Four Fingers" Capone, or giving one of your own fingers to Joey.

 Third. Use your circumstances to your advantage. It's your first night at the table so people will call you when you bet, but eventually you'll be dealt a good hand. When this happens, play aggressively, and if you're certain you're on a winner don't be afraid to bully the other players with big bets.

 Fourth. Bluffing rarely works. If you want to give it a go, don't try to bluff more than one player at a time because you're more likely to get caught out.

 Last, but not least. If you know someone's got a better hand just fold. It's the person with the most money, not the biggest ego, who goes home happy.

The art of the quickie

Shuffling across the living room floor with your trousers and underwear wrapped around your ankles as your dad's front door key rattles in the lock was humiliating enough on your lonesome. Throw a mascara-smeared, rosy-cheeked lady friend in to the mix, and you've got yourself a wedding day story the whole congregation will hear before the honeymoon car rattles over the horizon.

Quickies are an art form many never master. Here's how to do their name justice:

The time and place aren't of paramount importance. Stalled elevators, empty stairwells, isolated cars, dirty alleyways and clothing shops' dressing rooms are all possibilities. Wham-bam-thank-you-ma'ams don't require a scattering of rose petals, just a stiff wall or a firm floor and you're good to go.

Be sure she's up for it. Don't just wait for her to bend down to pick up a coin and attempt to mount her like a goat. Gauge her reaction by suggesting that you'd like to rip her underwear off right now. If she blushes, kiss her passionately from her lips down to her neck, while showering her with gentle caresses. Whispering seductively in her ear won't hurt either. "I've been thinking about being inside you all day" is a good place to start (unless you're at breakfast or her great-aunt's funeral), but not in Hannibal "I want to wear your skin" Lector voice.

Don't hang about and get too romantic or prolong the experience. You both know it's a quickie so pull her underwear to one side, lower your trousers and get the job done with gusto. Grunt and groan, by all means, but be prepared for the funny looks when you emerge two minutes later from Starbucks' bathroom.

Time-saver tip:

Stick to one position. Now's not the time to be swinging off the chandelier. If she's on top, she stays on top. If you enter her from behind, stay there. Don't whip out the *Kama Sutra* and say, "Want to give 'The Beaver' a crack?"

Don't forget to give her a kiss and a cuddle afterwards as you normally would. You don't have to get into exuberant declarations of love and marriage, but a peck here and a heartfelt squeeze there will make her think it wasn't all about you. Even if it was.

Give your partner the once over, adjust your own clothes accordingly, make sure your hair doesn't look like Albert Einstein's and go back to your daily business.

Quickies are a great way to spice up any relationship, so don't ruin the vibe by stepping back out into the big wide world without first warning your girlfriend that her skirt is stuffed up her underwear.

How to keep a wallet in your suit pocket without an incriminating bulge

A fitted suit and a fat wallet go together like a drag queen and a beard. Squeeze it into your breast pocket and you look like you're wearing a wire for the NYPD; stuff it in the back of your trousers and you look like you've soiled yourself; place it in your front trouser pocket and you look like you're enjoying the vol-au-vents a little too much. There's only one choice: thin it out. Here's how to banish the bulge.

Clear the debris. Old receipts including the one for the toaster you know you'll never return, coppers so old they'd turn a profit on the *Antiques Roadshow*, photos of Kim Kardashian, business cards from long-gone parties, and the obligatory out-of-date "emergency" condom all need to go.

Fold your bills in the same direction to reduce ruffles. Only keep one form of ID. Keep your credit card and cash card in slots on opposite sides of your wallet. If you have loads of cards and need to carry them all, invest in two wallets and place an even amount of cards in each wallet; put one in either side of your jacket.

You'll now weigh about 5 pounds less and can walk tall, safe in the knowledge that if anything's bulging, it's not your wallet.

Facial grooming for grown-ups

One day you're staring up at your dad's chin covered in shaving cream, longing for the day when you too will have a whiskered chin of your own. The next, you're staring in the mirror at your sprouting nostrils wondering when the hell you morphed into Chewbacca. Nobody wants to be that hairy.

Here's a step-by-step guide to taming your face and extraneous body hair:

Eyebrows

While you're still young, if you are lucky this will mainly be a case of plucking the odd unruly long and wiry ginger hair every now and then.

But if your brows verge on morphing into one, continuous brow, you might need more remedial treatment:

1. Plucking: pluck after a warm shower. This opens up the pores and makes it less painful. Use clean, slanted tweezers and pluck between the brows to eradicate the mono-brow. Tweezer a single hair at a time, grasp close to the root and pull, not yank, in the direction of growth.

2. If your eyebrow hair is unusually long, trim back with scissors.

3. Pluck out the odd stray hair above and below the eyebrow line, but don't overdo it—you don't want to end up looking like Boy George.

Waxing

Ideal if you sport the my-father-married-his-sister-and-I'm-the-result look. Done by a professional it will prolong the time your mono-brow is banished for. On the other hand, if you don't want to enter a salon and say, "Will you wax my unibrow today?" you can do it yourself in five minutes.

* Use small wax strips specifically designed for facial hair.

* Place the strip between your eyebrows.

* Smooth over and, pulling your forehead taut, whip the strip off in an upward motion.

* Wipe the waxed area with tea tree or aloe vera lotion to calm redness and prevent spots.

Ears and nostril hair

Hair trimmers work wonders and most cost under $5. And much less painful than tweezers! Always blow your nose first.

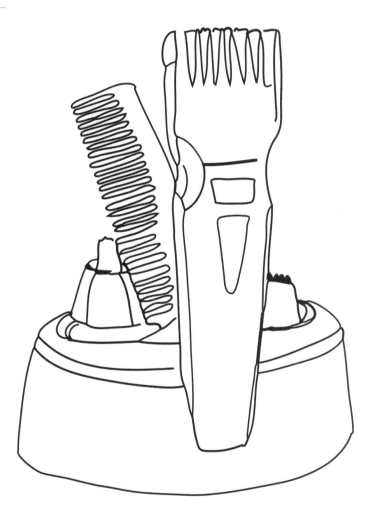

How to save money as well as the environment

Saving the world can save you money. Make your house an energy-efficient paradise without living in a box room lined with tin foil eating the flotsam and jetsam leftovers of the fast-food tide.

* Lower your central heating thermostat by just one degree and knock 10% off your total heating bill.

* Don't leave the TV, computer, stereo, etc. on stand-by.

* Unplug phone and iPod chargers when they're not being used.

* Dry clothes on the line outside or fit an old-fashioned clothes airer to the ceiling. Tumble dryers should only be used on rare emergency occasions.

* Energy efficient light bulbs might take a while to heat up and leave you feeling like you're standing in a dungeon for fifteen minutes, but they do **save you about $15 a year and last about ten times longer.**

* Check that your roof is efficiently insulated.

* Take showers rather than a baths. An average bath uses 40 to 45 gallons of water, whereas taking a five-minute shower uses only about 15 to 20 gallons of water.

* PCs use more energy than laptops, so get a laptop.

* Get a high efficiency, condensing boiler which could cut your heating bill by up to a third.

* Install a wind turbine, heat pump, or wood-burning stove.

* Recycle everything you can and make regular trips to the local recycling bank.

* Use rechargeable batteries.

* Wash your clothes on a low-temperature 86°F wash and invest in Eco-balls rather than using traditional detergents.

* Gray water systems, whereby the water from your washing up and shower gets transferred to your toilet cistern, can also be installed. The world and your wallet might be the least of your worries however, if you get the pipes mixed up.

How to live on $50 a week and still have a social life

How often do you find yourself scrabbling down the side of the sofa in the hope of finding a stray dollar or two? And desperately searching in old coat pockets for the odd quarter? Counting pennies isn't much fun for anyone. But sometimes needs must, so here's how to live on the breadline or the dole and still have a life.

Assuming rent, bills, and council tax have already been paid, and you don't own a car, fifty bucks a week can go a long way.

Be strict. Every Sunday night go to an ATM and withdraw $50. This is a good way of keeping track of your money—if you haven't got any in your wallet you won't spend it. This should be the only time you visit the bank all week.

Next up, first thing Monday, it's the supermarket. Be careful what you buy. Meat is expensive so limit yourself to one portion of streaky bacon or sausages and make them last. Cutting down on meat will do wonders for your waistline, too. And vegetarians live longer, apparently.

Keep your store cupboard stocked up with durable items such as rice, canned tomatoes, or dried pasta. Baked beans and eggs are also good staples. **Always opt for the supermarket's own brand or "basic buy" range.** Having base ingredients means you only have to buy fresh vegetables and the essentials such as milk, butter, and bread. Also, bargain hunt and freeze any reduced pieces of meat for the following week.

Shopping like this will cost you between $15 and $25, leaving you up to $35 to play with.

Planning is the key to optimizing your pennies. If there's a good game on TV, buy six cans for about $5 and spend a night in. This will leave you about $20 to spend out on Saturday night. That's a good weekend of entertainment. Not bad for $50.

Alternatively, save the thirty-five dollars for a big night on the town. Start the night out with some cheap beer before you go out so you have enough to pay the extortionate prices in the bars and clubs.

Two more tips to remember. Take your lunch to work and utilize all the free stuff in this country. Art galleries, libraries, books, TV and radio, let alone the Internet, all provide free entertainment. Follow these rules and $50 can feel like $5,000…or $500 at least.

BEER

BE

6 for $5

CHEAP AS CHIPS, UNLV CHEAP BEER

GRASHERS

How to surf on blocked websites at work

Getting caught with your hand in the cookie jar, or your pants, can have disastrous effects on your professional life. Those evil I.T. administrators have ways and means of knowing your every online move...but all you need to know are a few sneaky tricks to cover your tracks and ensure that the I.T. cat never catches your mouse logging on to off-limit sites.

Proxy sites—these are anonymous and allow you to enter the URL or Internet address of any site without recording or sending the information to your hard drive. The computer thinks it is surfing wherever the proxy is based, so it is essentially wearing a disguise. Proxy sites don't stay active for long because the bandwidth required to run them is expensive and they provide no advertising revenue. News of a fast one spreads quickly and the cost of keeping it running increases with its popularity, so sites that work one week will have often crashed and burned the next. However, proxy aggregation sites listing all the recently discovered proxies regularly reveal new ones, ducking and diving through cyberspace like the Artful Dodger. Google "proxy sites" with the date or "latest proxy sites" and you should find thousands of as yet undiscovered proxy gems.

Email bypass—an email bypass provides you with basic webpage viewing. Certain sites let you send an email to them with your required site in the subject box. After a minute or two you'll receive an email with the site you want to visit pasted in HTML format. If anyone asks, you're just checking your email— cue penis enlargement pop-up.

Take your own laptop or Smart phone to work—using your own wireless connection allows you to surf all day without being blocked.

Tips:

Depending on where you work and how strict your company's code of practice is, you could be sacked for breaking administrator rules.

Don't overstay your welcome. Your system administrator will notice a peculiar site shifting up through the ranks of sites visited regularly and investigate. Maybe save your "pretty lady" searches for the comfort of your own home, eh?

How to prepare your CV for a job application

CV, or Curriculum Vitae, comes from the Latin, "course of life." This is the perfect way to remember what it is you're writing about. Your CV should be a record of your occupational and educational life but also give an impression of the general direction your life is taking. "Course of life" incorporates previous achievements and future potential, so bear this is mind when constructing your CV.

First impressions

*   Keep it simple—a heart-shaped 30-page embroidered felt booklet might stand out from the rest of the pack but it will also make the manager think you're an egomaniac from hell with a fetish for felt.

*   Keep it brief—two pages maximum, typed on clean and unfolded paper.

*   Use black ink, so it can be photocopied, in Arial or New Times Roman size 10 and 12 font, and number the pages.

*   Put your name at the top in larger font.

*   All headings in bold and sub-headings in italics.

*   Leave spaces between each heading. Anal? A little. Job-worthy? Certainly.

*   Use short paragraphs, bullet points, and simple language. Not slang, innit?

Add your contact details to the bottom of each page—email, address, home, and mobile number. If you live at home inform your parents you're expecting some calls about work. Don't forget to help your father off the floor.

* Use a sensible-sounding email address. Bigballs@aol.com or similar is perfect.

* If emailing your CV use Microsoft Word. This is the format nearly everyone on the planet uses and if prospective employers can't open your document they'll just move on to the next one.

* Photos—especially that one of you being violated by a blow-up sheep in Ibiza—should not be included.

* Personal details such as marital status, age, and disabilities are not required unless you are requested to fill in an Equal Opportunities form.

* Double-check dates and spelling. Then double-check again. Bad grammar and spelling are not selling points.

Tailor the order of your CV to the position you are applying for. An entry-level job should detail education, then previous employment and interests and hobbies. For more experienced positions, lead with jobs, then education, with hobbies last. Use your initiative and give yourself the best chance to stand out. Putting your hobbies first will also make you stand out. As a lunatic.

Mission or personal statement

This is a paragraph declaring who you are, what you have to offer, and where you see yourself in the next few years. Think about your experience and skills which are relevant to the job you're applying for.

Example: "Qualified electrician with three years experience as an apprentice seeks corporate company offering large contracts."

* **Don't overplay your achievements and never lie on your CV.**

* List your job history, from the present back. Include the month and year you started and finished, then the company name and job title e.g. January 1999–August 2002—Boddiswell House, Hotel Porter.

* Under each job title, list a summary of core skills. Prioritize according to the job you're applying for. Plumbing firms are probably not going to be interested in cake decorating skills. List all key skills, from most important, e.g. management, to more secondary, e.g. basic Quark training.

* Negotiating, presentation, touch-typing, cash handling, public speaking, stock ordering and rota organization are all skills—so list them where appropriate.

* Fill in any unemployment periods with some information, e.g. "Went travelling around Africa" or "Took a break from work to reassess my life." Don't put "Won 'Championship Manager' twice in a row with Scunthorpe FC."

* Reduce the amount of info for older and less relevant jobs. Temping jobs for example can be reduced down to "Temping" with basic skills.

* Include unpaid or voluntary work. This gives an insight into your personality and perseverance.

* Anything that might be relevant is worth jotting down as long as you put it in its rightful place and keep it brief and informative. Working for a corporate company in your teens—such as McDonald's or Spar—shows you can pull your weight in an international organization.

* Read the job descriptions and pick out key words and attributes. If it says "Looking for adaptable person" include the word "adaptable" in your CV and back it up with proof from past roles.

Education history

* Follow the same format as your occupation history with achievements you gained in each institution.

* Include extra-curricular feats: rugby captain, contributor to student magazine, annual "Guitar Hero" competition organizer, etc.

* Other courses such as food hygiene and first aid should also be included here.

Hobbies and other activities

* Use your hobbies to paint a three-dimensional picture of your life. Sports show you can work in a team, blogging shows a good understanding of modern media and running the local bar trivia can show good presentation skills.

* Be selective about which interests you disclose. Personalize your CV, by all means. But stay within acceptable limits. If you wouldn't tell a bartender, you probably shouldn't include it here.

References

* Include a work reference and a character or academic one. Don't put down your Aunt Agnes, even if she does think you're a lovely boy.

* Include job titles, company name, company address, email, and phone number of your references.

Cover letter

* You should have an introductory paragraph much like the one at the start of your CV.

* Include a longer, middle paragraph expanding on the skills you've acquired from jobs, education and hobbies.

* The final paragraph should refer to your possible relationship with the company and state how and why you would be an ideal candidate for the job. Use "I" freely here. For example, "I consider myself a very competent person able to perform under pressure as my experience with the fire service shows."

* If your career path has changed radically over the years, now is a good chance to explain why.

How to put a condom on in less than ten seconds

There are some things our moms can show us: how to iron a shirt, how to fill out a job application, how to put on a condom…can you imagine?? This is one of those things you're going to have to master all by yourself.

First of all remove the condom from the packet by tearing off one of the sides—don't use your nails because you might rip it. And not your teeth as mostly they taste revolting. Once removed, hold the teat between your thumb and forefinger and make sure the rolled up part of the condom is on the outside. Next, get the old chap as hard as possible, ask for assistance, oral or manual if necessary, pull back your foreskin—if you have one of course— and still pinching the teat, so no air is trapped inside, place the condom on to the tip of your penis, then unroll the condom downwards in one smooth, swift motion. Don't worry if some of the condom is still rolled up before it reaches the base, just make sure it doesn't roll back mid-shag. When you're finished, grip the base of the condom, pull out, slide the condom off, tie a knot in it and pop it in the trash. One more thing: don't rinse and reuse it; that's just weird.

What to do if you cheat on your girlfriend

Before the Xbox, the PS, the Wii, and the Mac, youth clubs relied on a pool table and a pack of playing cards. After a game of Killer and a few rounds of Shit-Head, the obligatory hour-long game of Cheat ensued. Strategically shuffling and bluffing your way to victory, getting caught was half of the fun. It didn't matter. You'd be dealt the next hand no matter what the crime. But cheating on a girl isn't like cheating in a game. There are consequences, painful questions, and very few answers.

Even if your girlfriend wakes you up each morning with a knee to the groin, there really is no excuse for sharing your bed, let alone your heart, with another woman. But fluttering eyelids and skimpy dresses are not easy to ignore, especially if your girlfriend makes you feel as loved as your 12-year-old, broken down Taurus. Cheating can often be a form of self-assertiveness, a way of saying, "Look. Someone else finds me attractive, even if you don't." Low self-esteem and emasculation are the main culprits when temptation becomes inflation, as it were. A good old-fashioned talk might smooth out the creases in your heart, but be warned: a single kiss with another girl is not enough to start the fire but in your girlfriend's eye it's all that's needed to put one out. Mistakes don't always need to be confessed. If you know why you did it, and you know it isn't going to happen again, don't drag your girlfriend through the mire to appease your own guilty conscience. Keep it to yourself. If it becomes a regular thing, do the decent thing and finish with your girlfriend. That said, sometimes cheating can be a blessing in disguise.

It can spark reconciliation and strengthen the foundations of your relationship. Other times it can bring resentment and distrust and break the bond beyond repair. Love is not a game.

So the next time you think about calling for another card, have a look at your hand. You may never be dealt one so good again.

The man's guide to pornstars

America's porn industry earns the state an estimated $14 billion each year. That's $5,000 every two minutes. Or in other words $2,500 per average man's wank. Who says you can't put a price on single life? However, going blind is the least of your worries when you're spending all your savings on self-pleasure, so here's a guide to the factions of pornography to ensure you get what you pay for.

Classic. Blonde, big-breasted, and babelicious, these are the women you wish were your missus. Headed up by the greatest porn star of all time, Jenna Jameson, the heavyweights of porn include *Stepford Wives* wannabe Brianna Banks, old pro Jill Kelly and Misty, the strangely seductive girl with a face like she's just eaten a whole jar of mustard.

Gonzo. If Jameson's ladies do luncheon, the gonzo girls eat razor-blade sandwiches in shark-infested waters. Leader of the pack, Belladonna, is no stranger to a baseball bat and joining her going off on a tangent are the Romanian-born—and completely bananas—Sandra Romain, the human sprinkler Cytheria, and self-proclaimed existentialist Sasha Grey.

Lipstick Starlets. This lot look like fairies but play like little devils, and the horniest of all is new queen of porn Jenna Haze. Joining her, crossing realms but never legs, is ex-high school honey Hilary Scott, one-expression wonder Ashton Moore and, cough, "innocent" Bree Olsen.

Other odds and bods. Educational videos from giving perfect cunnilingus to spanking for dummies are presented by Silicon Valley stalwart Nina Hartley. Straight sex at its best stars Tera Patrick. For porn with a sprinkle of glamour, Sophie Moon is your woman. If, like your beef, you like it British, the pick of the current bunch is Lolly Badcock. Although watching women reaching climax calling out "cor blimey" or "oh by gum" should really be reserved for your private life, not your perving one.

The man's guide to writing a girl a poem

Cupid's arrows don't always hit their targets. Sometimes a little more effort is required to pierce the heart of the one we love. Writing a poem for the object of your desire, for example. But, if your middle name isn't William Shakespeare, fear not. Follow these simple guidelines and you won't get it calamitously wrong.

First, choose a style which matches one of your key characteristics. Sentimental or cheeky, charming or erotic. Next, think about what you want to say and how you're going to say it. For example, you might want to compliment her good looks. The poem should be simple and short. Two stanzas containing four lines each with the traditional ten syllables, give or take one or two, makes your message compact and foolproof. As does using rhyming couplets.

Here are a couple of examples:

Sentimental:

> You have pink cheeks like the first rose in bloom,
> Your eyes bring the dawn into every room,
> Your lips hold the secrets of many a ruined man,
> But I'll pay the price if that's the price of your hand.

Cheeky:

> It's as fun as a kid's bouncy castle,
> Admired by Princes as well as by rascals.
> Its cheeks are as red and as warm as the sun,
> The truth is simple: I'm in love with your bum!

Subtlety is the best policy when handing over this rather sticky slice of love. Think handwritten note placed under the pillow, not ancient papyrus wrapped around a unicorn horn. The very fact that you've penned an ode just for her will strike straight to her heart.

Where to put things in the fridge

The male mind short-circuits at the thought of housework of any kind. Vacuum cleaners make us weak at the knees. Feather dusters bring us to tears. But nowhere is this more evident than in the case of a man's fridge. Though he opens and closes its smelly door a hundred times a day, hoping that perchance some new tasty snack will have miraculously been beamed in from Whole Foods, a young male will remain blissfully oblivious to the gruesome sights and malevolent smells issuing from every festering cranny...Until the day, perhaps, when a new girlfriend delves in, and has to undergo trauma counseling before coming round for toast ever again.

Keep your fridge in order and keep your girlfriend out of therapy. Here's how.

* First, undertake a major overhaul of your fridge hygiene.

* Remove everything from the fridge. Be brutal and dispose of anything that looks unpleasant or is past its sell-by date.

* Put all the shelves and detachable vegetable drawers in the sink and fill with clean, warm water. Add detergent. Wash thoroughly. Add a cupful of white vinegar to the last rinse for extra squeaky cleanness and to remove bad odors. Allow to air-dry.

* Clean the inside of the fridge thoroughly using a clean cloth and a bowl of warm water. Again, add a splash of white vinegar or lemon juice to the final rinse to kill any bacteria and remove odors.

* Once dry, replace all the shiny clean shelves and drawers.

FOOD LIFE

- Mushrooms—1–2 days

- Asparagus, berries, cherries—2–3 days

- Plums, kiwis, French beans, peas—3–5 days

- Melons, cauliflower, cabbage, green beans, chilies, peppers—1 week

- Beetroots, radishes, carrots—2 weeks

- Cranberries, lemons, limes, and grapefruits—more than 2 weeks

- Apples—1 month

- NB: eggs, potatoes, tomatoes, mangoes, avocados, bananas, garlic, onions, squash, lemons, oranges, and apples do not need to be stored in the fridge.

Cut out and stick to front of fridge

Now start as if you mean to go on:

Vegetable drawer. Make sure air can circulate around the drawer—don't keep it packed full or you risk your greens going limp. Preferably use two separate drawers—or divide your drawer in two. Keep fruits, salad, and other leafy vegetables such as broccoli, spinach, celery, and rocket in one, as they lose moisture faster and will soak other veg. Use the other side for any other vegetables listed below (with a rough guide to how long they will keep the fridge).

Door shelf. Keep milk and fruit juice here, as well as ketchup, mayonnaise, and mustards. An open bottle of champagne and white or rosé wine lasts about four days in the fridge; add a silver spoon to keep bubbly bubbly.

Bottom shelf. The coolest part of the fridge. Store raw meat and fish here, wrapped in their packaging straight from the shop. Keep all raw meats separate to avoid contamination, and never mix raw and cooked foods on same plate. Wrap raw meat in tin foil and place a plate under larger joints—such as a leg of lamb—as an extra precaution to keep the fridge clean. Blood running over your salad is probably a step too far for most.

Beer shelf. Lay beer cans on their sides carefully to rest and to maximize shelf space.

Cheese box. Pongy Stilton gets everywhere so seal it up with cling wrap, as tight as Tutankhamen's tomb.

Top shelf. This is the warmest part of the fridge, so remember, food which isn't in jars or wrappers might not last as long here. Store opened jars of jam, butter, and any left-overs to be eaten soon on this shelf.

Advanced tips:

*   Don't let food touch the sides or back of the fridge as this can make it freeze.

*   Don't store certain foods together. Apples turn carrots bitter because of the ethylene gas they give off. Potatoes should be kept in a paper bag on their own as they can rot onions. Store garlic on its own or everything else will smell like a vampire slayer's neck.

*   A brown paper bag will stop vegetables becoming sweaty and wet. Vegetables or fruit kept in plastic packaging will last longer if taken out and stored loose in the fruit bowl or vegetable drawer in fridge. Don't keep fruit and veg in airtight containers.

*   Line your vegetable drawer with paper towels to quicken the annual—if you bother with one—clean.

*   Never keep food in an opened tin as this can cause serious illness and several trips to the loo. Store the remaining contents in a covered bowl or your grandma's hand-me-down Tupperware.

*   Anything bought from the chilled section of a shop should be kept in the fridge.

*   Warm food should be allowed to cool before being put in the fridge. Cover with cling wrap and store in the fridge for up to two days.

*   As a general rule, anything you can't remember putting in the fridge should be taken out and disposed of immediately.

*   Baking soda gets rid of any odors hanging about; pour into a small glass or egg cup, and make sure you change the baking soda regularly to keep pongs at bay. As long as you don't take a short cut past the local sewage works.

*   Check your manual and keep the fridge temperature at the optimal setting.

The man's guide to knots

Tying up a boat, a rock-climbing rope, or possibly even the girlfriend requires a steady hand and a keen eye. But if you don't know what knot to use or how to tie it, you could end up with a shattered starboard, a comatose climber, or a bitter bride-to-be.

From light bondage to scouting skills, here's a guide to knots.

Boating knots:

Bowline:

This knot forms a secure loop making it ideal for mooring a boat to a pole or ring.

Allowing for the size of the knot, form a loop at the end of the rope. Slot the end of the rope through the loop, round the back of the main rope and down through the loop to finish.

Cleat hitch:

Used for tying a rope to a dock cleat.

Pull the rope round the left-hand side of the cleat. Loop the rope round the horn— ohhh, matron—and cross over the cleat. Pass the rope under and over to form a figure of eight. Round the cleat once more and finally pull tight between rope and cleat.

Climbing knots:

Double Fisherman's knot:

Considered by many climbers to be the best knot to tie two ropes, or two rope ends, together.

Place the two ropes alongside and then over each other. Dealing with one rope first, pass its end under both ropes. Wrap the rope round twice. Pass through the ends and pull tight. Repeat the process with the other rope so you have two symmetric knots. Pull both ropes tight so the knots fit snug together.

Prusik knot:

A slide and grip knot, this knot tightens when pressure is applied and can be slid up or down when under no strain.

Get a piece of cord or rope tied together using a Fisherman's knot and pass it over another rope. Pull the Fisherman's rope back through the loop. Repeat this two more times until you're left with six loops around the rope. Pass the Fisherman's knot through the loop and pull tight to finish.

Fishing knots:

Palomar knot:

Strong and reliable, this knot is used to secure a fishing line to a hook.

Looping the end, push the rope through the eye of the hook. Pass the loop under the rope and through the second loop you've just formed. Pull the loop over the hook. Tighten the knot and snip the end off.

Arbor knot:

One of the most common knots used to attach the fishing line to the reel. Loop the line around the reel or arbor and back and under the line. Tie a standard or overhand knot. To prevent the first knot from slipping, tie a second overhand knot with the same end to finish.

Reef knot:

Used to join two equal length ropes together.

Cross two rope ends over. Pull the ends up—one under, one over. Tie the two loose ends together and pull tight.

Double Overhand Stopper knot:

Frequently used to secure a rope to stop it slipping through a pulley, another knot, etc.

Loop the rope round itself. Repeat. Slot the end of the rope through the turns and pull snug.

How to buy a suit without getting ripped off

There will come a time when one of your friends gets married, and when it comes you don't want to be the loser who turns up in Bermuda shorts and a Hawaiian shirt. You'll need to wear a suit. But before you go out and buy one there are a couple of things you need to do.

Firstly, set yourself a budget and, secondly, measure your collar, chest, waist and leg length. When you've done that, have a look in several shops and see what styles you like.

When it comes to trying on the suit, be wary of several things. The shoulders should hug yours; if you stand sideways against a wall your arms should touch the wall before the shoulder pads do. Also, you should be able to button up the suit without straining and there shouldn't be too much space between buttons and chest; about a fist's worth is a good guide. The trousers should rest on the top of your shoes and you should be able to put your hands in your pockets with ease.

Finally, lift your arms above your head. The suit shouldn't ride up at the back and the cuffs should meet the palm of your hand when you curl your fingers back.

One extra tip: Buy a spare pair of suit trousers; the jacket always outlives the trousers, and the last thing you want is to wear a jacket and jeans—unless you want to look like your "trendy" dad.

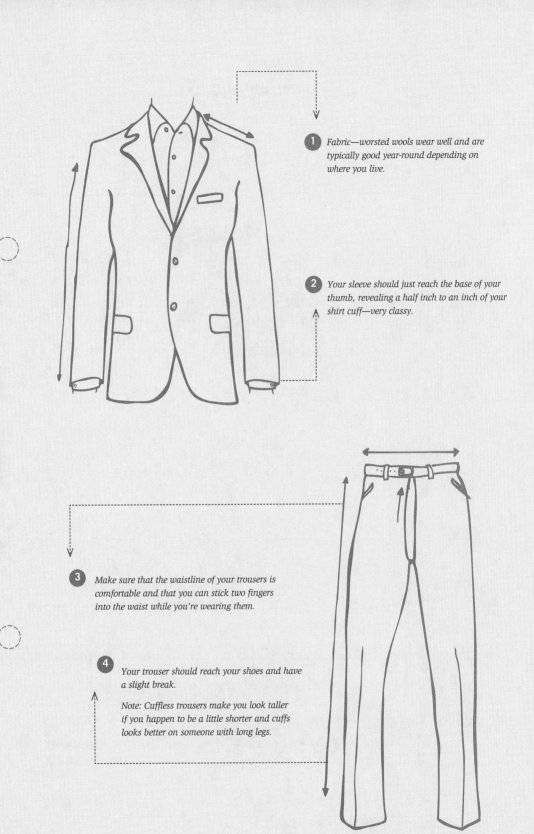

1 Fabric—worsted wools wear well and are typically good year-round depending on where you live.

2 Your sleeve should just reach the base of your thumb, revealing a half inch to an inch of your shirt cuff—very classy.

3 Make sure that the waistline of your trousers is comfortable and that you can stick two fingers into the waist while you're wearing them.

4 Your trouser should reach your shoes and have a slight break.

Note: Cuffless trousers make you look taller if you happen to be a little shorter and cuffs looks better on someone with long legs.

"THE FIRM HANDSHAKE"

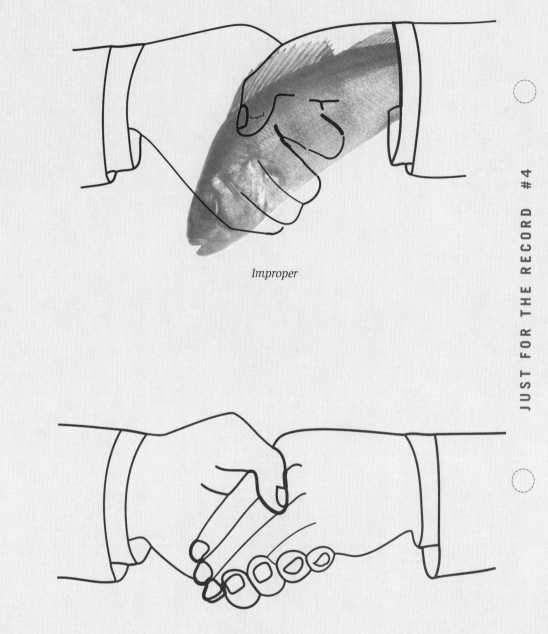

Improper

Correct

How to give a handshake like the perfect gentleman

International greetings are varied and bizarre practices. The Zen Japanese bow. The exuberant Italians air-kiss. The exciting and brash Americans high-five. Then there's the reserved and overly sensible British handshake. You couldn't beat it with a big stick.

Here's how to stay within the acceptable limits of reserve:

* Make initial eye contact with a broad smile.

* Face the person head on, shoulders to shoulders.

* Wait until they are at least an arm width away and extend your arm, with your hand stretched out vertically and your thumb pointing straight to the sky.

* Break eye contact to ensure your hands have met—groping their groin area with a big cheesy smile isn't good—and make eye contact again throughout the handshake.

* Place the palm of your hand against the palm of theirs so the web—the bit of skin between your thumb and forefinger—meets their web. Sliding your fingers along is also an option, although this can be a little creepy especially if your hands are clammy.

* Keep your forearm parallel to the floor and fold your fingers around their hand, laying your thumb over the top.

* Apply comfortable pressure. The same strength of grip you use to lift a mug of tea.

* Shake smoothly but firmly downward twice. Do so from neither your shoulder nor your wrist. One is overbearing, the other limp. Be a good chap and always shake from your elbow. Your arm should be tensed but the shake shouldn't cause the cuffs of your shirt or jacket to quiver.

* The handshake should last between 1 and 3 seconds and be over with before the introduction is complete.

Advanced tips:

---

* A firm grip shows strength and sincerity. An energetic shake gives off an air of professionalism. A limp or weak handshake declares low self-confidence. Fingers-only handshakes are reserved for social reclusives and baronesses.

* The glove handshake—when you cup both your hands with your redundant hand—should only be saved for close friends on rare congratulatory occasions.

* A crushing grip should be reserved for fathers whose daughters are dating older men and macho men trying to intimidate you.

* At work, always stand to offer your hand and greet people in front of your desk.

* If offered a handshake always accept it.

* If you get stuck in handshake limbo, and the handshake has turned into a holding hands situation, squeeze their hand and release. Old people will often do this if they haven't seen you in a long time. It is common courtesy to allow them to hold your hand for as long as they like but shake free if they start dragging you towards the toilet.

* Wipe clammy hands discreetly on your trousers pre-shake.

* Cold hands can be warmed in your pockets.

* If you get sweaty hands, carry an icy drink or don't close your fists.

* Never try a *Top Gun*-style high-five when meeting an important person.

* Always shake with your right hand even if you're left-handed. If you're carrying something, shift the goods and shake away.

* If someone tickles the underside of your palm, they're not coming on to you, they're letting you know they're a member of the Masons.

* Shake women's hands in the same way.

The handshake originated in Roman times when men would clasp arms to prove they weren't armed. With the onset of concealed daggers and backstabbing, medieval knights would grab the other person's hand and shake firmly in the hope of revealing any weapons. But a word of warning: never substitute a handshake for a good frisking.

What all the abbreviations in porn stand for...

There are so many abbreviations in porn, it sometimes feels as though you're trying to decipher the Enigma code and not, as truth would have it, download a video to crack one off to. Here's a quickie guide.

Let's start with something simple:

BJ = *Blowjob.*

MILF = *Mom I'd like to f**k.*

GILF = *Granny I'd like to f**k.*

POV = *From the point of view of the man.*

BBW = *Big beautiful woman*—for the man who likes his lady to be able to eat a KFC Family Feast in one sitting.

Here's where it goes a little off center:

DP = *Double penetration.*

DDP = *Double double penetration*—has to be seen to be believed.

ATM = *Ass to mouth.*

DV = *Double vaginal penetration.*

DA = *Double anal penetration.*

DVDA = *Double vaginal penetration, double anal penetration.* Not, you might be surprised to learn, the place where you apply for your provisional driver's license.

Love on a budget: cheap but romantic dates

There's nothing more romantic than holding hands with the woman you love, sunlight dancing in her hair, lips aquiver in the breeze, safe in the knowledge you haven't opened your wallet once. Here's how to tighten your belt on a date without reducing the chances of your lady unbuckling it later.

2 for 1 deals

Crash an art gallery opening

Home cinema with popcorn

Or see massage tips, page 141

Head for a beach. Pack a romantic picnic for two. Cucumber sandwiches and a silver platter are probably a little over the top, but a miniature bottle of her favorite wine, a rug, and a basket of ripe strawberries, and a selection of nibbles might result in a nibble of a different kind. Linger until sunset, then wrap her up in a shawl and take a moonlit stroll along the deserted beach.

Art gallery or museum. Impress her with your range of cultural knowledge spanning from Byzantine murals to Warhol's *Soup Cans*.

Go boating. Rent a boat for the day and watch her eyes twinkle with delight as you attempt to untangle yourself from your fishing line for the umpteenth time.

Night in the city. Wrap up and take a moonlit stroll along the lonely city streets at midnight. Romance will blossom in your isolation and before long you'll be discussing the names of your future children and picking out the curtains for your family home in the country.

Late and great gift ideas for girlfriends

Your girlfriend's birthday is one week away and you still don't know what to buy her. Well, you had better act fast if you want to avoid a swift kick to the testicles.

YEAR 1

Ask yourself how long you have been together. If you've only just started going out, play it safe. Be flirtatious and fun. **A "Stay Over Kit" with pajamas, toiletries, and her favorite CD** (unless her music taste causes you sleepless nights of worry) is a good start, as is a pampering pack including moisturizer, soap, scented candles, and the offer of a massage from you—yes, you! Cuddly toys, flowers, and chocolates are a last resort, but she won't care how little you've spent if the presentation's right. If you're really struggling for inspiration, ask her best friend if she's dropped any hints about what she'd love.

YEAR 2

The same can't be said if you've been together for over a year. No, sir. She's going to want to see not just the thought but the hard cash you've put into the gift. A nice piece of jewellery isn't enough on its own, so combine it with her birthstone or matching earrings. **A night in a hotel or a weekend away** will put a smile on her face—and yours—and framed art and perfume (bottled, not framed!) is always a winner too. One last word of warning: avoid clothes. Unless you want the words, "But darling, I don't think you're frumpy...or fat" to become your catchphrase for the year.

How to get away with staring at other women

Love's puritans and fundamentalists believe in wearing blinkers in a relationship. But any healthy chap knows that full-blooded males are designed to find the opposite sex attractive—and besides your missus will be doing a little window-shopping of her own.

If, however, your lady is of a jealous nature, here are some subtle hints for "looking but not touching" without getting a slap on the wrist.

Girl-scope up. Be sneaky. Use short sharp glances rather than long wide-eyed stares. This is the technique girls use to register facts about a man's body—a ring on his finger, fashion sense, hair length, etc. Get in touch with your feminine side and practice glancing, not drooling.

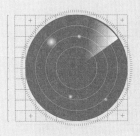

Hottie at ten o'clock. Be cunning. Comment on girls' negative aspects and give your girlfriend the chance for a good old bitching session, giving you the chance to take a longer look. Girls in short skirts and/or skimpy tops are an easy target. "She must be freezing" translates into "look at the nipples on her!"

Babe alert. Be cheeky. If a particularly well-endowed female of the species catches your eye when you're driving, a sure-fire giveaway is to sharply crick your neck round to cop a look at her as she retreats. This will usually result in a minor traffic offense as you take your eye off the road. Glance subtly in the wing or rear-view mirror instead.

Shwing! Be devious. Point at things on display in shops and ask stupid questions: "Look at those jewel-encrusted shoes, darling. Are they by Aloe Voile?" The ensuing diatribe on your fashion faux pas should cater for some covert SAS perving. If she doesn't take the bait, point to something behind the girl that's taken your fancy and comment on it so you can both look in the same general direction—she won't realize you're getting an eyeful at the same time. But be warned, this can send her girlie sense tingling and if it ever reaches Def Con One you'll be praying for the Puritans to come and take you away.

How to get over a girl

No man is immune to having his heart broken and a man is not a man if he hasn't felt the pain of a love gone wrong—even Johnny Depp's been dumped.

But, if that's no consolation, here are a few tips to help relieve the pangs and make the sense of loneliness go away. At least for the time being:

✓ When the news first comes, hit the bar with some friends, but don't sit there dolefully with your snout in your pint all night, wondering what "she's" doing now. Play a game of dominoes, darts, or pool. Take part in the bar trivia. In short, do everything you can to keep your mind occupied and your mood lighter.

✗ Don't drink yourself into a stupor, then pour your heart out to your mortified friends before sobbing loudly and hugging them.

✗ Don't be tempted to drink and dial, or take a cab round to hers to stare up at her window till the early hours.

✓ **If she has left any belongings in your apartment, put them in a box and return them to her as soon as you can post break-up.**

✗ Don't have sex with the ex. Although it is often the best sex you'll ever have, just don't. OK, just once if you have to but, if she is the dumper, accept the fact it probably means more to you than it does to her. If you dumped her, you could be setting yourself up for a whole world of pain.

✗ Don't do the "just good friends" thing, at least not until a good year has passed.

✓ Ultimately, the best way to get over someone is by not seeing them at all. This will feel weird to put it mildly as you've just spent pretty much every day together, but it's the first step to truly getting over her and accepting that she's no longer a part of your life. It never feels like it at the time, but time does heal. A total break will be better than renewing painful feelings by staying in touch.

✓ Unless the split was an amicable one and you're 100% sure you won't contact her for anything other than a friendly catch-up call, take precautions before you do or say something you'll later regret. Erase all her numbers from your phone and from your address book. Delete all texts from her or sent to her—and, yes, get rid of even those kept for sentimental reasons. If they're on your phone, then you still have her number. And if you have her number you'll give in to temptation and start texting her when you're low, needy or—worse—angry and bitter.

✓ The same applies for emails and letters—once sent, a long, self-pitying or bitter communication can't be retrieved. So don't send it. Delete all emails from or to your girlfriend and delete her email address too.

✓ Once you've said goodbye for good remember to stay active and keep yourself busy. Take up the activities you let slip while you were in a relationship. If you can, take a vacation abroad. Accept every invitation offered. Even if you don't want to go to your third cousin's second child's christening, go. If you're out of the house, you're less likely to be thinking about your ex.

✓ After a few months have passed go over the relationship in your head. This is the hardest thing you'll have to do and it might be upsetting or humiliating, but once you're clear on why it ended you can start thinking about moving on.

✓ Most important of all, keep telling yourself you're free to get out and enjoy exploring pastures new. And do just that.

Survival guide to living at home with the folks

What with free rent, home cooked meals, and fabric-softener-smooth boxer shorts, KIPPERS— Kids In Parents' Pockets Eroding Retirement Savings—have it made. That is until the day they walk in on their folks getting it on on the kitchen table. In an instant the dream is gone. Blasted to smithereens by a little pill called Viagra and a dusty old Barry White album.

Here's how to live with the parents and still be your own man:

Live independently in their home, buy your own food, and offer to pay rent.

Keep your self-respect, focus, and drive. It sounds like something your dad might say, but just because you're staying in the same room you did as a kid doesn't mean you have to act like one.

Don't be lazy. Your mom might not mind you hogging the sofa and remote all day long in nothing but your boxers, but soon enough your dad will make your life a living hell. Pick a chore to do daily—tidy the kitchen, for example, take the garbage out, empty the dishwasher—something your dad will notice and he won't have to do when he or your mom gets in from work.

Use the opportunity wisely. If you're moving back after a graduation or break up, set a time limit of six months to a year. Find a job, save some money, and think about your next move in life.

Accept your circumstances. A lack of independence and a feeling of emasculation can make meeting a lady friend problematic. But if you do, be up-front about your situation. Invite her over and introduce her to the folks. Don't tell them to head out for the night (unless she's bringing a buxom blonde friend along for your dad, in which case you better book your mom into the local Travelodge).

Respect your parents. Don't lie about playing your Xbox in your room all day. Integrate your parents into your life. Eat with them; go out with them and generally treat them like roommates.

Talk to your parents. If you feel like your folks are still treating you like a kid, sit them down and tell them so. Don't forget your parents were young once and they'll have some pearls of wisdom you'll never learn about if you never ask.

Perfecting the hug and roll technique

Cuddles before bedtime can have uncomfortable consequences. With your girlfriend in a deep slumber and her head rested on your chest it's not long before you want your arm and your side of the bed back.

Here's how to deploy the hug and roll technique and reclaim your right to a good night's sleep:

Step 1. Ensure your other half is zzzzzzz. Discuss Tom Brady's total passing yards for the season. If she doesn't tell you to shut up, she's asleep.

Step 2. Give her a tight hug. Don't crack a rib, but let her sleeping-self know you intend to hold her all night long.

Step 3. Hold her close and gently roll both of you towards the edge of the bed—not off it. Even if she made you watch the latest Nicholas Sparks chick flick, revenge is not a dish best served in bed.

Step 4. As you begin to roll back, release the hug, gently pull your arm out from under her and shift your body weight to your side of the bed.

Step 5. Breathe a sigh of relief and congratulate yourself on a perfectly executed hug and roll.

Trapped Arm Syndrome, or TAS for short, is something many men in relationships suffer from. The symptoms occur during a spooning session. Dead arm, pins and needles, fear of amputation are all symptoms of TAS. Avoid the crushing sensation all together with this bed-commanding cuddle. Rather than having your sleepy loved one lie directly on your arm, slide it under her pillow. When you want to roll over to your side of the bed, pull your arm out carefully with the pillow acting as a buffer zone. The perfect cure for TAS. And you can both fall into a deep sleep—limbs intact.

How to give yourself a haircut

Step 1. Buy some quality clippers.

Step 2. Use two mirrors—one at the front, one at the back. Once you're confident enough you can switch to one.

Step 3. Pop the clippers on to grade one or two and shave all over.

Step 4. Prefer the Bic look? Wet your head all over or take a quick shower before you wield the razor.

Step 5. Apply some shaving oil or gel attentively—the more you work the foam in, the better the shave and the less sore your head.

Step 6. Shave the areas of little hair or light fluffy hair first. Save the coarser areas until last.

Step 7. Go slowly and smoothly with the grain, letting the shape of your head dictate the path of the razor.

Step 8. When you're finished, wash your head with some soap and water and pat it dry with a towel. Apply a moisturizer to your head, preferably one with aloe vera or vitamin C, as alcohol-based ones can dry your scalp.

Step 9. You'll have to shave your head roughly every three days.

Step 10. Don't forget to apply a high factor sunscreen in summer—or wear a hat. Nothing worse than a bright red and painful bald head.

Penis exercises: how to maximize your erection

Despite what the emails in your dad's inbox say: PENIS EXERCISES WILL NOT MAKE YOUR PENIS BIGGER! Your penis has no muscle therefore it cannot be fattened up like a turkey before Christmas. It is what it is.

However, you can train and enhance the muscles around your penis that are responsible for maintaining and getting an erection in the first place. If these muscles are primed you can hold your erection for a prolonged time. You might even be able to act as a mobile coat hanger at your next office party.

Here are five exercises you can try to maximize your erection:

Jelqing:

Used by nomadic Arabian tribes, this exercise involves milking your penis like a cow teat. If they did this out in the open, it's no wonder they had to keep moving house so much. Advocates say jelqing increases the volume of blood able to be held by the corpora covernosa—the spongy tissue of your penis which becomes engorged when you have an erection—ultimately making it bigger.

How to jelq: become semi-erect. Soak a face cloth in warm water and wrap it round your penis for a few minutes. Repeat three times rewarming the cloth each time. Rub some baby oil on both hands and make an "OK" sign with your fingers, encircling your penis with your thumb and forefinger at the base. As you reach the end place your other hand at the base in the same way and repeat to build to a rhythmic continuous milking motion. Each "milking" stroke should take up to two seconds. Apply the warm and wet face cloth at the end of the exercise.

Precautions:

Use a light grip. Always "warm up" with the face cloth before and after. Never do the exercise with an erect penis.

HEALTH WARNING: there is a risk of bleeding and infection, and also of long-term erectile dysfunction.

(Some suggest that jelqing is a hoax as there are no sources to confirm its history.)

Penis stretches:

Allegedly this makes the cells in your penis grow, increasing your length and girth. But there's as much chance of scientific proof coming to light as there is a PE teacher recommending this during gym class.

When it's at rest (i.e. not erect) hold the head of your appendage and pull it forward. Don't yank it or you'll do yourself an injury. Hold the stretch for up to 15 seconds and repeat 10 times.

Weight hanging:

HEALTH WARNING: Avoid at all costs. You really could do yourself harm with this one, not to mention leave your roommates wondering where the Yellow Pages has disappeared to.

Ballooning:

This exercise involves increasing the circulation of blood to your groin area and can make your erect penis larger and increase staying power during sex.

While masturbating, stop when you're close to ejaculation. Do this for as many times as is humanly possible, massaging your penis and testicles to stimulate blood flow. This needs an iron will, or the will of God, to master.

Pelvic floor or "Kegel" muscle exercises:

The pubococcygeus muscle—technically referred to as the love muscle—is used to control the flow of urine and semen. It is responsible for the firmness of your erections, the power of your ejaculation and staving off premature ejaculation.

Locate the muscles by stopping mid-pee; the muscles you can feel tensing are your pelvic floor, or PC, muscles. You can do these exercises at any time. Clench for five, ten, or thirty seconds depending on how strong your PC muscles are to start with. Exercise three times a day clenching between 30 and 50 times; with a ten-second break between each tense. Clench in short sharp, one-second bursts to give you control over premature ejaculation or hold the clench for up to two minutes for enhanced firmness.

A trained penis equals increased sensation, prolonged bedroom stamina, and even the added bonus of being able to flex your erection. Amaze your friends, astound your partner, by using your new flexible and sturdy friend to catapult peanuts into your mouth at your next barbecue. As for the office party, that's up to you.

How to test for testicular cancer

The phrase "I know it like the back of my hand" should, for this instance at least, be replaced with "I know it like the back of my scrotum." If you're going to safeguard against testicular cancer, you're going to have to familiarize yourself with your balls.

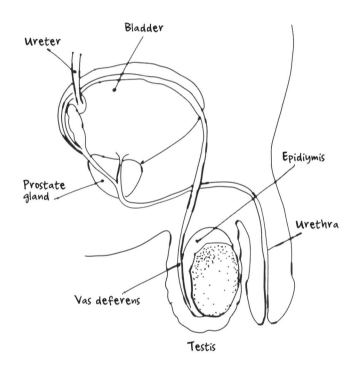

Get naked and have a look. Look in the mirror too. Notice how one ball differs from the other, observing which hangs lower or is larger. Now have a feel and note their usual weight and shape. This is the key to noticing any major differences in the future. Check them once a month after a warm bath or shower. Lift your right leg onto something like the sink—bathroom not kitchen—and gently cup your right testis in the hand you don't write with. Then, using your other hand, roll your ball between your thumb, forefinger and index finger. Swap legs and do the left testis. You'll

notice a soft bump at the top and back of each testis: this is a tube called the epididymis. Other than these two bumps there should be no lumps or swellings. However, if you think you have found a hard, bone-like lump don't panic. First of all compare it with the other testis—it's very rare for cancer to develop in both testicles at the same time. If there isn't a similar-feeling lump in the same place make an appointment with your doctor and he'll check it for you. If you're feeling shy about this, don't be. A doctor has seen a lot of men's meat and two veg so he's not going to take one look at yours and laugh. However, if he does laugh he's probably not a doctor and you should zip up and leave the "Doctor's Surgery" right away.

How to engineer a threesome

Benito Mussolini. Italian dictator, fascist leader, scaredy cat. The day before his triumphant march on Rome, the coup d'état which shifted power into his hands, Mussolini booked a train ticket to Austria in case his intimidation did not succeed. Announcing this to the crowd upon his arrival wouldn't have roused the troops, but this live-to-fight-another-day mentality was indicative of Mussolini's opportunism. He rode his luck, took his chances, and rose to power. And that's the perfect formula for three-in-a-bed fireworks.

Be lucky. Getting accosted by two women who aren't police officers is rare, but if Lady Luck provides you with the opportunity don't miss your chance. Kiss both women for a minute or so in quick succession and read their reactions. You'll know soon enough if they're outraged. If, however, the signs are positive, jokingly suggest taking them home. No means no but a timid

smile or an eager grin and you're in. Get a taxi and go home or to a hotel immediately. Forget your parents' house. Once in private, things will take their natural course—use protection and enjoy it.

Got a girlfriend? You're halfway there. Tactfully discuss fantasies but remember, have a get-out clause. If she's not interested tame your feral fantasies and move onto what's on the box instead of what's in your pants. If she seems keen, don't get over-excited and start drawing diagrams; this is a threesome, not a Boy Scout project, so be patient.

Searching for a third party should be a shared experience. **The Internet enables you to break the boundaries together and in a secure environment.** A mutual friend is also a possibility but precaution is required. Drop hints for a considerable amount of time before popping the question; if possible be certain your chosen friend will say yes. But also be warned your future friendship may be uncomfortable, uncontrollable or just plain Single White Female weird. Anonymity is normally the best choice for all concerned.

Once you've found someone get to know one another for a week or so via email and eventually, when the time's right, invite her over. She'll be as nervous as you so don't welcome her in with a camera crew, pop open a bottle of wine and go with the flow.

Threesomes are great fun but they can ruin relationships. Make sure your girlfriend's not doing something she doesn't want to just to please you or you might suffer a fate worse than Mussolini: having your penis cut off and stuffed in your mouth. Celebratory cigar anyone?

How to stay alive when you go shopping with the lady in your life

Women are programmed to find shopping displays fascinating. From nylon tights to diamond slippers they can't resist a little browse here, a little gander there. But when she picks up a pair of shoes you know she wouldn't wear in a month of half-price Mondays, feel free to show your impatience...but only if you want to spend the night on the sofa with a packet of frozen peas hugging your nether regions.

At times, being the shadow-boyfriend is essential. When her face becomes ingrained with the look of intense shopping contemplation, stand well back. If interrupted at this point, she could hit out. Once she's picked out her clothes she'll want your opinion. At this juncture you need to remain as calm and appeasing as a peace envoy to the Middle East. Never lead with "You look..." Always blame the clothes or brand. "That skirt doesn't look..." etc. Be confident and positive in your answer. Too nonchalant and she'll think you don't care, too involved and she'll think you're trying to mold her into a Barbie doll. Keep it simple. "That looks lovely on you" is spot on. Never say, "Jesus love, you look like John Travolta in *Hairspray.*"

At sales time, enlist a fellow couple on your mission. You boys can wander off and have a pint while the girls catfight over who saw the half-price cork wedges first. Alternatively, wander off on your own, but arrange to meet her back in *her* shop after half an hour or so.

It takes men five minutes to make a decision on an item of clothing. The same decision can take women five millennia. For this very reason, NEVER agree to a shopping trip with more than two women at a time. For each additional woman, add another hour on to each decision made. Be warned, however, no action beyond an arson attack—and even that's questionable—will speed a woman up. Patience and tact are your only tools. Despite the fact that every daintily hung belt is becoming a possible noose at this point, offer to play packhorse and carry her bags. At five o'clock, she'll show mercy on you and you'll be back in time to get the game scores.

How to get rid of sweaty armpits before a big meeting

Armpits can smell fear. They pick up the scent of trepidation and pounce on it. Their aim: to send the new CEO running from the office, mentally scarred from the sight of sweat patches the size of saucers and the whiff of body odor redolent of rabid camel.

Here's how to banish the sweat monster before that important meeting:

Dress to suppress the sweat. When the last shake of the antiperspirant can or the final smear of the roll-on isn't enough, you're going to have to disguise the problem. A black or white shirt will go some way to conceal the patches, but as an extra protection, wear a high-quality cotton vest or undershirt to soak up any perspiration, leaving your shirts bone-dry and sweat-patch free. Always wear loose cotton or linen shirts to allow the air to pass between your clothes and your body. Invest in a light linen suit for summer.

Avoid coffee, drink lots of water, and don't power-walk to work. Leave plenty of time to get to your meeting so you don't have to rush or panic. Keep your body temperature low, reduce the amount of heat your body gives off or receives.

Take off your jacket and loosen your collar and tie on the way there.

Take two shirts to work. Nip off shortly before the meeting starts and change in the gents. As for the odor, carry a little stick of body spray in your pocket or buy one specifically for your desk at work.

In severe cases, dab cider vinegar on your armpits before you go to bed, and wash them thoroughly in the morning. Drink a cup of green tea at night, as this dries your body of oils. Avoid spicy foods and alcohol. Carry a hand fan and cool yourself down at regular intervals.

Some home remedies you can try:

Drink sage tea instead of your usual brew.

Dust your armpits with baking soda—it absorbs the sweat and acts as a deodorant.

Add two cupfuls of tomato juice to your bathwater and soak the pits for at least 15 minutes.

Drink a cup of tomato juice every day. You can do this while you soak in your tomato juice bath.

Slice a potato and rub the juice on your armpits, then apply deodorant as usual.

Extreme measures:

Lift your arms in front of the hand driers in the bathroom every hour. Have an auxiliary Botox injection pre-meeting.

How to cook breakfast in bed

So you're not the mushy, poetic type. If you're semi-intelligent, interesting, and employed, you may be able to get away with being your non-romantic self around her most of the time. But every once in a while something in the female brain snaps, and she starts fantasizing about having an affair with a muscular guy with a sexy accent. In these instances, it becomes necessary to go full-out guy from The Notebook *on her if you want to stay on her good side. Cook her a breakfast in bed that will make you look like the hottest man alive and guys with accents look as attractive as Danny DeVito.*

1. Figure out what you're going to make. Forget that box of Cheerios or anything else in your kitchen that would take less than thirty seconds to prepare. Try to remember breakfast foods she likes to eat. If you can't think of anything, French toast is fairly easy to make and impressive-looking on a plate. A fruit salad on the side is also a safe bet.

2. Consult a recipe. Look in a cookbook, search online, or call your mom.

3. Make a list (including items you need and how much of each item you need) and go to the grocery store.

4. Do a dry run. Cook the breakfast for yourself one day to see how it'll turn out. Learn from any mistakes you make. If you really screw it up, now's a good time to call your mom again.

5. Prepare as much as you can the night before. If it takes hours for you to ball a melon, it's best if you do it the night before so she's not eating breakfast in bed at 4:00 p.m.

6. Sneak down the morning of, and try your best not to make a racket while you cook. Use the good plates and silverware (nothing dingy, dirty, or plastic), and plop it on a tray with flowers. You'll be a winner for life in her eyes, or at least until the next time you accidentally call her fat or make fun of her cat.

The man's guide to Internet chat room slang

We've come a long way from telegrams, smoke signals, and paper cups with string. Thanks to the Internet, communication has never been so easy. If you're about to eat a packet of prawn cocktail crisps, you're only a click away from letting the world know on Facebook. With so much to say, and so little time to say it, heaven forbid Generation Instant Messenger should type twenty keys when only two will do.

Acronyms:

WUU2? = **What you up to?**

NM = **Not much**

LOL = **Laughing out loud**

ROFL = **Rolling on the floor laughing**

FOCL = **Fall off chair laughing**

LMAO = **Laugh my ass off**

PMSL = **Pissing myself laughing**

WTGP? = **Want to go private—for the cybersex obsessive**

FYI = **For your information**

GR&D = **Grinning, running, and ducking**

IMO = **In my opinion**

AAR = **At any rate**

AFK = **Away from the keyboard**

BAK = Back at keyboard

F2F = Face to face

ASL or a/s/l = Age, sex, location

IOW = In other words

AFAIK = As far as I know

JAS = Just a second

GAL = Get a life

LTNS = Long time no see

NIMBY = Not in my back yard

GBTW = Get back to work—one for the boss

OTW = On the way—file sent

PMJI = Pardon me for jumping in

BRB = Be right back

TTTT = These things take time

SOTA = State-of-the-art

TRDMF = Tears running down my face

IWSN = I want sex now—don't we all

FITB = Fill in the blanks

TTFM = Ta-ta for now

POS = Parents over shoulder

WTF = What the f**k?

ADIH = Another day in hell

ADIP = Another day in paradise

NIFOC = Naked in front of computer— often responded to with TMI, too much information

BOFH = Bastard operator from hell

PTKFGS = Punch the keys for God's sake

FOAF = Friend of a friend

JK = Just kidding

KISS = Keep it simple stupid

MTFBWY = May the force be with you

NSFW = Not safe for work—i.e. "I'm sending you porn."

MUSH = Multi-user shared hallucination

MYOB = Mind your own business

PITA = Pain in the ass

SOHF = Sense of humour failure

TANSTAAFL = There ain't no such thing as a free lunch

OMG = Oh my God

ZOMG = Zoh my gawd—a way of mocking those that use OMG all the time

JC = Just chilling

YAA = Yet another acronym

Random symbols:

XOXO = Hugs and kisses—one for the girlfriend

^5 = High five

?^ = What's up?

_/? = Cup of tea?

Emoticons:

Sideways faces showing emotions following the guidelines:

Colon = Eyes

Semi-colon = Winking eyes

Brackets = Lips

Hyphen = Nose. Some cyber-rebels kick cyber civilization to the curb and don't even bother with a nose. Crazy. And they said the Internet wouldn't change a thing.

;-)~~~~~ = Giving someone raspberries

:-) = Smile

;-) = Wink

:-/ = Perplexed

:-(= Sad—probably because they don't have any friends. Real ones at least.

:,-(= Crying

;-0 = Shouting

:-D = Big grin

<:-| = Curious—because all curious people obviously wear paper sailor hats

---

:-o = Surprised

:-| = Bored

:-x = Keeping mouth shut

;-)~ = Drooling, drunk, or massive seizure

;-P = Sticking tongue out

;-{} = Someone with a moustache

8-) = Wearing glasses or being clever—in short, being a smartass

Toolbox essentials

A good tradesman never blames his tools. But as you're a DIY amateur, inserting profanities before naming each tool is an essential part of your duty. Here's a must-have list for your f**king toolbox.

1. *A heavy claw hammer with a wooden handle.*
2. *Three varying sizes of Phillips screwdrivers.*
3. *A flat-head screwdriver.*

A cross-point screwdriver—a two-in-one screwdriver will suffice.

Screws—all types and sizes.

4. *Needle-nose pliers—cutting and gripping pliers, also called "snipe-nose" or "pinch-nose" pliers. Handy for reaching awkward cavities where wires can't be reached with your fingers.*
5. *A medium-size wrench.*
6. *Retractable tape measure with lock feature.*
7. *Cordless or corded electric drill.*
8. *Angle square.*
9. *9" torpedo spirit level.*

Pencil or chalk.

10. *Small hacksaw.*

Old toothbrush.

Nails.

11. *Putty knife.*
12. *Utility knife with blades that can be replaced.*

Electric current detector.

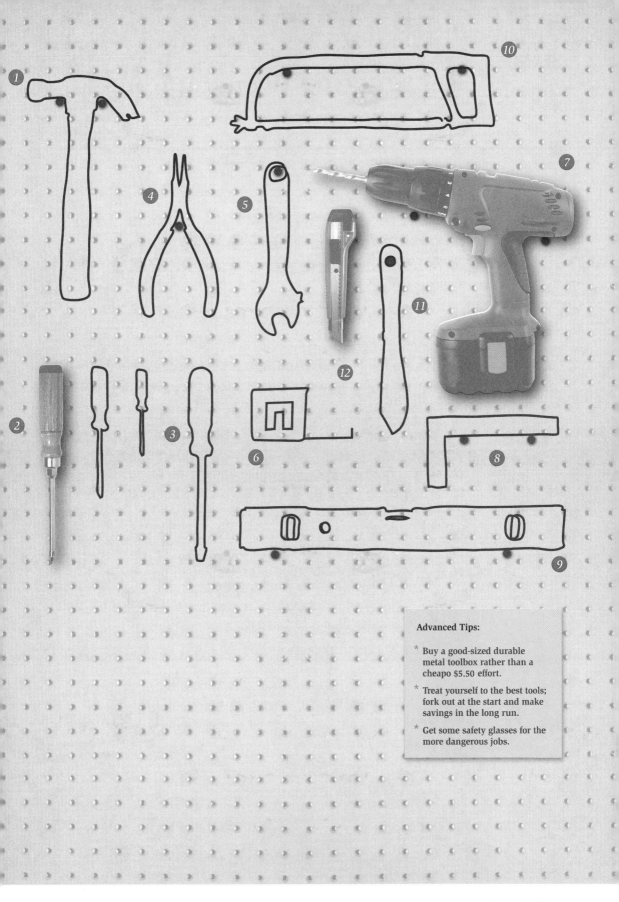

Recognizing the symptoms of depression

Boys don't cry. Or so we're told the first time we fall off our bikes and scrape our knees. From then on we only blub behind closed doors or after our hometown team's crushing defeat in the Super Bowl.

Even when our grandparents pass away, we trace our fathers' footsteps to the front pew and stoically stare ahead. We bottle it up, thinking crying shows weakness; a lack of strength and control.

When we don't feel strong we often feel like we are failing at being men. But the true failing is in not recognizing that something's up.

We all feel low every once in a while. Sometimes we feel the heavy touch of depression, and if we don't recognize the symptoms and do something about it, it can swallow us up.

Here are some signs of depression to take notice of:

* A lasting feeling of low self-esteem and self-confidence, not the odd day here and there.
* Overwhelming sadness.
* Lack of hope for the future.
* Worrying about everything.
* Catastrophic thinking—usual worries taking on abnormally negative implications.
* Apathy towards activities you normally enjoy.
* Abnormal fatigue and exhaustion.

* Abnormal sleeping patterns—more or less than usual. Insomnia, or waking up in the early hours of the morning.

* Extremes in eating habits—eating more or less.

* Lowered sex drive.

* Difficulty in concentration and motivation.

* Thoughts of self-harm or self-destructive tendencies, including excessive drinking.

* Thoughts of suicide and death.

* Unexplained and unpredictable periods of crying.

* A sense of fragility.

* Lethargy.

* Guilt and worthlessness about everything, even things not directly related to you.

* Social reclusiveness—not taking calls, avoiding friends and family, inability to face social events.

If you're experiencing five of the symptoms shown above for over two weeks, the best thing to do is to try and combat them. Incorporate some of the behavior listed below in to your life for at least two weeks.

Talk to a close friend or relative about how you are feeling and your worries, no matter how trivial they might seem.

Stay active. Force yourself to see friends and family, even if you really feel you can't face it. You'll often find your mood lifting once you are in their company.

Exercise. Go for a swim, or a walk round the park or in the countryside.

Eat well.

Don't take drugs or alcohol—even though they might make you feel better for a short time, drugs and drink only make depression worse.

If you can't sleep, sit up and read until you nod off. Or get up and do something—a crossword can take your mind away from circular negative thoughts—until you feel sleepy again. Don't lie awake staring at the wall and agonizing about your life.

Take a chill-out period from work or school.

If the symptoms persist for another two weeks, see your GP. Be clear and honest about your symptoms; don't beat about the bush.

Your doctor may suggest you start taking an antidepressant to help you through the bad patch. Don't worry, you probably won't have to take them forever, but antidepressants can be very effective at lifting the fog and allowing you to see things clearly again. You may be offered counseling or therapy, which can be very helpful too.

For some, depression can overshadow a short period of their life. For others it's an illness, part of their existence they learn to live with. There are many types of depression and an equal number of methods to combat it. Asking for help is the first step to finding a solution. There's a lot of truth in the saying, "A problem shared is a problem halved."

How to dress up as a convincing woman

Smelling of roses and sporting suspenders, you'd think the alpha male in us would be suppressed. But no, our competitive spirit remains intact. When another man strolls into the fancy dress party looking like a Bangkok pre-op and smelling of Old Spice we can't resist the temptation to gloat. Stroking a smooth chin and blowing smoke through silver-glossed lips we utter a comment in consternation, "P'ah, five o'clock shadow; you'd never catch Ms. Edwina making such an amateurish mistake!"

Donning a skirt and blouse for a fancy dress party is all very well, but why not go the whole hog? Here's how to be the best-dressed tranny in the room.

First off you've got to get rid of your Adam's apple. That doesn't mean re-enacting the botched tracheotomy from last night's *Grey's Anatomy*; tie a nice silk scarf around your neck, with a loose knot resting on your apple.

Your beanbag should be next on the list. A "gaff" is a specific garment designed to smooth out that particularly bumpy part of the body, but an athletic cup is a cheaper and less embarrassing alternative. If you've rather a lot to stow away, Sellotape the offending weapon under your legs and put on a tight pair of underpants.

Breasts. These can very tricky. If you're fortunate enough to have a pair of man-boobs you're laughing. A push-up bra and you're away, sister. If not you need to stuff the bra with cotton wool or tissue paper. Another possibility is to fill two balloons with exactly the same amount of water, and place them in your size D cups. As a last resort a couple of oranges are your best bet. Coconuts are an absolute no-no—unless you're going for the hairy Mary look.

Outfit. Put a lot of thought into what you wear when dressing like a lady. Chucking on the first thing you find in your mom's wardrobe won't convince anyone, apart from your dad after a couple of beers. Work out what suits your body. Some general rules: dark colors make you look thinner, long sleeves cover up hairy arms and tight-fitting clothes should be avoided if you don't have the body for them. V-necks distract from broad shoulders and large skirts give thin buttocks more curves. Mix and match; because you're worth it.

Legs. Wear two to three pairs of stockings. Two pairs of white stockings will cover your horsehair legs and a pair of fishnets on top of that will give the impression of feminine legs, pale and smooth. Choose flat shoes or small kitten heels—your height advantage will serve you well and prevent you from falling down a flight of steps and breaking your womanly little neck.

Shave. Just before you go out shave, to limit the five o'clock shadow.

Make-up. The chances are you won't have put make-up on before so ask a girlfriend to come over and work her magic. You don't want to look like Coco the Clown after several brandies. If you haven't got any girlfriends, or the idea of opening the door looking like Norman Bates sends shivers down your now beautifully accentuated spine, do it yourself following these rules. A thin layer of brown blusher along your jawline and chin will soften your features. Apply blusher by smiling and stroking your cheeks with upward brushstrokes. Emphasize your eyes *or* your lips. If your lipgloss is striking, tone down make-up on your eyes and vice versa. Not both.

Wig. Choose one that won't make your face look manly. Straight hair will accentuate your Desperate Dan jawline, so opt for a curly or wavy-haired wig. Not an Afro wig—that will only make you look more like a clown. Put the wig on and tuck any of your own hair away, then pull down on the two tabs just in front of your ears. Brush out your wig until you get the desired look. Don't rush putting it on, stand in front of the mirror until it looks real. Apply make-up before you put the wig on. Don't bend over and throw the wig on to your head, place it gently for maximum effect.

Accessorize. Wear dainty clip-on earrings, don't go the Pat Butcher route and hang chandeliers off your earlobes. Carry a delicate handbag or clutch and leave your rucksack at home. Talk like a lady. The best way to do this is by talking incredibly softly and quietly. Suck your stomach in and practice walking in a slightly mincing, bottom-wiggling step. Don't hunch and walk with your legs apart.

Extreme cross-dressing. Pluck your eyebrows and thin them out to a wispy layer of hair. Shave your legs and arms. For the hourglass figure purchase hip pads and a girdle for your beer belly. Wear a corset. Learn to walk in high heels or buy some decent boots. Apply for a sex change.

How to get out of paying for a parking ticket

Parking tickets are #1 on the list of Pointless Things You Don't Want to Waste Your Money On. If you're one of the brave souls who'd rather fight the ticket than fork over the cash, try following these steps, being sure to also note specific laws and procedures in your state. Then you just might be able to claim that you fought the law and you won.

* Look for mistakes on the ticket. Wrong dates, times, and addresses on the ticket could get you off the hook. You may have to prove the discrepancy, so hunt down any evidence that backs up your case, including invitations to events, receipts, or anything that would prove your whereabouts at the time of the ticket.

* Take pictures. If the meter broke or the no-parking sign was somehow knocked over, misplaced during construction, or covered with graffiti, take pictures to demonstrate that you had no way of knowing you were parking illegally.

* Take up another reasonable defense, which may include: the vehicle did not belong to you and was not in your name the date the parking ticket was issued, the vehicle experienced mechanical failure, or a passenger in the vehicle was in need of immediate medical assistance.

* Contest the ticket. Check specific laws in your state on how to approach the situation. You'll have to contest within a certain time period after the ticket was issued, so stay on top of the situation to avoid incurring more fines. You'll most likely need to either write a letter or appear at a hearing. Remember: it's your story versus the police officer's story, and in most cases, the police officer will be right. Do your best to respectfully explain that the ticket was a misunderstanding.

* Don't get a ticket in the first place. Look for and read signs. Download parking apps on your smart phone like Parking Mate or Pocket Parking Meter to help keep track of time when the meter is running. If your friends say you can park in a certain spot but you have your doubts, follow your gut rather than your friends. If a broken meter's the issue, leave a detailed, dated letter somewhere on your car that explains that you attempted to pay the meter.

How to give the perfect best man's speech

Winston Churchill might have been a great orator, but he is not a great role model for your first public speech. After all, you don't want to send the wedding guests or business partners to the buffet with a war cry echoing inside their heads.

Follow these guidelines and you won't have a riot on your hands:

Order:

* Have a funny opening line; a cocky icebreaker that sets all the guests at ease, but also lets them know this might be a little embarrassing for the groom.

* Point out some things about the wedding—be positive, don't say the food is garbage and the service stinks.

* Set out your feelings about being best man. If you're a confident sort make a show of being nervous and vice versa. Send yourself up, but let everyone know you're in control.

* Give some hilarious and/or touching insights into your relationship with the groom.

* Lead into a character assassination—but don't be nasty or cruel. If he was still a virgin at 33 don't share this with the assembled guests.

* Mention the impact the new wife has had on your best friend's life. Be positive! Crying into your beer because she wouldn't let him come to the pub last Thursday shouldn't be mentioned. He'll have told you what she means to him—now's the time to let everyone else know.

* This is the bit you've been dreading—the honest appraisal and moving tribute to marriage. No matter what your views, congratulate the bride and groom on their nuptials and wish them all the best for the future.

* Finish on a sincere or humorous, but not offensive, note. Whatever you do don't wink at the bride's mother and make an overt sexual advance. Wait until the dancing gets going for that.

* *Raise a toast to the happy couple.*

Advice:

* Don't get pissed before the speech.

* Be open and talk frankly about the couple, but don't embarrass them. If they're looking uncomfortable change tack and move onto something else. It's their wedding, not your debut stand-up show.

* Thank the parents of both the groom and the bride—add extra thanks to the bride's dad for getting a decent amount of booze in and guarantee him you won't be letting any go to waste.

* Balance out your speech, don't just witter on about the groom, know your stuff about the bride too.

* An original and apposite quotation can be worked in to the speech to either humorous or dramatic effect, but avoid clichés and anything too obvious, or you'll fall flat on your face.

* Write out notes for your speech on the back of some cards. Use the notes to keep you on track, but engage your audience by making eye contact in a charming manner.

* Speak slowly and calmly; don't rush in a nervous desire for it to be all over. Breathe and remember to smile as you speak. Before you know it you'll be back in your seat with a crescendo of applause ringing around your ears.

How to get rid of shaving cuts in a hurry

* Run a washcloth under very hot water for a few minutes and press it on the offending bleeder.

* Press sugar or salt onto the cut to stop the bleeding.

* Apply some Vaseline to the spot. It won't heal it but it will stop it bleeding.

* Push a piece of toilet paper on to the cut; let some blood soak up into the tissue so it sticks. Leave for ten minutes, remove, and the cut should have clotted. Remember to remove tissue before you leave the house.

* Press an ice cube against the cut to make the capillaries constrict and stop the bleeding.

* Spray some deodorant on your fingertip and press on to the cut. The aluminium compounds cause blood to clot more quickly.

* Dab some urine on your face. Shaving cut or smelling of pee? That's a tough one.

How to beat that Monday morning hangover from hell

With a brain feeling like the victim of a sensory deprivation chamber saboteur and a stomach doing the hokey-pokey, hangovers make Monday mornings even moodier. The main culprit of a hangover is a toxic chemical called acetaldehyde, the by-product of alcohol metabolism and breakdown. This chemical works on your brain and makes you sweat and feel nauseous.

The headache comes from your brain rattling around your head.
Because all the cerebrospinal fluid (the stuff that your brain likes to take a dip in) has been sucked out to replenish your dehydrated body. What a lovely image.

The trick to preventing a hangover is to do all you can the night before the morning after arrives. The problem is that you are usually too drunk to remember what you should do.

Before you go drinking:

1. Take two tablespoons of olive oil and eat a baked potato before leaving the house. This will line the stomach.

2. Alternatively, swallow some milk thistle tablets. They help the liver deal with serious alcohol consumption and can help reduce after-effects.

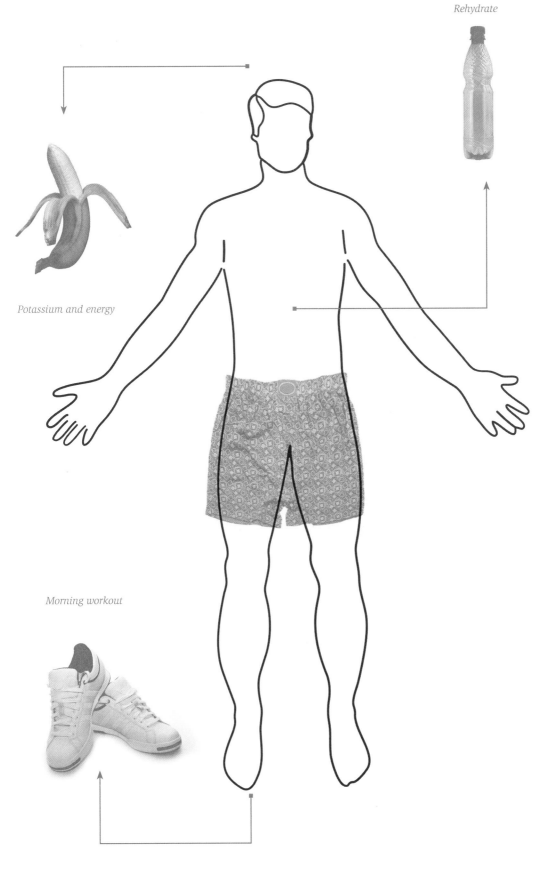

Rehydrate

Potassium and energy

Morning workout

Later, after the drinking session:

3. You should try chugging pint after pint of water just before you collapse. This will help you rehydrate and prevent a devastating headache the next morning.

4. Some swear by Diarolyte, a diarrhoea remedy which helps to rehydrate and restore mineral salt and sugar levels in the body. Drink a packet with water before bed.

If you still wake up with a headache and the need to vomit:

5. Acetaldehyde's nemesis is cysteine, which can be found in eggs, meat, and honey. So, if you can face it, a poached egg on toast, or even better the full fry-up, is the perfect remedy.

6. Try the traditional *Prairie Oyster Recipe.*

7. Other cures include: eating bananas, lemons, and limes. These will settle your stomach and give you carbohydrates and potassium, which give you energy.

8. Tomato and orange juice boosts your body's vitamin C as well as helping replace lost electrolytes.

9. A nice long, hot shower, or a trip to the local steam room and sauna will revitalize your skin and help you sweat out the evil toxins.

10. A morning workout banishes toxins from your body and increases circulation which gets essential oxygen to your brain.

11. Pulling your hair gets blood to your head, reducing your headache and getting you some funny looks on the bus to work.

12. Beware the caffeine monster. Coffee will dehydrate you even more.

Prairie Oyster Recipe

- A Traditional Hangover Remedy -

---

2 dashes of white wine or malt vinegar

1 egg yolk

1 tsp Worcestershire sauce

1 tsp ketchup

Black pepper

Directions:

Mix the vinegar, Worcestershire sauce, and ketchup in a glass.
Separate the egg and carefully add the yolk to the glass, taking care
that it doesn't break. Grind in some fresh black pepper.

Down in one go.

The hangover from hell sent straight back from whence it came!

The real man's guide to the *Kama Sutra*

The Hindu God Shiva and his wife Parvati were no strangers to a bit of hanky panky. But they didn't bank on their trusty noble steed and doorkeeper, Nandi the sacred bull—and distant cousin to Nando the chicken—being a peeping Tom. He spied on their carnal antics and, believing these two had a thing or two to teach mankind, sketched out their various moves. These doodles and scribbles were indecipherable at first—have you ever tried writing with hooves?—but over the years they became the ancient Indian scripture that is now known as the Kama Sutra.

Sprinkle a little spice onto your bed with these positions.

Are you sitting comfortably? Sitting positions:

The Tortoise/Kaurma. An easy one to start with. Sit with your legs spread out in front of you and get your girlfriend to straddle you with her thighs on top of yours and her legs spread out behind you. Hold her with your arms to support her as she lifts herself gently up and down. Tense your buttocks and leg muscles to aid her elevation.

The Swing/Dolita. Cries of "higher, higher" won't be forthcoming but get this right and she won't be able to speak for a week while her throat recovers from the incessant screams of pleasure…or something like that anyway. Sit face to face, chest tight on chest, locking your feet behind one another. Lean back, and holding on to each other's wrists, rock slowly backwards and forwards building momentum to a monumental crescendo.

Look behind you! Rear entry positions:

The Deer/Hirana. On all fours, your partners arches her back, her bottom up into the air. Enter her from behind on your knees or, for those with steadier legs—stand on one foot or both feet with your weight on your thighs and enter her from a higher position.

The Cat/Marjara. She lies on her stomach and you hold her ankles in one hand. Kneeling, penetrate her, lifting her ankles high up in the air—don't bend them forward. With your other hand reach forward and gently lift her chin.

Stand to attention. Standing positions:

Face to Face/Sammukha. Also known as the "knee trembler." She leans with her back against a wall and separates her legs as far as possible. With bent knees, enter her supporting your weight with your hands against the wall, or hold her close round her waist or bum. Perfect for a quickie in the alleyway, you old romantic.

The Tripod/Tripadem. Grasp one of her knees from underneath, lifting it above waist height. Steady yourself by holding behind her thigh with your other hand. A tricky balancing act—get it wrong and you could end up looking like two drunk students after a naked Twister game went horribly awry.

Girls on top:

The Swan/Hansabandha. Lie flat on your back and get her to sit upright on you with her head leaning back and both feet brought together on one side of your body. Yells of "Ride 'em cowgirl" and/or humming the *Rawhide* theme tune—not recommended. Good for hitting the G-spot.

The Sacred Thread/Upavitika. This position is not for the faint of heart (literally) and requires your girlfriend to have a little bit of leg strength and a whole lot of balance. She lowers herself onto you with one foot spread out on the bed and the other spread across your heart. She lifts herself up and down gracefully while trying not to puncture one of your lungs.

First date survival guide

Playground romance had its charms. A "first date" consisted of a quick squeeze behind the bike shed, commemorated with a chorus of K-I-S-S-I-N-G from your friends. And once you'd written her initials in White-Out on your pencil case, you were as good as married. Out of the playground things get a little trickier. Show up to a date with a bottle of White-Out and a map to the nearest bike shed and the only thing you'll be kissing is the tears on your pillow.

Here's how to survive the first date:

The time and the place.

Gigs, the theater, or a film all sound good but there's one problem: none involve talking. You'll want to get to know her in a relaxed environment where you can work your charms without distractions.

Go for a drink or a meal before the gig or film. You can calm those first-date nerves with a couple of pints, or if the outlook is grim, get hammered.

Mid-week is the best time for a first date.

If you're picking her up, knock twice, take a step back, and look around outside. Don't stare dead ahead and wait for the door to open; don't bang on the door and shout, "Come on darling. Get a f**king move on!"

Make eye contact. You don't want to look like a shifty weirdo.

Give her a light kiss on both cheeks, like a real Casanova.

Don't grab her hand the minute she's out the front door. She'll think you're possessive, or sappy. Or that you're taking sniper fire.

Pay her a compliment to set the tone—tell her she's looking lovely or amazing, or admire her dress.

First impressions.

Take a shower beforehand and arrive clean-shaven or with decent designer stubble.

Clean your teeth. Twice.

Dress to impress, but if you don't normally wear a suit and tie during the day, now is not the time to start. Just wear what you normally do when you go out on the town—some decent jeans, an ironed shirt, and a jacket. Sometimes a T-shirt and pullover will look good if you look the part.

Give yourself plenty of time so you're not late and flustered. You'll already be sweating profusely so don't exacerbate the situation by running for the bus or your crotch area will feel like someone's just poured a jug of water on it.

Relax. Tell yourself you're just two good friends hanging out. So what if you goof up and make a fool of yourself? Women like men who can laugh at themselves; if you're too serious she'll have wished she'd stayed in with a good book.

Women like strong-looking men. Keep your back straight and your shoulders broad and don't slump over your pint (or curry if you're eating).

Be a gentleman, but don't go over the top. Hold the door open for her, buy the first round of drinks, and possibly pay for the meal, but don't refuse if she offers to pay half.

Conversation.

Don't brag about yourself. Mentioning your job and where you grew up is one thing, describing in slow-mo the overtime jump shot you scored last weekend is quite another.

Before you go out think about some topics you feel confident talking about. If there's an awkward silence—and there is always an awkward silence—nip into your memory bank and pull out a topic you prepared earlier.

Get the balance right between aloof and interested. Be playful and flirtatious and a little elusive at times. Don't give her every morsel of information; it's up to her to find out about you. Ah, the thrill of the chase.

Let her do some of the legwork. Smile when she's talking and let her finish before speaking.

Enjoy yourself. Even if the conversation is mundane, consider that she might be bored too, so change tack and talk about something else.

Banter is good. Let her know you'll give as good as you get, but don't be afraid to let her have the last word.

Be confident but not overbearing. Don't be afraid to show weakness or ignorance on certain subjects. And if she's the intellectual type, don't pretend to have read the whole of Proust in the original if you haven't.

Avoid religion, politics, money, sex, the ex, or how children should be raised. Leave these until the fourth or fifth date.

Look at her, not at the hot waitress who keeps brushing past your table.

Pick up on her body language. Open palms towards you, shoulders lifted and leaning towards you and smiling at you while looking into your eyes are all signs she doesn't find you repellent.

At the end of the night.

Walk or drive her home if you live nearby. Even if the date has gone badly and you pretty much want to vomit when you make eye contact it is common courtesy to make sure the lady gets home safely.

Wait for her to go indoors before you either walk away or drive off, but don't loiter about staring up at her bedroom window.

If she's played with her hair, kept up eye contact, and sounded interested and giggled with you—not at you—generally speaking she's enjoyed your company and wouldn't turn down an innocent kiss. If it turns into a full-on makeout, that's a bonus, but she'll admire your gentlemanly restraint. Leaving her wanting more is much better than a face full of Mace.

If she asks you if you want to come in for a coffee, she actually genuinely means a coffee despite what your friend in your pants is telling you. Stripping down to your underpants when she pops into the kitchen to put the kettle on will scare the living daylights out of her.

When saying goodbye, only say you'll call her if you really want to.

How to sell your car

Between rolling out of the showroom and death in a scrapyard a million miles from home, a car will have many owners. Some will put their feet up on the dashboard, some will cut off the feet of those who dare. All will shed a tear when the day comes to say goodbye.

Here's a step-by-step guide to selling your car:

Step 1. Know the market. Family cars are always in demand because—yes, you guessed it—people are always having babies. 4x4s will be easier to sell in the countryside. Convertibles and sports cars in the summer. Vans will always sell at competitive prices due to the never-ending evolution of the apprentice. But collector cars will have particular buyers.

Step 2. Price your car. Check the ads in local newspapers and used car websites. Note the mileage, condition and price. How many other cars like yours are on the market? Work out a realistic value of your car and add on a couple of hundred quid for good measure.

Step 3. Make your car buyable. Dents, scrapes, and ex-girlfriend's key markings should all be taken care of prior to sale. Get a close friend to take the car for a test drive; they can often hear any unusual noises that you have got used to. A mechanic can then give your car a once-over and give you a report. You can either pay for what he suggests—and keep the receipt to show the buyer—or factor it into the price, informing the buyer of what extra work needs to be done.

Step 4. Spruce it up. First impressions are crucial. Take the car to a good hand car wash and pay for a valet clean, or do it yourself. Properly. Don't forget to wipe the dashboard with polish cleaner, empty the ashtrays and vacuum the carpet thoroughly. Make sure the registration and latest inspection certificates along with owner's and stereo manuals are all in the glove compartment. Top up all fluids. Check the spare, jack and all the light bulbs. Remove old copies of the newspaper strewn across the back seat and the pair of pants dangling from the gear stick.

Step 5. Sell to a local dealership. It can be the perfect solution if you don't have time to go through the whole rigmarole of advertising and viewings. Garages offer roughly 20% less than the actual value of the car—that's how they make their profit. However, a garage might be the best way to go, if you know your car needs repairs. Less money but also less hassle.

Step 6. Advertise. Newspapers ads cost $50 or so, online ads $25. Online ads include more space for photos and information and also reach a wider audience. However, research the company first so you know they're not pulling a fast one and remember to read the small print. Notice boards in local shops, word of mouth and parking your car at a decent location, i.e. outside a university with a sign in the window, are also options. Your ad must include: year, model, make, color, number of owners, automatic or manual, mileage, and condition.

Some selling slang:

---

* **Must sell**—your price is low because you're getting out of town.

---

* **OBO**—"Or best offer." Lets buyers know you're open to negotiation.

---

* **Asking price**—you'll waiver a little on the price but not by much.

---

* **Firm**—no rush to sell. You'll wait for the right buyer.

---

* **As is**—the car will be sold as it is with no further repairs done.

Step 7. Viewing. Once the ad is placed, be ready to receive calls. If you answer the phone half-cut and slurring over prices the person on the other end is hardly going to feel comfortable going on a test drive with you let alone be happy to buy your car. Be friendly, polite, interested and accommodating. Answer any questions honestly and if they want a test drive check their driving license and accompany them. A request for their mechanic to give the car a once-over is acceptable as long as you don't have to pay for the service. If you doubt their integrity, refuse. Last but not least sell the car. Point out all bonus features—CD player, electric windows, your extensive collection of Page 3 clippings, etc.

Step 8. Negotiate. Know your lowest acceptable price and stick to it. Use the buyer's eagerness to push them to the price you're looking for. Don't rush the sale. Be willing to wait for a few viewings so you get the right price. However, if you get what you're looking for first time out, do the deal. If you don't get any buyers at all, be ready to drop your price to a more realistic one, you greedy git.

Step 9. Finalizing the sale. Shake hands and organize the transfer of funds. If they want to pay by cheque, be polite but say you'll have to wait for it to clear before you let them have the car—if they say no they're trying to pull one. Check the car once more to make sure you haven't left any prize magazines in the trunk and record the mileage on the dial. If the car breaks down after the sale you are not legally bound to accept responsibility. However, it is common courtesy to try and fix the problem if the breakdown occurs on your driveway. Be sure to transfer the title, adjust your insurance as needed, and fill out all other relevant paperwork.

How to hold a baby like a mother of three

At family functions up and down the country, there's always an exhausted mom who needs a helping hand. Here's how to step into the breach by holding the baby.

Hold your palms flat and, in a soft scooping motion, place one under the baby's bum, cupping gently, and place the other hand underneath the neck and head. A baby has incredibly weak neck muscles from birth to three to four months, so the head and neck needs to be supported at all times. Without support, the baby's head could loll back and result in spine damage. Having a boiling cup of tea spilt over your lap, watching the greatest goal ever, or even getting hit by a truck, don't excuse you not supporting that head. Once lifted up, and after a little practice and confidence, the little bundle's neck will eventually snuggle into the crook of your elbow, with its body stretched out on the line of your arm. And both your hands should meet underneath to give level support. Once past four months or so, the neck and head control will be stronger and they will want to have a look around. Lift the baby up over your shoulder—but not a fireman's lift just yet—and support the bum with one hand. Use the other hand, placed flat with your fingers pointing towards the sky, to support the upper back and neck. Lift up so the chin is level with the top of your arm, and as you walk around the child will nose about or rest its head in the hollow of your shoulder. This is a good position for

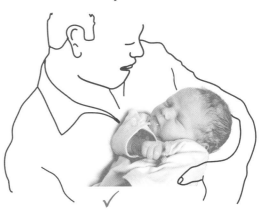

babies who are a bit windy and upset—gently patting them on the back while in this position can help "wind" them or, in simple terms, make them burp. You might want to cover your shoulder with a clean towel or muslin cloth in case of milky regurgitation—uhm, delicious.

One of the most important things to remember when handling newborns is that the bones on the top of their heads stay soft to enable passage through the birth canal. The bones fuse and the skull grows tougher after nine months to two years. So until they've shuffled up the mortal coil a bit more, be wary of their soft little heads. Next up, diaper changing.

How to build a campfire like a Boy Scout

Tip:

To keep your fire alight overnight, simply remove all large logs which are still burning to the edge of the fire. Cover the glowing embers with ash, then carefully pile large stones over the top. Next morning, remove the stones (caution: they might be hot enough to fry an egg), add fresh kindling and logs from the edge of the fire. And voila!

If you've never had the sensation of biting into a half-cooked sausage you've never lived. Or, nearly died of food poisoning, more like. So if your attempts at building a campfire result in a dwindling flame, leaving your sausages on the pink side, follow these rules for campfire glory. Roll on the roaring blaze.

Choose an area with no overhanging branches that's shielded from the wind. Next, forage for wood. Avoid green or wet wood. The rule of thumb for the perfect fire is DEAD BUT STILL ON THE TREE. The wood will be perfectly dry and will burn magnificently for cooking.

To start a fire, you need to collect:

* *Tinder*—Twigs, shavings, strips of dry bark (birch is perfect), dry leaves, grass, and thistle tops. This forms the base of the fire, which burns quickly and ignites the larger pieces of wood.

* *Kindling*—Thin, small, and very dry sticks about 6" long. When properly placed, these keep the fire alive while allowing oxygen to enter.

* *Fuel*—Larger pieces of dry dead wood and little logs, along with some green or live wood. The live wood is wet with sap and is slower burning than the dead wood, giving a well-balanced fire. This wood fuel makes for a long-burning and enduring fire.

Now it's time to build.

* If the ground is wet, lay a base using lengths of green or live wood.

* Grab a handful of tinder and ball it together to form a nest at the center of your chosen area. Place some kindling on top in the form of a tepee, or pyramid, making sure to leave gaps for the fire to breathe. Poke some birch strips or dry bracken in among the kindling to help it catch. Next, place four kindling sticks in a square around the tepee, followed by five or six sticks on top of them, to create a miniature wooden fence. Place two larger pieces of dry wood on opposite sides and build a partial roof of wood fuel, propping up the sticks between the fire and the wood with clumps of tinder.

* Sit with the wind on your back and light the fire by poking a match through a gap. Light the tinder first and the flames should spread to the tepee, the fence, and finally the larger pieces of wood on top. Long, slow blows from the depths of your lungs will keep the fire ignited, as will adding the remnants of your forage.

* Let the fire die down to an even flame, with lots of smoldering embers, then prepare your cooking pan and let the sausage sizzle commence. Anyone for a round of "Kumbaya?"

Getting the most out of being the designated driver

Whether you're standing stone-cold sober in the middle of the dance floor surrounded by strangers screeching Robbie Williams's "Angels" or cowering in the corner trying to avoid the advances of an AARP member, one Diet Coke-fueled evening is often enough to make you wish you'd never passed your driving test.

However, there are ways to make those Saturday nights of sobriety a little bit more bearable. First of all, rule with a Red Bull fist. Be firm, and don't put up with any nonsense. You're saving your friends countless pennies on the taxi ride home, so it's not entirely unreasonable if you want to leave a good half an hour or so before the bright white lights scatter the revelers like vampires at dawn.

After midnight, things usually get messy, so make the most of your friends' company at the start of the evening; get them to pay for your alcohol-free cocktails and enjoy yourself. Being sober doesn't mean you can't joke or flirt. In fact, turn it to your advantage. Let's face it, not punctuating every sentence with a belch enhances your chances of scoring rather than limits them. Stepping in to "rescue" a damsel in distress from one of your drunken friends' loutish slurring chat-up attempts will make you seem like a knight in shining armor. By comparison, prospective girlfriends will find you articulate and erudite. What's more, the promise not to redecorate the interior of her bathroom with Gastric Yellow, let alone freak her out of her skin by dancing like you're having some sort of fit, should (at the very least) get you a phone number or two by the end of the night.

The answer to the question: "How much can I drink and still be under the limit?" is simple. Either don't drink at all or, if being seen in a bar brandishing anything but a beer is tantamount to walking down your local street naked, two 12 oz. bottles of

4% beer spread out over the night, or a couple of pints of weak bitter shandy, will keep your dignity and faculties nicely intact. Tell the bartender that you're the designated driver—this should guarantee your drinks are measured correctly and your pint of shandy won't send you and your car the wrong way down the highway. It will win you his sympathy and someone sober to talk to when the rest of your party become incoherent or preachy.

When closing time arrives, rounding everyone up can be tricky. Most stragglers will quicken their pace with a few short, sharp thwacks to the back of the thighs, but if you haven't got a bamboo cane at hand, shouting over the crowd that you're leaving, marching to your car and revving the engine like a 17-year-old at his first set of traffic lights normally spreads panic.

Once the cries of "Shotgun!" have died down, feel free to overrule the verdict and elect the least drunk or most sleepy of your comrades to ride up front. Wind down the windows—a blast of good cold air could help hold any nausea among your passengers at bay.

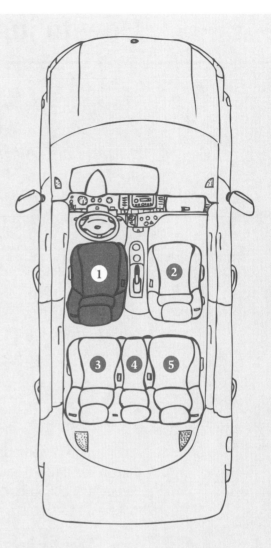

KEY	3. Most drunk
	(window down)
1. You	4. Most chatty
2. Least drunk	5. Most sleepy

As you approach the witching hour and the embers of the night begin to fade choruses of "I love you" and "You're a star, you are" will echo around your car like a stuck CD. This is the perfect time to drop a few hints about gas money. Silence will ensue but soon enough the drink-induced guilt will kick in and you'll be showered with money from every quarter of the car.

How to juggle a soccer ball

Despite the ridiculousness of a sport in which it's possible to have a final score of 0–0, women cannot help but instinctively flock to even the least impressive soccer players. Their tan complexion, toned physique, and association with names like Donovan and Ronaldo gives soccer guys an advantage that you just can't match sitting on your couch eating Cheetos and watching Sports Center *for the fifth time in a day. Thankfully, you don't have to like the game (or even know the rules!) to use a soccer ball to impress the ladies.*

The basics

Step 1. Pick a warm day to practice, pull on some board shorts or, if it's a particularly humid day, Speedos, and make sure you're on a flat surface.

Step 2. Drop the ball onto your favored foot and kick it back from whence it came. Don't hoof it. Elevate your toes higher than your heel so the ball spins towards you and tap it about knee height in the air.

Step 3. Rather than trying to juggle twenty times in a row straight off, concentrate at first on mastering a straight kick. Catch the ball, drop, kick, catch, drop, kick, catch, etc.

Step 4. Once you've perfected your balance and can kick the ball vertically, practice juggling twice in a row.

Step 5. Continue to practice until you can do five or six without the ball touching the ground.

Step 6. Now it's time to start with the ball at your feet. Put your favored foot on top of the ball, quickly roll it back and with the speed of Road Runner on heat slip your foot behind it. As the ball rolls over your toe kick it up and start juggling.

Step 7. Mix it up with a bit of a knee or thigh action and switch feet once in a while. When you've done about fifty in a row you're a freestyle funkster.

Mastered the juggling? Try your hand at these advanced moves:

Around the world

The aim of the ATW is to knock the ball up slightly, circle it— hence the expression around the world—and then catch it on your toe before it touches the ground.

Step 1. Balance the ball on your favored foot.

Step 2. Let the ball shift a little to the outside of your foot.

Step 3. As the ball begins to slide off your foot, lift your foot up the inside of the ball, over the top and down the other side. Don't brush the ball as you circle it.

Step 4. Catch the ball on your toe.

Rai Flick

This trick lifts the ball up and over your head. It's a great skill for flicking the ball over defenders on the field or old people in the park.

Step 1. As you dribble towards the defender, move your body over the ball.

Step 2. Clinch the ball between both feet and lift the ball up into the air. Attempt to flick the ball with one of your heels for added height.

Step 3. Run around the defender and control the ball on the other side.

Headstall

Not the best trick to pull off mid-game or you might get a mouthful of studs, but a classic to impress the ladies.

Step 1. Bend your neck so your face is towards the sky.

Step 2. Place the ball in the middle of your forehead just below your hairline.

Step 3. Keep your hand on the ball until it is balanced then peel your fingers away one by one.

Step 4. Relax your body, keep your eyes on the ball and use your neck and shoulder muscles to level out the ball's slight movements.

The man's guide to Texas Hold'em

Wild Bill Hickok. Gunfighter, professional gambler, and all-round figurehead of the Old West. In 1876 he was playing poker when a past loser shot him in the back of the head. Legend says Wild Bill was holding a pair of aces and a pair of eights at the time. The infamous Dead Man's Hand.

Old Wild West tales aside, assuming you've got at least four friends, here's how to have a go at stealing their pocket money:

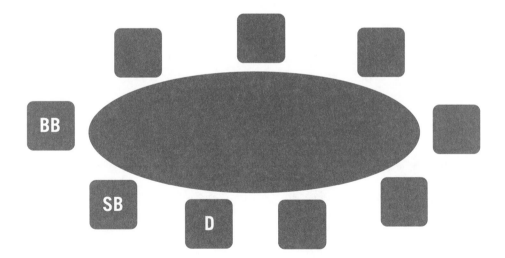

D = Dealer
SB = Small Blind
BB = Big Blind

The object of Texas Hold'em poker is to create the best five-card hand using any of the seven cards available. The two "hole" cards are dealt to each player at the start of the game, which only they can see and use. And the five cards which are dealt in the middle of the table throughout the game are called "community" cards because they can be seen and used by everybody.

Step 1. Set a minimum and maximum bet, shuffle the cards and put on some smooth jazz.

Step 2. Use an empty beer can, ashtray, etc. to mark player 1, the dealer.

Step 3. Before the cards are dealt, the two people to the left of the dealer, player 2 and player 3, place "blind" bets—so-called because the players make them without seeing any cards. Player 2 bets the small blind, half of the lowest limit. Player 3 bets the large blind, the complete lowest limit.

Step 4. Each player is dealt two "hole" cards—one at a time— face down on the table. The dealer receives the last card.

Step 5. Pre-flop round. Player 4 begins the betting round and betting continues clockwise round the table. Your options for each betting round are as follows:

*   Call the bet—in the first round each player, bar player 3, must call the large blind bet to enter the game. In later rounds, when calling the bet, a player must equal the previous amount of money placed in the pot. For example, if player 3 raises the bet to $8, player 4 must therefore call the $8 to stay in the game or fold.

*   Raise—place at least double the previous bet in the pot to up the stakes and put pressure on the other players. For example, a previous bet of $2 must be raised to $4 or more; bets can only increase, not decrease.

*   Fold—opt out of the game. Give your cards back to the dealer due to a bad hand or a raise in the bet you're not willing to equal.

*   Check—don't bet but stay in the game. Checking is not allowed on the first round because you must bet to enter the game. Each new round, once someone has raised the bet you can only call, raise or fold, not check.

Step 6. The first betting round ends with player 3—although player 2 and 3 placed blind bets, these don't count as their official first bet: they are a way of ensuring each hand played has some money in the pot. However, if no one has raised the bet, player 3 can check without calling his original "big blind" bet.

Step 7. It is important to note at this point that each betting round only ends when every player has either folded or called the largest bet. Rounds must end with everyone still in the game having an equal stake in the pot.

Step 8. The flop. The dealer deals the first three "community" cards face up in the middle of the table.

Step 9. Another betting round begins from player 2, or if player 2 has folded the next player still in the game to the left of the dealer. This is the starting point for all subsequent betting rounds post-flop.

Step 10. At the end of that round a fourth community card, or the turn card is dealt.

Step 11. Play another round—in this and the next round the minimum bet is equal to double the large blind bet.

Step 12. The last community card, the river card is dealt.

Step 13. Final betting round.

Step 14. The showdown. All remaining players show their cards and the winning hand takes the cash in the pot. If only one person remains and all other players have folded, the last man standing scoops the pot.

Step 15. Move the dealer/player one marker clockwise one place and start another game.

* Pennies, quarters, or even matchsticks will suffice as chips if you don't want to bankrupt your best friends.

* You do not have to use both your hole cards when making your five-card hand.

* If you like your chances, go all-in and dramatically throw all your chips into the center of the table. If you lose, however, you'll be out of chips and out of the game for good.

* When all other players have folded by the showdown you do not have to reveal your hand; if you've won by a two pair, however, this is the time to gloat.

* The card ranking always determines the winner. The highest pair wins—two 7s trump two 5s, for example. The highest-ranking straight wins and the highest card at the end of the flush determines tied flushes.

* With regards to straights, cards cannot "wrap"—go from Q, K, A, 1, 2, for example.

* If a game is tied, decide the winner with the "kicker" card. This is the card next in line in your hand. It is common to use only one card in your hand to make a winning hand and therefore in the event of a tie, use your second card as a kicker—if it is more than your opposition's kicker card you take the pot.

* In the rare occasion that ties cannot be determined—as sometimes happens with straights—divide the pot among all winners.

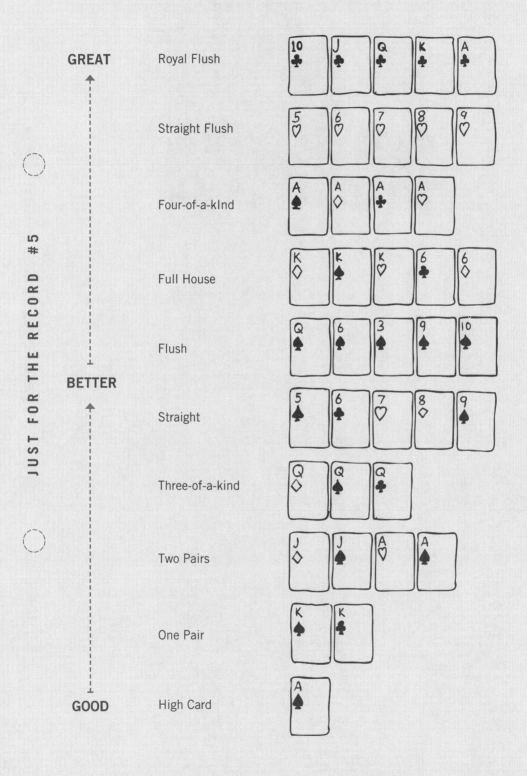

GREAT — Royal Flush

Straight Flush

Four-of-a-kInd

Full House

Flush

BETTER — Straight

Three-of-a-kind

Two Pairs

One Pair

GOOD — High Card

The Indispensable Garbage Bag: A Rough Guide

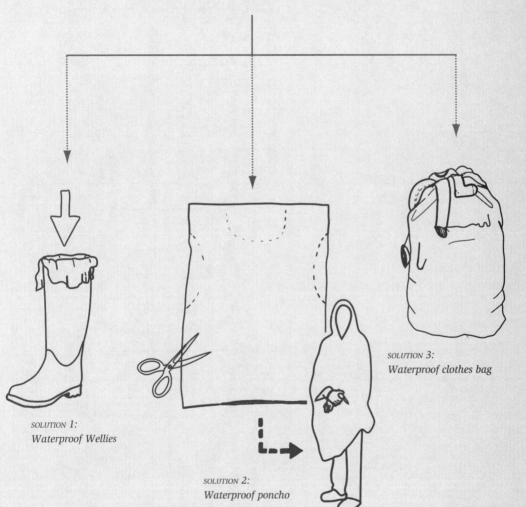

SOLUTION 1:
Waterproof Wellies

SOLUTION 2:
Waterproof poncho

SOLUTION 3:
Waterproof clothes bag

Festival essentials

As the summer sun rises and the days roll into one, it's only a matter of time before festival season arrives. The key to festival-going nirvana is to forget about fashion and concentrate on necessity.

The obvious ones first: tent, sleeping bag, clothes, lighter, large water container (full, obviously), wellington boots and/or old sneakers, rainproof anorak, hat, money, sun lotion, penknife, condoms, flashlight, toilet paper, Immodium tablets, toothpaste and toothbrush, and wet wipes.

If you've still got room consider these: a battery-powered radio to keep the music going when the lights go out, some firewood and firelighters—so you don't spend three hours in a drunken haze rubbing two sticks together—and a cooking stove and pan for those morning fry-ups.

Take some trash bags; their uses are endless. Cut a hole for your head to make a poncho, use them as waterproof mats, wear them inside your wellies for extra-dry protection, wrap and tape them around your shoes or boots, and keep your spare clothes dry in one.

If it's one of those festivals where there is a monitored gate between the sleeping area and the music arena, and where there is security checking that no alcohol goes in to the arena, make sure you have several small water bottles as big ones won't be allowed. You can sneak gin or vodka past security in the small water bottles.

Take two sweatshirts and put one in a pillowcase to use as a pillow. Also take something to make your tent stand out. A distinct flag from a rare country will work, but be prepared to meet some strange people. Mind you, that's what festivals are all about.

CHECKLIST

Essentials:

☐ Tent
☐ Sleeping bag
☐ Clothes
☐ Lighter
☐ Large water container
☐ Boots / old sneakers
☐ Anorak
☐ Hat
☐ Money
☐ Sun lotion
☐ Flashlight
☐ Penknife
☐ Immodium tablets
☐ Condoms
☐ Toilet paper
☐ Toothpaste
☐ Toothbrush
☐ Garbage bags
☐ Wet wipes

Luxuries:

☐ Battery-powered radio
☐ Firewood / lighters
☐ Gas stove
☐ Frying pan

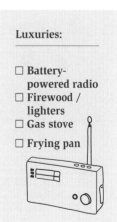

Tip: A few luxury items you might consider: anti-bacterial gel for washing hands, a shooting stick to lean on when everyone else is getting coated in muck, head-flashlight, hand-cranked phone charger, solar-powered backpack with MP3 plug-in, tent locator and homing tag, and last but not least, spoil your girl with a Shewee which enables her to pee standing up.

How to negotiate a pay raise with the boss

In the current economic crisis, wading into your boss's office and demanding a pay raise will probably be met with arched eyebrows and incredulous laughter. But if you think you're worth more than you're earning, argue your point with sound judgment and provide adequate reasons. The corporate purse may spring open just for you.

Here's how to stake your claim for a seat on the gravy train.

Think about why you deserve a pay raise:

*	How long have you been at your position? Have you taken on new responsibilities? Or trained new employees?

*	Consider your value to the company. Be honest about what you're worth and what your boss will think you're worth.

*	Gauge the "supply and demand" of your position. If someone else could easily supply your skills the company won't pay you more to do something a chimp could do.

*	Everyone moves up the rungs of the ladder; wait your turn, don't attempt to leapfrog others.

* Don't ask for a pay raise if others are being laid off. The best time to negotiate your salary is after you've been consistently working at a high level for several months and preferably when your department or company as a whole is not in decline.

Compile evidence to back up your claim:

* Research salary surveys online, question contacts in other companies, browse job advertisements, and find the going market rate for your position.

* Write a list of any new responsibilities you have taken on since joining the company.

* List the skills which make you an important asset to the team. Awards and exceeded expectations should also be listed.

* Letters or emails of praise from colleagues—not including the doorman—or clients will back up your claims of importance.

* Consider your main accomplishments. Securing a new client, finalizing a deal, or consistent sales all point towards an indispensable member of the team.

* Make sure your information is well-presented and in a logical order.

Prepare yourself for the big showdown:

* Arrange a meeting with your direct line manager or boss. Under no circumstances go above your boss's head by going straight to his or her boss.

* Request a meeting either via his or her secretary or send an email. Say that you'd like a career review, rather than bluntly stating that the meeting is to ask for a pay raise.

* Plan what you want to say in advance. Make notes, and have a practice run with a close friend or partner. Don't tell everyone at your workplace you're going to "milk the boss dry."

* Set a clear objective in your head. Know what salary you would like and what you'd be willing to settle for. Give yourself room to negotiate within those boundaries.

*   Prepare responses to any questions or concerns your boss may raise. Remember, he'll have to defend any pay increase to his or her boss as well.

*   When you enter the office, thank your boss for making time to see you.

*   Take a deep breath, don't enter in to small talk or start to stutter. Be factual, professional, and straight to the point and present all your information in a concise and articulate manner.

*   Clearly state you're happy at the company and that you're not looking for a new job but you'd like to discuss your pay.

*   Don't simply bombard your boss with stats, give brief examples of your achievements, and hand over the documents you've prepared. If necessary, give your boss some time to think over and consider your case.

Negotiating and leaving with what you want:

*   If your boss is open to your request for more pay, never start the bidding. Let them make the first move. Remain silent for at least 30 seconds after his first offer; this may provoke him or her to offering you more.

*   On the other hand, if you are pushed to state a price, always ask for more than you actually expect—within reason. Don't ask for a million dollars in brand new bills.

*   Take an active part in the discussion and be respectful of your boss's position. However, don't talk too much or you may end up agreeing to something you don't want.

*   Negotiate. The final package may not incorporate money alone; your boss may want you to go on a training course or work extra hours. You could also ask for more vacation or take on more responsibilities—be flexible.

*   Be friendly but in control. Don't come over all emotional and mention your need for a plasma TV in a flood of tears.

*   If your request is declined on monetary reasons alone, ask your boss to review your pay at the next possible opportunity.

The man's guide to fishing

Man versus fish. The age-old battle. Homer Simpson vs General Sherman, the legendary and elusive 500 lb. catfish. Richard Dreyfuss and Co. vs Jaws senior. Ah, the thrill of the chase. A thrill the fish hardly experiences, having been hooked, whacked over the head with an oar, and cooked on a red-hot skillet.

You will need:

Fishing rod and reel. You can buy these already strung with a line from fishing shops or department stores. Preferably the line should be 4–16 pound test—how strong the line is, called poundage—and the rod medium light, between 5 and 6 feet long.

Bait. Bait and tackle shops are widely available in fishing areas. Choose worms for your first time; live bait is widely considered the best form of bait for fishing novices.

A pack of hooks. Size 6 covers most fish, unless you snare a Great White.

One or two bobbers or floats. Brightly colored for easy observing.

Non-lead split-shot sinkers. Small weights to make sure the bait sinks and the line doesn't float on top of the water.

A friend. So you don't a) go mad from isolation, b) starve from male pride.

Bucket. To keep the fish in once caught.

Optional: *fishing net.*

Optional: *fishing knife.*

Sea fishing requires no license whatsoever, but lake or river fishing will. You may also need to pay for the right to use a landowner's body of water.

Step 1. Ask local fishing shops for tips on good fishing spots. Other anglers are likely to keep their special little places secret, so there's no point asking them.

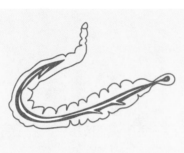

Step 2. Tie the hook to the end of the rod (see page 179 for knots). Thread the hook all the way into the worm.

Step 3. Place the bobber or float on the line about 3 feet above your hook. And leave about 10 inches of line between the bobber and the tip of your rod.

Step 4. Clip a split-shot to your line slightly above the hook. Add more according to the conditions; strong currents require more weight than calm water.

Step 5. Set the drag on the reel. The drag is the amount of line that is released by the reel from the fish's end. Too tight and the line could snap, too loose and the hook might not catch the fish's mouth. As a general rule, set your drag to 25% of the line's poundage.

Step 6. Cast your line. Hold down the button on the reel. Keep your elbow still and draw the rod back until your hand is level with your ear and your wrist bent back at 2 o'clock. Quickly "whip" the end forward and release the button as your forearm sticks out at 11 o'clock. Follow through to 10 o'clock. WARNING: make sure no one is behind you when you cast or you might end up hooking a human instead.

Step 7. Monitor the bobber and/or keep a finger rested on the line. You'll need to stay patient and relatively quiet. Metallica banging out on the radio isn't music to a fish's ears.

Step 8. When you feel tension on the line, the bobber or float submerge or drift away upstream slightly, a fish may well have fancied a nibble of your worm.

Step 9. To "set" the hook in the fish's mouth jerk the rod back and up. If the line goes tight and starts to follow the movements of a fish you've got him.

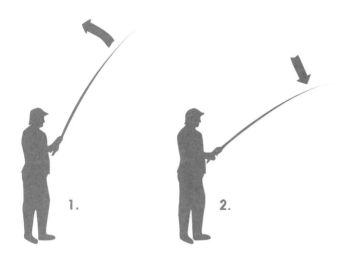

1.

2.

Step 10. Once hooked the fish will start to fight like Rocky in round 12, so steady your grip, let him have some drag and lift the rod vertically—so your arms and rod take the brunt of his fisticuffs. Wait until he begins to tire, lower the rod to a 45° angle and reel him in until your rod is horizontal with the water. Lift and lower again and repeat. If he makes another run for it, lift and let him go. Once the drag stops coiling off, reel him in once more. Remember, always keep the line tight to ensure the fish doesn't shake off the hook.

Step 11. A net is handy at this point to catch the fish. If you haven't got one, grasp him by hand—be warned, many a fish has escaped the dinner plate due to slipping away, so cradle rather than grip.

Step 12. Once on shore, hold the fish away, avoiding the fins— they can be sharp—squeeze so its mouth opens to locate the hook. Look at the way it has gone in and try to "back" it out in reverse—don't yank or you'll rip the fish's mouth.

Step 13. Decide whether to eat or free the fish. If it's a tiddler, it won't amount to more than a mouthful so show some mercy; slide the fish back into the water.

Step 14. If it's for the frying pan, kill the fish quickly. Do not leave it to suffocate. Hit it firmly at the back of head with a blunt instrument—the handle of your fishing knife should do the trick— and put it in a bucket of cold water.

Extra tips:

* If the fish are not playing ball, shut up shop and try another spot.

* Many beginners mistake the pull of the current for a bite; only over time and through trial and error will you be able to tell when a bite is a bite.

* If you're fishing for sport rather than for the plate, crush the barb of the hook with pliers so you can easily remove the hook from the fish's mouth without causing trauma.

* Research the area you plan to fish in. Some places have restrictions on live bait and others have restrictions on fishing itself.

* Check for knots in your line: they hamper your cast and weaken the line.

When to fish:

✓ Sun behind clouds—good   ✗ Hot sun—poor

✓ Clouds—good   ✗ Thunderstorm—poor

✓ Rain—good   ✗ Cold front—poor

✓ Warm front—good   ✗ No wind—poor

✓ Light wind—good

How to gut a fish

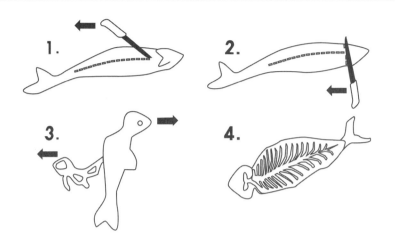

Step 1. If possible, gut the fish outside—the smell and scales get everywhere—or spread plenty of newspaper on the work surface.

Step 2. Rinse the fish thoroughly under cold running water.

Step 3. Remove the fins with a sharp knife or kitchen scissors.

Step 4. Descale the fish. Hold the fish at the head or tail; use a blunt knife, butter knife or the edge of a spoon and scrape from the tail towards the head at a 90° angle, using firm, quick strokes away from your body. Pay special attention to the gill area.

Step 5. Run your hand up from the tail end to check all scales are removed, then rinse the fish in cold, clean water.

Step 6. Place the fish belly up and use a small sharp knife to make a shallow cut from the soft bit of the belly near the tail to the gills. Don't insert the knife too deep or you'll split the guts open.

Step 7. Spread the cavity and pull out the entrails by grabbing the main connecting tissue at the base of the head and pulling it loose.

Step 8. Rinse inside and outside the fish.

Step 9. Remove the head behind the gills and the tail where it connects with the body.

Step 10. Plonk your fish on the grill or campfire.

How to dry your jeans in 15 minutes

Wet jeans. They cling to your legs like a superhero's spandex, smell of damp newspaper, and have a crotch damper than a boy's pants on his first day at school. Whether you're running late for a date or just picking Mom up from bingo, here's how to get comfortably dry jeans in a jiffy.

Step 1. First of all, while your jeans are still in the wash you've got a bit of pantaloon preparation to do. Pinch your mom's or girlfriend's hairdryer, turn the central heating on—or at least one radiator—and whack the iron on its highest setting.

Step 2. Remove jeans from the washing machine. Turn jeans inside out, take outside and, gripping them firmly at the waist, give them good airing. Dash back into house. Grab your leather belt and place lengthwise on hot radiator.

Step 3. Plonk jeans on ironing board and run the hot iron over both front and back. Concentrate on the thicker areas—waistline, pockets, ankle cuffs and crotch. Press iron onto these sections and leave for a few seconds until they steam. If you smell burning you've overdone it.

Step 4. Turn jeans right side out and run iron all over again, front and back. Switch iron off and grab hairdryer. Crank hairdryer up to hottest and highest setting and push nozzle into either pocket. Rotate nozzle and blast crotch area with hot air for up to two minutes per pocket.

Step 5. Put jeans on—if not bone dry, they'll at least be nice and warm, in a damp way, especially round the waistline. Feed the hot belt through the loops and by the time you arrive at your destination your waistline will be warmer than toast.

Wet jeans? What wet jeans?

Coping with premature hair loss

For some, BALD is the ultimate four-letter word. But while losing your hair at an early age isn't a laughing matter, it isn't the end of the world. Here's how to deal with the early onset of hair loss.

Men can start to lose their hair from the age of 15 onwards.

Some men are bald by the time they're 25, for others it can take up to 20 years. So, don't panic and shave your head at the first sign of hairs on your pillow or in the drain. If you notice thinning or wispy hair, a receding hairline and/or a developing bald patch on the crown of the head, avoid using a hairdryer as it can damage your scalp, wash your hair every day to keep it healthy and lay off your dad's Just For Men.

If you do continue to lose your hair, and the balding makes styling problematic—comb-overs are a no-no— visit the barber and have your hair clipped really short, or buy some clippers and ask a friend to shave your head. With practice, you'll be able to use the clippers yourself. (Think of all the money you'll save on barbers and hair products.) Put all your worries about big ears and shiny pates to one side and embrace your new look.

Look in the mirror, and think Thierry Henri, Samuel L. Jackson, Andre Agassi, and Bruce Willis. Not Dr. Phil. You may have changed on the outside and, as a man, lost one of your major areas of self-expression, but you're still the same gorgeous, sexy dude inside. In fact, research shows that many women find men without hair far more attractive than men with hair. Get yourself buffed up down the gym to remove any puppy fat from your cheeks, giving you a chiselled jawline to rival Batman. A goatee is also an option, but a full Michael Eavis beard that looks like your head's upside down is a step too far.

Some men who start to lose their hair early on can't imagine themselves without it. But within months of shaving your head people will be saying they can't imagine you with hair.

Some words of wisdom:

Accepting you're going bald is better for you in the long run than denying it to yourself for years. However, if it's really affecting your self-esteem talk to other family members who may have experienced the same thing.

How to survive your first Starbucks experience

When you first enter a Starbucks the bright lights and painfully jovial staff will be enough to make you feel nauseous, so the quicker you order the sooner you can get out of there.

Step 1—Select your size. No matter what some people may say size does matter, in the world of coffee at least. The size simply means the number of caffeine or espresso shots—the stuff that makes you wide awake—each coffee has in it. There are three sizes:

Tall—one shot

Grande—(pronounced gran-day) two shots

Venti—(Ven-tay) three shots

Step 2—Choose your type of coffee.

*   ESPRESSO—Slightly more than a thimble's worth of coffee. A pick-me-up for those on the go.

*   LATTE—Pronounced la-tay, this is the choice of the coffee novice. Roughly 80% hot milk, 20% espresso, the latte comes with a thin veil of tasteless milky foam on top.

*   CAPPUCCINO—The cap-a-chi-no is exactly the same as a latte only with a mushroom cloud of foam topped with a sprinkling of cocoa powder and the promise of a milk moustache Magnum P.I. would be proud of.

*   AMERICANO—Steaming hot water and espresso. Simple and effective. No surprise then that it's most men's weapon of choice for an early morning wake-up call.

* CAFÉ MOCHA—A latte hybrid with a spoonful of hot chocolate and whipped cream instead of the layer of foam. But sadly, no cocktail umbrella.

* CARAMEL MACCHIATO—For a man with a sweet tooth. Foamed milk, espresso, vanilla, and caramel. Look out Tooth Fairy.

* FRAPPUCCINO—Milkshakes aren't just for kids, as this strong and frothy coffee escapade proves. Ice-blended versions of espresso, mocha, caramel macchiato, and even a Starbucks special of strawberries and cream.

* VIVANNO—Feeling nutritional? Try a smoothie. Choose from orange, mango and banana, or banana chocolate. Asking for an espresso to be added to the chocolate one is seen as respectable experimentation; ask for one to be added to the fruit one, however, and you're committing coffee blasphemy and could find your beans in the blender.

* TEA—From the spicy Tazo Chai that will tickle your nostril hair to the pot of Earl Grey straight from the pages of an Evelyn Waugh novel. If the complexities of coffee are getting you down, plump for a cuppa instead.

Step 3—Practice your pronunciation. And use of the terminology. Many of the baristas or servers may not be native English speakers, but they do speak the language of coffee. You need to be quick, as any inept mumbling or poor pronunciation can result in misunderstanding and humiliation.

Step 4—Make the order. Keep it simple. Say the size followed by the type. For example: "Tall latte, please." The person behind the counter might try and catch you out at this point by saying, "Would you like a pastry, sir?" Say "No" in your kindest tone, grab your coffee, and with "Have a nice day!" ringing in your ears, get back among the grumps on the street.

How to convince your girlfriend to have sex with you when she has a "headache"

Six months is a long time. You leave the toilet seat up, belch, fart, and even keep the bathroom door ajar when you're pinching a loaf. But at bedtime try and remember: romance is timeless. Clean your teeth, do your hair, spray on some aftershave, and walk across the room like Tom Cruise's ass-double.

*   ***Sex is psychological for women.*** If you've passed the non-stop sex = honeymoon period, understand that for women, sex can become a duty to perform like the washing-up. Your girl needs to know she is loved and appreciated—and desired—in subtle ways. So, jumping on her after she's just put the trash out and breathing, "Want to go at it?" might not sound like her dream dish. She's had a hard day at work, no doubt. And you're trying to seduce her, not buy her a bag of chips.

*   ***Rub her temples.*** Listen to her problems at work. Empathize. Light a scented candle and run her a deep hot bath. Add a few drops of ylang-ylang essential oil. Rub her back and trickle hot water down her neck while she's bathing. As you are gently drying her legs, smoothly murmur, "According to some neurologists, if you have sex within thirty minutes of the onset of a headache you can nullify it completely."

*   ***If the headache persists.*** Back up your remedy with hard scientific facts. Endorphins and oxytocin are released by the body during sex. These chemicals have similar effects to morphine and relieve pain, including headaches…She'll be ripping off your white coat in no time!

How to perform the perfect golf swing

Yellow and red tartan bottom-hugging trousers, a gaudy sun visor, and a woolly tank top you wouldn't even wear as a dare on Christmas day...On the golf course, however, it's not your sweater that will stick out like a sore thumb. Oh no. It's a bad swing. Perfect your swing and you can get away with any sartorial no-no.

Grip. Grasp the club with both palms facing one another. Place your left hand towards the top of the club grip, with your thumb pointing down, and place your right hand below but slightly over your left. Grip firmly but not too hard; hold the club in your fingers not your palms. Relax your wrists and keep your hands evenly matched on the club.

The three main grips:

* ***Overlapping.*** The little finger on the right hand sits in the groove of the index finger on the left hand. Good for those with strong forearms and wrists.

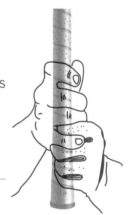

Fig. 1. Overlapping

* ***Interlocking.*** The little finger on the right and the index finger on the left intertwine with each other. Suits those with fat and short hands.

* ***Baseball.*** All your fingers grip the handle like you're holding— funnily enough—a baseball bat. Fingers do not overlap or interlock but run alongside each other. For those with weak arms and strong wrists, or knitters.

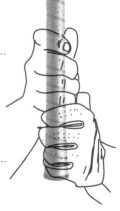

Fig. 2. Baseball

Fig. 1.

Stance. Stand with your hips and feet positioned directly below your shoulders, with your feet pointing slightly out, not directly forward. Bend your knees as though you're perching on the edge of a table and lower your hips. Keep your back straight at all times. Your hands and arms should hang down from your shoulders with the club at the center of your stance and your weight evenly spread.

Target alignment. When you are practicing your swing, pick a target in the distance; something you can see out of the corner of your eye when you line up to the ball. A tall blade of grass, a tree, something immovable. You will need to concentrate on getting the target and aim correctly aligned, but with practice this will soon become second nature. Facing slightly to the left, align your body alongside the ball with the club and ball facing your target.

Backswing. Bend your elbows slightly towards you and slowly draw the club back over your shoulder. Shift your weight to your right foot. Simultaneously drop your left shoulder and lift your right. Don't consciously move your head, but allow the natural movement it makes to the right. Your right foot, your hip, and your head should be vertically inclined behind the ball. Your back should be facing the target and your shoulders at a right angle to your spine like a capital T. Keep your elbows close together. At the apex of the backswing your left arm should be stretched to the max across your chest and your right bent like a waiter's when carrying a tray on his shoulder. Your wrist should be hinged towards your neck with the club behind your head, pointing off in a straight line towards the ball.

Fig. 2.

Downswing. Allow your hips to run the show as they dip into the swing and pull your arms, which in turn will pull the club downwards. Don't move any other part of your body. Shift your weight from right to left early in the swing. Don't drag the club down; allow momentum to build until impact. The club should hit the ball at its maximum speed, thus optimizing the impact. Don't force it. Relax and be willing to let go and soon your swing will occur naturally.

Impact. At impact your right elbow should be pointing at your right foot and pretty much all your weight should be on your left foot. Rotate your hips through the motion. Your left arm will be straight by this point and your hands should be slightly in front

Fig. 3.

of the ball. Your body will look like a K at impact, your left side straight and your right side bent in at the hip. Don't try to hit the ball hard—simply swing through it.

Follow through. Rotate your hips towards the target and let your upper body follow until all of you, apart from your feet and knees, face the target. Both arms stay straight at the beginning and then mimic the backswing in reverse, with the left arm bent more than the right. All your weight should be on your left foot. If you resemble a twisted Stretch Armstrong you know you've got it right.

Remember, practice makes perfect. Once you feel you're getting somewhere with your swing, congratulate yourself with a trip to the clubhouse shop and bag some tartan socks. It'll be the trousers next, and you know it.

Fig. 4.

When you first start to practice your swing, place a club on the ground, pointing the way you want the ball to go. Line your feet up with the shaft and strike the ball. This will help you avoid playing "regimental golf"—hitting the ball left, right, left, right, left, right—rather than hitting it right up the middle of the fairway, where it's supposed to go.

Internship survival 101

Whether you're in finance, advertising, or IT, being a gofer during your internship is part of the essential rite of passage on the path to becoming a major player in the company's future. Menial tasks such as fetching coffee and dry cleaning will be commonplace as you log long hours, likely without pay, in pursuit of your dream job.

But if you're lucky enough to have a boss who harbors a particularly large grudge against the young and enthusiastic, you can also expect to:

* *Run luxury errands.* There are few things more demoralizing for a young, eager intern than walking into Hermes wearing a three-season old H&M suit to pick up gold monogrammed pages for your boss's personal planner.

* *Book reservations.* It's likely your boss isn't important enough to demand a last-minute table at the hottest spot in town, but are you going to be the one to tell him? Be prepared to negotiate, argue with, and (if it comes down to it) desperately beg hostesses and hotel receptionists to secure that 4-star spot your boss has his eye on.

* *Call the doc.* If your boss is too busy to keep up after his own health, you may be required to call his doctor's office and relay a list of symptoms…no matter how strange or wildly personal they may be.

Recreational drugs: the short-term and long-term effects

With DARE's Say No to Drugs campaign at one end of the spectrum and hippy liberalists screaming for legalization on the other, it's often hard to tell what's what in the world of drugs.

Here's a no-nonsense guide to the short- and long-term effects of taking drugs:

Stimulants: **Increase brain activity.**

Cocaine.

Usually sold in "wraps," white powder sometimes with a grainy texture, not dissimilar to baking soda. The powder is usually rubbed on the gums or snorted through the nose.

Alternative names. Coke, charlie, blow, chang, snow, sniff, white.

Short-term effects. Feeling hyper-alert and incredibly confident for a short amount of time. Talking like a twat. Inability to sleep for several hours afterwards. Rapid pulse, palpitations, and confusion. Bad "come down" the day after with low mood, anxiety, tearfulness, anxiety, and paranoia.

Long-term effects. Strong psychological dependency. The need to have more and more hits. Cocaine addiction and overuse can cause irreversible damage to the nasal membranes and collapse of the septum. Heart problems including heart attack and stroke, depression, mood swings, anxiety, paranoia, confusion, and memory loss.

Celebrity casualties. Whitney Houston and Lindsay Lohan; David Bowie attributes his memory loss to long-term cocaine abuse: "My mind is like Swiss cheese. Unbelievable holes in my memory."

Crack cocaine.

Crack is cocaine in the form of small lumps, or rocks, roughly the size of a raisin. Crack is usually burned and the vapor inhaled through a pipe, plastic bottle, a glass tube, or in foil.

Alternative name. Rocks, snow coke, candy, base

Short-term effects. The "hit" from crack cocaine is very intense but very short-lived. Strong risk of psychological dependency.

Long-term effects. As for cocaine, but higher risk of addiction. Lung and heart damage. Heart failure, depression and serious mental health problems, loss of sex drive.

Celebrity casualties. Pete Doherty. Say no more.

Speed.

Usually sold in wraps. Off-white or pinkish powder, with slight grainy texture. Like cocaine, taken by dabbing on gums or snorting through nose. Wrapped in cigarette paper and swallowed, this is called a speedbomb.

Alternative names. Whizz, meth, base, poor man's coke, billy, uppers, glass.

Short-term effects. Increased heart rate, respiration and increased energy and chattiness. Heightened senses and loss of inhibitions. A long "come down" of up to two days can include depressive and dark thoughts, tiredness, and disconnected feeling. Taken in combination with alcohol or antidepressants speed can be fatal.

Long-term effects. Damage to the immune system and heart, paranoia, anxiety, depression, irritability, and aggression as well as more severe mental illness and psychosis.

Poppers.

Usually sold in small glass capsules which are "popped" open and inhaled.

Alternative names. Liquid gold, rave, rush, kix, TNT, snappers, thrust.

Short-term effects. An intense but momentary hit, with increased flow of blood to the brain and heart. A head rush of massive proportions and a heart beat like you've just run the 100-yard dash. Said to increase intensity of orgasm if sniffed during sex. Hit only lasts a couple of minutes and can cause nausea, dizziness, and severe headache shortly afterwards.

Long-term effects. Loss of erection in men. Can be dangerous for anyone with heart or lung problems.

Ecstasy.

Sold in pill form in various colors, often stamped with a smiley face or other popular symbols. Pure ecstasy is sold in a white crystalline powder form and known as MDMA.

Alternative names. E's, pills, beans, disco biscuits, mitsys, yokes, doves, echoes.

Short-term effects. Heightened emotions, empathy, and senses, colors seem brighter, sounds more intense. A buzz of "coming up." Feeling like you rule the world. Loving everyone in sight.

Long-term effects. Those with heart conditions, epilepsy, blood pressure concerns, and asthma can have fatal reactions to the drug. Dehydration can cause death. Anxiety, panic attacks, psychosis, and paranoia and possible long-term serious mental health problems. Impotence or/and damaged urinary system resulting in incontinence. Liver, kidney, and heart disease.

LSD.

Lysergic acid diethylamide, originally derived from ergot, a fungus found growing wild on rye and other grasses. On the street LSD is usually sold as tiny squares of paper or "tabs" with pictures on them. Can also be sold as a liquid or tiny pellets.

Alternative names. Acid, stars, trips, Lucy, rainbows, L, smileys, paper mushrooms, tabs.

Short-term effects. Powerful hallucinogenic effect or "trip" which can last up to 12 hours. Trips can be pleasant or very bad. Strange objects can appear and you can believe you're seeing things that aren't actually there, or "hallucinate." A sense of seeing the whole of the world as connected and feeling at one with nature in true hippy fashion. Until you take a tab of acid you can't tell how strong it is or how it's going to affect you. Your experience can be affected for good or bad by who you are with and how you're feeling when you take the drug. Bad trips can be dangerous and terrifying with people being known to fatally self-harm.

Long-term effects. Some LSD users say they experience trip flashbacks years later without even taking the drug. Serious long-term effects for anyone with a history of mental illness, and also may be responsible for triggering previously undetected illnesses such as schizophrenia and depression sometimes years later.

Magic mushrooms.

Semilanceata, or liberty caps, are small and tan-colored, when touched they bruise blue. Fly agaric (Amanita Muscaria) look like the traditional red and white spotted toadstools of fairy tales. Mushrooms can be eaten raw after picking, cooked in a soup, or dried out and stored. Most people take between 1 and 5 grams.

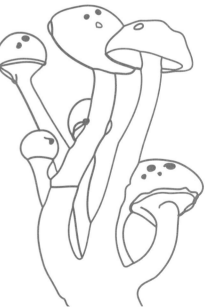

Alternative names. Agaric, mushies, shrooms, buttons, magics, happies.

Short-term effects. "Trip" lasting up to four hours. A good trip will normally include sporadic periods of intense giggling followed by feelings of contentedness or euphoria accompanied by visual and auditory hallucinations. Bad trips similar to those described for LSD use. Eaten raw, agaric mushrooms can cause severe nausea.

Long-term effects. Can exacerbate or trigger latent mental health problems.

Cannabis.

Cannabis is sold in different forms: hash, a black or brown slightly malleable lump, is made from the resin of the plant. Cannabis oil is a dense, sticky, dark caramel-colored oil. Herbal cannabis (grass or weed), made from the dried leaves and flowering parts of the female plant, resembles densely packed dried green herbs.

Skunk is a stronger form of herbal cannabis with a very strong, distinctive smell and is usually locally grown using hydroponic methods with artificial lighting. Contains two to three times the amount of the active compound, tetrahydrocannabinol or THC, compared to the traditional herbal cannabis.

Alternative names. Grass, skunk, weed, blow, dope, pot, green, wacky backy.

Short-term effects. Feeling of being incredibly relaxed, giggly, or chatty. Heightened senses. Or adversely, feeling of nausea, anxiety and paranoia. Later, increased appetite and urge to eat everything in sight, known as the "munchies."

Long-term effects. Lack of concentration, total loss of motivation, mood swings and dependency. Short-term and long-term memory loss. Paranoia—from the playful, like finding yourself up in the attic at two in the morning searching for a sound that didn't exist in the first place, to the debilitating, such as hearing voices. May exacerbate mental health problems and there is evidence of links to onset of schizophrenia.

Heroin.

If pure (diamorphine) sold as a white powder. On the street heroin is cut with other substances and can range from a brownish white to brown powder. Can be smoked or dissolved in water and injected or, if pure, snorted.

Alternative names. H, horse, brown, gear, skag, china white, smack.

Short-term effects. A rush followed by an overwhelming feeling of well-being and bliss. With larger doses, sleepiness or drowsiness.

Long-term effects. Heroin is highly addictive, both physically and psychologically. Risk of death by overdose is very high, as is coma and respiratory failure, or choking on one's own vomit. Injecting heroin can cause gangrene and infection, and increase risk of contracting HIV, Hepatitis B and C. In other words, kiss good-bye to a normal, happy life.

How to behave in a job interview

You slave over your CV for days on end. Send it out to a hundred companies and after months of waiting, finally land that elusive interview. You buy a new suit. New pair of shoes. Get a haircut. And blow it all in an instant by swearing the minute you step through the door.

Here's how to make sure you raise a toast by getting the post:

Preparation:

*   Research the company—products, services, market, trends, competitors—in B2B (business to business) magazines, on their website and in literature you can request prior to the interview.

*   Prepare yourself for the generic questions. Why you want the job, what your strengths are, your best achievements, what you'd do if you got the job and a question to rival, "To be or not to be"—"Where do you see yourself in five years?"

*   Find out the exact name of the person or persons who will be interviewing you. Arrive early and be polite to everyone in the building when you enter, especially the secretary. Her duties might go beyond the secretarial in nature. Wink, wink, nudge, nudge.

*   Prepare a few questions for the company. Where they plan
to be in the next few years shows an interest in their future.
Also, take at least three spare copies of your CV in case
you're asked to produce one.

---

*   Dress smart. A suit and tie and shined shoes are a must no
matter what the position. Casual dress gives the impression
that you're a casual person.

---

*   If you smoke, don't smell of cigarettes on arrival and, it goes
without saying, don't light up mid-question.

During the interview:

*   Walk in with a straight back, don't slouch, don't chew gum
or look out of sorts; this is the moment you wished you'd
passed on that final whisky chaser. Give a firm handshake
on arrival to everyone in the room.

*   Body language. Face your interviewer. Don't cross your arms
or legs and keep your head up and your hands still. Look the
interviewer straight in the eye, thus making you look more
confident and trustworthy.

*   Turn your phone off. Never interrupt. Don't fidget. Don't look
around the room and don't, no matter how itchy, scratch your
groin.

*   Smile. Smiling is infectious and the chances are they'll
take to you immediately. Either that or think you're a smug
bastard who they'd never employ in a month of Sundays.

*   Don't use slang or go off on one. Control yourself and answer
concisely and lucidly. Acknowledge the importance of the
questions asked of you and relate each answer you give to
the company in question.

* Point out your strengths and don't be afraid to point out areas that you could progress in. If the position is a newly formed one, saying how you'd develop the role is paramount. Include innovation and invention in your ideas.

* Be prepared for the dreaded, "What would you say are your weak points?" question. Be honest, but not too honest. And answering, "Well, sometimes I'm just too hard-working and a perfectionist" is just creepy.

Make your own cider

According to folklore, an apple is so much more than a juicy snack. One bite and Adam and Eve learned all about forbidden knowledge. One nibble and the Norse Gods earned the gift of immortality. Master the skill of cider making and you too can receive mystical powers in the comfort of your very own kitchen—the mystical powers of the piss artist.

You will need:

Apples. A selection of cider apples (Kingston Black, Foxwhelp, Golden Russet, etc) and dessert apples (Cox, Red Delicious, Worcester Pearmain, etc). Any apples will do but use a mix of eating and cider apples or the cider will be too sweet. Avoid cooking apples. 7.2kg or 16 lb of apples will roughly make 3.75 liters or 1 gallon of cider.

Pulping device. A household blender or juicer, a Pulpmaster—a bucket with a rotating blade on the inside of the lid which attaches to a drill, they cost about $40—or bucket and heavy object.

Cider press. You can purchase a professional job online but homemade efforts are just as good. Four large clamps, two hard flat surfaces, some muslin and a tray larger than the press are all you need.

A couple of sterilized buckets. Or kegs with lids and either a makeshift or real bunghole and bung. One bucket and one large plastic bottle will suffice.

Siphon. Or sterilized plastic tube.

Plastic or glass fermentation air lock.

Plastic or glass bottles. To hold the end product.

Optional:

Crown corker. For putting tops on the glass bottles.

Packet of cider brewer's yeast.

Campden tablet. Used to aid the fermenting process.

Step 1. **Wash apples in clear water.** You can chop the apples in half at this point to see if any are rotten at the core. Discard bad apples.

Step 2. **Pulp.** Use your kitchen blender or juicer if you're making a couple of glasses for your grandma. Larger amounts require a Pulpmaster or if you don't have one, bludgeon your apples to a "pomace" in a large bucket.

Step 3. **Press.** Place the large tray securely under the press. Wrap the pulp in the muslin cloth, place in the press and screw the clamps shut. The cloth stops the pulp from squelching all over the place and the large tray will catch all the juice. Loosening and tightening the screws will produce more juice.

Step 4. **Fermenting.** Fill your bucket or keg to the brim with the juice. At this point you have two choices:

*   **Organic or Scrumpy Cider.** Leave the bunghole open. After 1–2 days wild yeast will naturally ferment the apples and white froth will bubble up through the hole. Organic can be hit and miss.

*   **Brewer's Cider.** Add a Campden tablet. Two days later sprinkle a packet of yeast in. Place the air lock on top so no extra yeast gets in.

After two days the frothing and scum production will reduce but the fermentation carries on and ends roughly three weeks later.

Step 5. **Racking off or siphoning.** Place the bucket with the cider on an elevated surface and the other bucket or bottle below. Put one end of your siphon tube in the bunghole, suck on the other end and place in the lower bucket bunghole or bottle opening. This process siphons off the cider liquid leaving the dregs at the bottom of the cider, called the "lees."

Step 6. **Maturation.** Remove the siphon tube. Place the air lock in the bunghole to keep flies etc. out but allow gas to escape. You can now leave your cider to mature for anything between three and eight months.

Step 7. **Bottle up.** Sterilize your bottles and siphon the cider into each one. If you want to seal each bottle use a crown corker to press the caps on. Store in a cool place.

How to complain in a restaurant (without looking like a complete jerk)

No one likes complaining to a manager, but sometimes the service is so bad, you can't avoid it. Here are some guidelines to make the process easier:

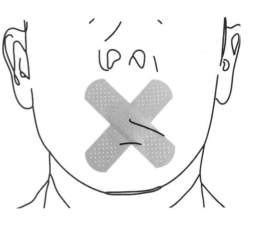

* Ensure what you're complaining about is valid. Getting angry because your starter is cold is a little sad if you ordered a chilled cucumber soup.

* Undercooked or missing ingredients are valid reasons to get mad and get even. Or just point the problem out politely.

* Voice your complaint ASAP. Eating half of your burger before demanding a new one will earn you a side order of "homemade" mayonnaise when your plate is returned.

* Express what the problem is calmly and clearly. If it's not the waiter's problem, don't take it out on them. If it is, try to be nice. Bankers earn enough to be yelled at, waiters don't.

* Normally the waiter will take your food back to the kitchen and change it for you; however, if he is not forthcoming ask him if he could ask the chef to recook or redress your meal for you. Pressure him a little but smile and be polite.

* Sometimes service can be dreadful. If this is the case ask to see the manager and explain the problem factually. Don't just say the waiter looked at your girlfriend funny, especially if you are dining alone.

* If there's a problem with the bill, ask them to add it up again and check it meticulously.

How to fry the perfect steak

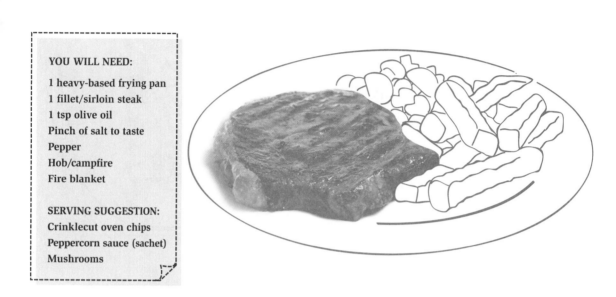

The steak is the Holy Grail of manhood, so take up the gauntlet and learn how to cook one like a trained chef. First of all, buy a filet or sirloin steak from your local butcher's and take it home, preferably securing it with a seat belt or, better still, a baby seat.

Step 1. If your steak has been stored in the fridge, take it out half an hour or so before cooking and allow it to come to room temperature.

Step 2. Put either a chargrill or a heavy-based frying pan on the heat, get it really hot, but not smoking.

Step 3. Brush the steak with groundnut or olive oil or drizzle about a tablespoon of oil into the pan. Grind some salt and pepper over the steak to season.

The Finger Test:

Little finger & thumb
Well done

Ring finger & thumb
Medium-to-well

EXPERT TIP: A good way of testing if the steak is cooked to your liking is to use a simple finger test by comparing the springiness of the steak with the fleshy pad on your palm beneath the thumb, as shown. The softness of this part of your palm should match the texture of the meat following these simple thumb and finger combinations.

Middle finger & thumb
Medium

Index finger & thumb
Rare

Open palm
Blue (i.e. completely raw)

Three fingers & thumb
Labrador steak

Step 4. Place the steak in the pan. Fry the steak on one side, to seal it off, for about one to two minutes, depending on how you want it cooked, and then turn it over to cook the other side. Meanwhile warm your plate in the microwave for about 15 seconds.

Step 5. Once cooked, remove the steak from the pan and place on a rack or warm plate. Leave to rest for about five minutes in a warm spot before eating—this gives time for the meat to relax and your mouth to water. Plate up and tuck into a tender steak fit for King Arthur.

How to tell if she's faking an orgasm

When it comes to orgasms, men and women were not created equal. With men, the unmistakable grunt after a few minutes of "love play" signals that it's all over till next week, but for women the road to sexual heights can be long and winding. We men do our best to follow the map but sometimes we get a little lost, and your companion may decide to abandon the journey without bruising your pride.

Don't be offended if she *is* faking; she's actually trying to be considerate. She might know that she's not going to come, due to stress or tiredness, and therefore simply pretends to. So, play along and forget about feeling like an emasculated weed. Again.

Here's how to tell if she's faking:

✓ At the point of orgasm her pupils may be dilated.

✓ Her lips (both sets) will swell a little, although kissing will also have this required effect so peck lightly to get a true indication.

✓ Her limbs may stretch out or twitch erratically, her back may arch, and her face contort. Slight "shivering" or "jerking" movements all over her body are also commonplace.

✓ She might be thrashing about the bed and quaking like Ellen Burstyn in *The Exorcist* but if her heart rate hasn't increased two-fold and her breathing isn't hitting the Richter scale she's not actually coming, only rehearsing her starring role in the 15th sequel.

✓ Increased heart rate, blood pressure, and muscle exercise will cause her to perspire, so if she sweats a lot the chances are she's not faking. She may become very wet elsewhere also.

✓ If she lies still breathing deeply or is floppy for a while after sex she's definitely come. If she jumps up and starts to do the ironing, she's having you on.

✓ Her face and neck will be flushed due to adrenaline coursing through her veins.

✓ Her clitoris will become really sensitive so she probably won't want you to touch her and will squirm away from all attempts.

Vaginal clenches will be strongest at the point of orgasm and happen between three and ten times afterwards as well.

Warning: this can also be faked with strong pelvic floor muscles, but when combined with all the other signs it takes a lot of coordination for the perfect bluff.

✓ Loud convoluted sentences are probably an indicator she's faking. A simple "Oh my God" or deep, seemingly uncontrollable moaning is normal but anything that involves the weather or sounds remotely like it was edited directly out of a porno movie isn't heartfelt.

✓ Her nipples will harden.

✓ An orgasm can last between 3 and 5 seconds, although if you're James Bond they can last up to 15.

How to taste wine in a restaurant

If the waiter asks if you want to taste the wine you can either say you're happy for him to just pour it or, if you feel particularly confident, nod suavely.

142

fig. 1. Nice Legs

* The waiter will pour you a quarter of a glass. Hold it up, tilt and check the color. Both red and white wines should be translucent and jewel-like—never cloudy.

* Swirl the wine in the glass. This adds oxygen to the wine—allowing it to "breathe"—and also lets you see the wine's "legs" (fig. 1). These are the thin lines of liquid clinging to the side of the glass—which indicate the body and alcoholic strength of the wine. Lighter, less strong-bodied wines such as rosés will have a thinner consistency, and thus lighter "legs."

* Bring your glass to your nose and take a good sniff—this is to test the aroma or "nose" of the wine. A slightly musty or dusty smell or a plainly unpleasant smell may indicate the wine is bad or "corked."

* Take a sip and let it get into the taste buds of your mouth. Swill it about your tongue and gums—but don't go all Jancis Robinson and start whittering about subtle blackberry and fire station overtones.

* Normally after tasting you'd spit the wine out, but not on this occasion. Just swallow and judge the "finish"—the lingering taste of the wine. Unless you truly don't like how the wine tastes, ask for a glass to be poured.

This is a quick process so don't take an hour over it; you're going through the motions—they know you're not a wine connoisseur. Lift, swirl, smell, sip, swallow. As easy as ABC.

Lap dance etiquette

We all say we won't go. It's not our sort of thing, not our cup of tea. Only perverts and old men pay women to dance for them. We're young and good-looking and we don't need to part with our hard-earned cash for an experience like that. Or so we say. Then the day comes when Spearmint Rhino opens in our local town. Now pay attention. Here's how to enjoy yourself when you finally give in and go.

First things first, prepare for your evening as though you were going on a date. If you want a lap dancer to get up close and personal with you, take care over your personal hygiene. Stinky breath and foul body odors will repel a professional dancer. Some girls also complain about their skin being scratched by rough jeans, buttons and zips—so leave the punk-zipped trousers at home. Opt for soft chinos or cords with a clean T-shirt.

Take as much hard cash as your budget allows with you. Lap dancing clubs profit from charging per dance and hiking up the price of drinks. There may also be an entrance fee, although some clubs have free entry before a certain time. Say hello to the bouncers as you enter. They're never going to be your best friends, but you want to keep on the right side of these bundles of beef.

Once inside the girls will be all over you, but take your time and relax; control yourself and don't pop your cork too soon. There will normally be a pole and a little stage at the center so kick back with a drink and watch the dancers work their magic. There is never an appropriate time for you to get up, remove you trousers and shimmy up the pole like you're on *The Krypton Factor*.

Going with a severely drunk friend is a good way to save money. A lot of the girls will proposition you for a dance and more often than not you'll feel obliged to accept. If you've got a friend who's the worse for wear and would probably say "yes" to riding a camel through central London naked, never mind a lap dance with a sexy girl, palm her off on him and wait for one you like.

Find out about the house rules—you can kill two birds with one stone and strike up a conversation with the girls by asking them wittily about the dos and don'ts. Treat them as you would any girl—with respect. Don't patronize them or talk to them as if they're brainless. They're just doing a job and for all you know are studying neuroscience in the daytime. **Remember that a) they're entertainers, artistes, or dancers, not strippers and b) they are the ones doing the exploiting. Of you and your overdraft, that is.**

Offer to buy one of the girls a drink and have a chat before she dances for you. But don't throw caution to the wind and order a bottle of champagne, as this will blow your budget in one fell swoop.

Costs vary from $25 to $40 per dance; most girls have a set price so clarify this before you're ready for lift-off. A booth with a curtain or a side room are the normal location, however, you can pay for a private dance which will normally be away from the main bar and last up to half an hour. These cost anything from $80.

Once the show begins, sit on your hands so temptation doesn't get the better of you. Never, ever, proposition, touch, or attempt to touch, a lap dancer. Nor should you try to sniff or lick any part of her body or clothing. And don't heckle or shout abusive words at the dancers even if they *do* turn out to be lady boys.

One final warning. Don't get infatuated with one of the girls and borrow loads of money from your friends to keep her dancing for you. The girls are working, they don't love you, and they will go home to their neuroscience text-books. Unlike you, they're not all sex addicts. And even if some are, they won't be interested in your little nubbin when someone beds them with a penis the size of a prize zucchini.

Covering your tracks...
how to get away with cheating

Some men aren't happy with a steak at home; they want to go out every once in a while and tuck into a nice juicy burger. Whether you're a cheetah who doesn't intend to change his spots or a once-only player who wants to make sure he doesn't lose what he's got, here are a few tricks of the trade to make sure you don't get caught out after the deed is done.

Some general rules:

*   All lies should be based on an element of truth.

*   Never write down names, emails, phone numbers, or addresses. Always delete your texts and call log and don't add your floozy as a friend on Facebook.

*   Store her name under a man's name or consider getting a separate pay-as-you-go mobile and keep it hidden in a safe place.

*   Long-term affairs involve taking up a hobby such as visiting the gym. It must be something convincing and credible to everyone.

*   Keep a spare toothbrush and toothpaste and some deodorant hidden in your car.

*   If your mistress has visited your house or been in your car, double-check for any incriminating evidence. A pair of frilly pants draped over the dashboard will put your cheating days to an abrupt end due to the severance of your penis.

* Air your apartment or car so no traces of strange perfume remain.

* Keep two packets of condoms in separate parts of your apartment. Never get them mixed up or let your girlfriend know you've got more than one packet.

* Never see your girlfriend directly after cheating; you'll give the game away with your after-sex smile. Allow for a buffer period of several hours or a day.

* When accused of cheating—and eventually you will be accused—don't get angry. Simply laugh, crack a joke about how she's more than enough for any man, and move on.

* Your girlfriend will never *know* you're cheating unless someone sees you, or you admit it to her. She only *thinks* she knows. There's a difference.

* Never ever, ever visit places you and your girlfriend go to together and don't drive around your local town with the bit on the side riding shotgun.

* Make sure your newly acquired lover knows the situation from the start. Don't play two women at the same time; if hell has no fury like a woman scorned, God help you if you piss two off simultaneously.

Excuses for staying out all night and not phoning:

* Tell her you fell asleep on your friend's sofa after the umpteenth bottle of beer.

* One of your friends had a mini-breakdown and you had to look after him.

* Your phone battery died.

* Rope a friend into the lie. Get him to pick you up from the other girl's house and drive you home. He can take the brunt of the blame and by arriving home with him in the morning you'll allay her suspicions.

Striking the cue ball in pool: how to generate different types of spin

The kid with the most kudos was never the kid who could run the 100 yards in a nanosecond, or swim a whole length without coming up for air. It was the kid who could con the bar lady into giving him a shot of rum in his coke, who could blow smoke rings and get the pool table to work with a well-positioned kick. Relive those halcyon pool days with some killer spin techniques the next time you're down the pub.

Topspin. This causes the cue ball to spin forward and run on after striking another ball. Strike the white ball a quarter of a cue tip directly above the center. Keep the cue horizontal and avoid downward contact upon striking. Hitting the ball the slightest amount to the side of center will also cause sidespin, so precision is the name of the game. **Hitting with more power won't make much difference. Follow through with the cue. (Fig. 1.)**

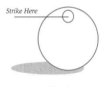

Fig. 1.

Backspin. Makes the cue ball spin back towards you after hitting a color ball. Strike the ball at the base, below center with some considerable force. Don't hit too low, about one-and-a-half cue tips is on the money. The greater the distance to the color ball, the harder you should strike. After striking the ball, don't yank the cue back abruptly, instead, try to snap the cue forward sharply to get maximum impact. **Follow through and keep the cue parallel to the table. (Fig. 2.)**

Fig. 2.

Sidespin. Generally used to change the direction of the cue ball when it hits the cushion. Sidespin also affects the direction a color ball will take after impact with the cue ball. Hit the ball left of center and the cue ball will move to the right slightly and vice versa. **The further out from center you strike the ball the more the ball will curve.**

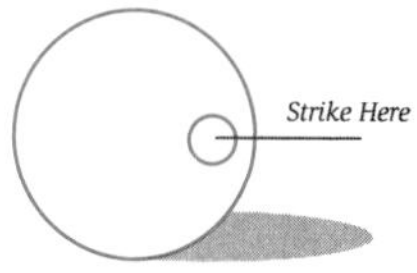

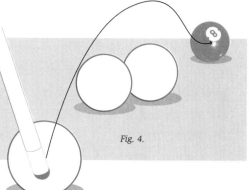

Fig. 3.

Stop shot. Does exactly what it says on the tin; when the ball collides with another ball it will stop in its tracks. Hit the ball slightly below center—about a quarter of a cue tip. This should only take a small amount of draw, so don't whack it or you risk knocking some poor guy off his bar stool.

Jump shot. Get the right cue angle and you will make the ball do a little bunny hop, possibly over another ball. Elevate your cue and hit downwards on to the cue ball.

Fig. 4.

Masse shot. This shot will make the cue ball curve round the color ball in front of it. Hold the cue almost vertically, directly above the ball. Strike the cue ball off center. A fancy move but probably best left to Ronnie O'Sullivan and friends.

Tip: you don't have to use these shots on their own. The real pro would be able to play a combination of top/back spin with sidespin. For example, by hitting the ball low—backspin—and to the right—sidespin— the white will come off the color ball back, and to the right.

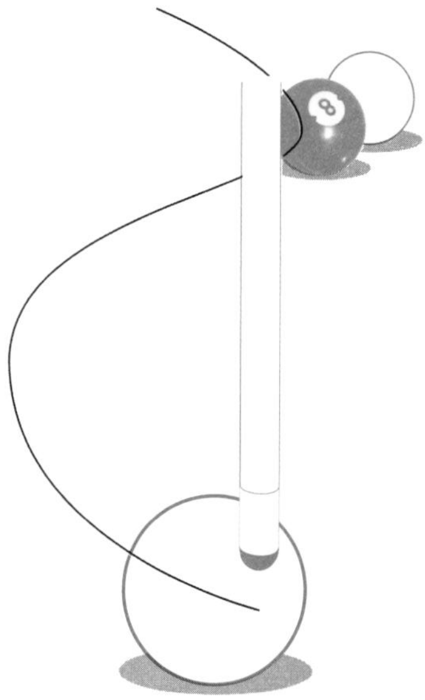

Fig. 5.

How to start a fire without matches or a light

Stranded on a desert island. Lost in the middle of a forest. Or merely messing around in the backyard after watching Survivorman *on TV. Men have an urge to master fire. And when there's no matches or lighters at hand you've got to do it the Neanderthal way.*

Here's a selection of techniques to make sure your cockles don't get cold:

Hand drill

You will need:

*   Fireboard. A dry, flat-ish piece of wood about a foot in length. Use a dry softwood such as willow, aspen, or juniper.

*   Spindle. A strong, thin, and two-foot-long stick, preferably the same type of wood as the fireboard.

*   Tinder nest. A bundle of super-dry small tinder such as grasses, seed heads, lichen, bark shavings from aspen, poplar, cottonwood trees. Form the bundle loosely to the size of a tennis ball.

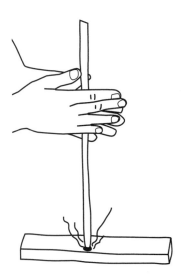

The hand drill method relies on friction to create heat. Cut a V-shaped notch out of your fireboard. Place a piece of dry bark or sturdy leaf underneath the notch. With the spindle wedged into the notch rub your hands either side of the spindle, up and down applying a good amount of pressure. Keep going until a glowing ember falls onto the bark or leaf and transfer it to your tinder nest. Cup your hands around the nest and blow softly to fan the flame. Transfer the burning tinder to your prepared campfire.

Fire plough

You will need:

*   Fireboard

*   Spindle

*   Tinder nest

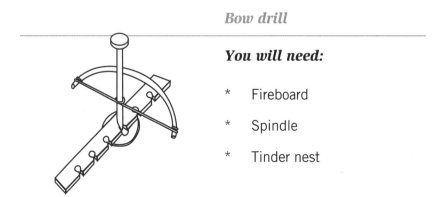

Another friction heat method. Cut a long groove down the center of one end of the fireboard. Rub the spindle up and down the groove in firm, fast movements. Place your tinder nest at the end of the groove and once an ember forms it will fall into the nest and catch fire. Continue as above.

Bow drill

You will need:

*   Fireboard

*   Spindle

*   Tinder nest

* Socket. A heavy rock of some kind.

* Bow. A bendy stick, at least as long as your arm.

* String. In true survival fashion a shoelace will suffice.

Create your bow by tying one end of the string to one side of the bow. Loop the string around your spindle and tie the loose end to the other side of the bow. Cut a notch in the fireboard. Place the spindle into the notch and apply pressure on top of the spindle with the socket. Saw back and forth with the bow. This rotates the spindle quickly and an ember should form as with the hand drill method.

Lens method

You will need:

* A pair of glasses, magnifying glass, piece of glass, etc.

* Sunlight

* Tinder nest

This technique will be familiar to anyone who cruelly burned ants to a cinder at school. By focusing the heat of the sun on one specific spot you can create fire. Place the lens under the sun and over your tinder nest. Tilt the lens until you can see a clear beam—a clear silver dot—on the tinder. Within a short amount of time the tinder will spark.

Can and chocolate method

You will need:

*   Coke or other drink can

*   Chocolate bar with foil wrapper

*   Sunlight

*   Tinder nest

*   Tweezers

Unwrap your chocolate bar and smear some on the underside of the Coke can. Use the wrapper to buff the metal. Essentially you're polishing the surface so it will rebound the sun. Repeat until you can see a clear reflection of your face in the can—have patience—this can take up to two hours. Point the bottom of the can at the sun—away from your eyes—and using a pair of tweezers (to reduce the shadows) hold a small piece of tinder directly in the reflected beam, about an inch from the center of your can bottom. Once the piece of tinder begins to smoke, transport to your tinder nest.

Tip: Toothpaste or ashes will work just as well to polish the can. Rub it in with a cloth.

Battery and steel wool method

You will need:

*9 volt battery

*Steel wool

*Tinder nest

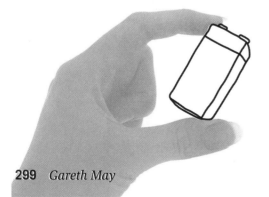

Stretch the steel wool out. Rub the side of the battery with the nub, or contacts, on the steel wool. The wool will glow as it gets hotter. Blow softly to keep the wool glowing—it will cool quickly—and place in your tinder nest.

Tinder fungus: This corky growth is found on birch barks and is one of the few naturally found materials that will catch a spark and glow readily.

Get hold of a chunk of "tinder fungus" and keep small dry bits in a small tin. Keep this in your pocket at all times, just in case you need to start a fire.

A whole large fungus will also retain a glow over a long period, so that it can be transported and used to make a fire in a new camp. Cut a large fungus in half, and use one half as a lid to keep the glow alight.

How to sharpen a knife using a whetstone

Whether you're in training for Top Chef *or just peeling a few spuds for tea, every chef needs a good sharp knife. Sharpening knives is all about angles—yet another reason why you should have paid more attention in math class.*

Here's how to do it like Mario Batali:

1. Your whetstone has a rough side and a smooth side. Rub the rough side with mineral oil or water to remove small particles that could clog up the stone and ruin the grind. (Water on a water stone, oil on an oil stone. Don't mix and match the two.)

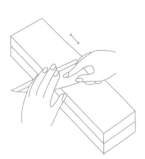

2. Place your thumb tightly on top of the handle of the knife and push the blade—lengthways—in a short and steady motion away from you at the preferred angle. Between 22 and 25 degrees—the angle your knife would be at if you were to rest it against a box of matches—is the standard angle for sharpening European knives. For Japanese and professional filet knives, hold the knife at an angle between 12 and 15 degrees. This scrapes away the metal to form a blunt edge, or burr, the first step to sharpening your knife. Never pull the knife towards you or you risk losing a finger or two.

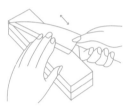

3. Feel for the burr every now and then. Put your thumb on the other side of the edge you've been grinding and gently slide downwards along the flat side. You should feel something scraping at your skin—this is the burr. The burr will form quicker nearer the hilt but take longer towards the tip. Keep grinding until the burr is formed all along the blade.

4. Once you establish a burr on one side grind away on the other so that the burr covers the entire length. You need to get a burr on either side.

5. Turn the stone over so the fine side is facing up. Slightly raise the angle of the knife and continue to grind away as before; this will remove the burr and leave you with an über-sharp micro bevel—the edge of the blade.

6. Take it slow and alternate sides moving from the hilt all the way down to the tip. Release the pressure as you go and once you've done ten strokes on either side check the sharpness by holding a piece of newspaper and seeing if it goes through it with ease.

7. Keep going until the blade is sharpened equally.

8. Finally, with no pressure at all, lift the angle ever so slightly and glide down the stone to finish.

9. Wipe the stone clean at the end of each sharpening session.

Understanding your payslip

For most men, the arrival of their payslip means one thing—time to hit the pub. But before you drink your way back into overdraft, why not open the envelope and at least attempt to understand what all those codes and jargon mean?

Every payslip layout differs from workplace to workplace. However, the essentials are as follows:

Employer	
Employee	Payment Date
Gross Pay	Overtime
Sick Pay	
Units	Rate
Method of Payment or MOP	
Deductions	Fixed deductions
Voluntary Contributions	401K Contributions
Net Pay	

Employer. Name of the company you work for.

Employee. Your name...unless you've mistakenly got your boss's payslip. Should also have your employee number, to quote to your accounts department if you have any queries re your payslip.

Payment Date. When you'll receive the money.

Gross Pay. Your full pay without any additional hours or deductions.

Overtime. Any extra hours you've put in out of sheer love for your chosen vocation.

Sick Pay. Days you've taken off sick because your team has an afternoon game.

Units. Hours of work you've done.

Rate. How much you earn per hour. Or the depressing bit.

Deductions. A list of deductions from your gross pay. Depending on your salary and tax bracket, you'll lose a percentage of your earnings to federal and state income tax, social security, and Medicare.

Insurance. Insurance can range from basic health to dental, vision, and life insurance as well. The amount you contribute to your insurance each paycheck will depend on the plan that your company has set up.

Voluntary Contributions. Savings scheme, charity donation, staff gym membership, sack the boss campaign, etc.

401K Contributions. A percentage of your income you put aside for your future.

Net Pay. Your take home pay, minus deductions. The total amount you'll receive on a paycheck, or paid directly into your bank account.

How to control your aggression: anger management for big boys

Despite being a useful tool on the sports field and at times as motivation to change the direction of your life, anger, if not kept in check, can only be a destructive emotion. Know when to show outward aggression and frustration by practicing inner strength and control.

Here are a few telltale signs that you're blowing a fuse a little too often:

* Overly irritable or stressed. You express this by shouting at people or throwing things.

* You regret getting angry shortly after an outburst and sometimes feel embarrassed by your actions.

* People close to you become scared and/or find your behavior difficult to understand and at times unforgivable.

How to deal with aggression and anger:

* When people are aggressive they move forward into other people's space. Take a step back and stand still.

* Stop talking. Instead concentrate on calming yourself down and clearing your mind of negative or angry thoughts

* If your body is pent-up with anger, tightly grip a desk or some other immovable object that you can't pick up and throw.

* As much as we might laugh when our fathers say, "Next time, count to ten!" it actually works. Take a deep breath— this relaxes your muscles, which are probably tensed by this point—and give yourself time to think with a ten-second time-out.

* If the rage is still coursing through your blood and you feel like you have to release it physically, do so by punching

something soft like a cushion or pillow. As a last resort punch a wall or door, anything other than someone else.

Some more things to consider:

Try and pinpoint what's making you so angry. Anger is often a secondary emotion triggered by fear, hurt, regret, etc. Recognize that you're angry, accept it's your responsibility and deal with the emotions that caused it.

Anger is often a result of feeling like you don't have a voice. Some people find it hard to express themselves and instead internalize their feelings and emotions. Learn to tell people how they make you feel and don't bottle it up—being assertive in the short-term means you won't become aggressive in the long-term.

Use "I" rather than "You" at the beginning of sentences. Compare, "I feel ignored" with, "You're ignoring me." By saying, "I," you're taking control of your feelings.

In the heat of an argument resist the temptation to apportion blame. Even if you feel you're innocent, it takes two people to argue. Apportioning blame only exacerbates the situation. Swallow your pride and apologize if you made a mistake.

Don't raise your voice. Even if the subject or situation is something you feel passionate about resist the temptation to shout. Articulate people rarely raise their voice; their words are far more productive delivered in a calm and assertive tone.

Take yourself away from the situation. If you're in an enclosed space with your girlfriend, family member, or friend often the only way to calm down is to get away. Go for a walk and return once you've rationalized your emotions.

Channel your stress and vent frustration through sport, meditation, long walks in the countryside, making time for yourself, shouting or singing (preferably in a wide-open space), eating healthily, having a regular sleeping pattern, and drinking less booze.

If you find your aggression persists and the methods above seem to have no short-term or long-term gain, go for a meeting with your GP and talk candidly about your problem. He'll be able to refer you to a therapist or local anger management class.

How to survive small talk about a game you didn't see

Even in the age of DVR, the unthinkable occasionally happens—we miss the big game. Nothing ruins your sports cred with your bros at the bar—or the suits at work—faster than being the guy who's out of the loop about last night's killer tackle or insane pass interference call. Admitting that you were at your niece's baton-twirling championship or a Michael Bublé concert with your girlfriend is not a valid option. Your one shot at surviving this socially unacceptable situation is to have a game plan. Follow these dos and don'ts to convince any pals that you were glued to your flat screen for every minute of overtime.

* **Do:** Remember that your best offense is a good defense. Think defensively and, if you can, prepare ahead of time. ESPN.com is your best friend. Make a habit of scanning it for game highlights.

* **Don't:** Change the subject. An immediate topic change is a dead giveaway. Resist the urge to talk about the Food Network, even if that's what you were watching instead.

* **Do:** Know your team and coach. Chances are that most conversation will be about your home team, so memorize a few random stats or some trivia about your coach and players ahead of time. Casually drop them into the conversation when you get a chance, but make sure that they are relevant. Trivia about favorite foods or shoe brands won't score you any cool points.

*   ***Don't:*** Go AWOL. Making up facts and hoping that no one notices is not an option.

*   ***Do:*** Get smart. If the conversation allows it, pretend to send a text on your smart phone and actually head over to a sports website for the headlines. Remember, this is not a good choice in one-on-one conversations.

*   ***Don't:*** Prolong the pain. You don't need to fake appendicitis, but if you can come up with a viable reason to hurry off, you should. With any luck, the guys will exhaust the topic while you're gone.

NOTES

_____

_____

_____

_____

_____

_____

_____

_____

_____

_____

_____

_____

_____

_____

_____

_____

_____

_____

_____

_____

Useful websites

Cancer Research www.cancer.org

Expectant Dads www.greatdad.com

Mental and Emotional Health www.helpguide.org

National Domestic Violence Hotline www.thehotline.org

Personal Finance and Budgeting www.mint.com

Speed and Online Dating www.8minutedating.com

YMCA—support for young people www.ymca.net

Acknowledgments

All the blokes in my life—and a few blokettes—who've filled out questionnaires, lent their words of wisdom and put up with my ego trips. They include: Dan Ward, Lenny Teehan, Joey Card, Dave McAllister, Luke Elms, Tony Ambler, Trist Earl, Andy Palmer, Katie Hall, Lambert Kleinjans, Amy Mann, Niki Khouroushi, Mikey "Man's Man" Holroyd, and everyone at Drake Circus Waterstone's, especially Clint "I hate Bret Hart" Jones.

For various gems of information from the sublime to the serious I'd like to thank, Olly Luscombe, Neil Parker, Phil Jane, Jayne Morris, the guys at Slow Dating, the Japanese waitress in Yukisan, numerous Starbucks employees, all at David May Motor Services, South Devon Women's Aid, the two very friendly women in Blackheath, and Daisy at the Spearmint Rhino in Sheffield. Also, all my ex-girlfriends—without whom this book wouldn't have had half the insight it does. Sorry for all the grief and thank you for all the patience.

To all those who supported me with my idea for "a manual for young men" from beginning to end a massive thanks goes to all the staff on the Professional Writing course at University College Falmouth. Including Tom Scott, Susy Marriot and Christina Bunce—this book wouldn't exist if it weren't for you three. For help with the website and various other bits and bobs: Matt Collins, Tony Bowry, Paul Matchett, Cam, Laura Sewell, Dena Blakeman, Merik Flynn, Luke Friend, Katy Moon, Kate Burt, Fiona "Iolaire" Campbell-Howes, James "DM" Henry, and everyone else I've undoubtedly missed out. An extra big thank you to Pat and Rog—we'll always have Whitstable.

At Random House I'd like to thank my editor Rosemary Davidson whose insight and vision has taken this book beyond anything I could have imagined. Thanks for backing me on the controversial issues and putting your faith in a young author. For Tom in editorial, Tom in sales, Louise Rhind-Tutt in publicity, Claire Morrison in marketing, and all the phantom proofreaders and supporters. Thank you to all the designers and illustrators at

Unreal who nailed the sentiment of the book from the word go and brought all the tips to life in a way just words couldn't have.

My agent Susan Smith deserves a singular thank-you. Thanks for putting up with my rants and raves whether work related or relationship related. You're not only a great agent but also a great friend. Just promise me you'll stay away from kayaks and Burgh Island!

A little thanks to my two A-level English Lit teachers, Ms. Daniel and Mr. Dart. Never be a writer, eh?

And last but not least my family. Uncle Col for his beard and horse racing advice, Auntie Biddy for her permanent interest and unfaltering support. Rex, Ad, Suzy, Catharine, Glynn, Cal, P, M, and B for always showing an interest. My sister and her three little boys—Ben, Wills, and Edward—for teaching me how to hold a baby not to mention all her invaluable advice at pivotal moments in my life over the past year. Her husband and my brother-in-law Mick for everything car, Beckham and beer-related. For my late Grandma and Nanny who taught me the importance of compassion with their tales of sandbags, American soldiers, and air-raid-shelter shenanigans. To my parents, who have supported me in every way, shape and form in achieving this and always encouraged me to follow my dream when most would have told me it was time to call it a day. "Golden Balls" would like to thank you and ensure you both you've passed the nursing home test with flying colors!

Gareth May

Penryn, Cornwall; August 2009

About the author

Born and bred in Devon, Gareth May is a twentysomething writer. In 2007, he set up the popular blog 21st-Century-Boy.co.uk, with the intention of giving young men an alternative voice from the lad mag generation, and his humorous but informative videos have had hundreds of thousands of views on YouTube. Gareth likes listening to the cricket on the wireless, drinking ale, and watching *Midsomer Murders.* And is well aware that all three make him an incredibly old git.